GREATER BOSTON

Park an

GUIDE

Each town should have a park, or rather a primitive forest, of five hundred or a thousand acres, where a stick should never be cut for fuel, a common possession forever, for instruction and recreation. We hear of cow-commons and ministerial lots, but we want **men**-*commons and lay lots, inalienable forever. Let us keep the New World* **new**, *preserve all the advantages of living in the country.*

Henry David Thoreau
Journal *1859*

GREATER BOSTON

Park and Recreation

G U I D E

by Mark L. Primack

The
Globe
Pequot
Press

Chester, Connecticut 06412

Text Copyright © 1983 by Mark L. Primack

Library of Congress Cataloging in Publication Data

Primack, Mark L.
  The Greater Boston park and recreation guide.

  Includes index.
  1. Outdoor recreation—Massachusetts—Boston Metropolitan Area. 2. Boston (Mass.)—Recreational activities—Directories. 3. Boston (Mass.)—Parks—Guide-books. I. Title.
GV182.P74   1983   917.44'61   83-80634
ISBN 0-87106-979-2 (pbk.)

Manufactured in the United States of America
First Printing

Photographs on pages 9 and 63 by Stan Grossfeld.

Cover design by Peter Good
Text design by Wendy Walden

To My Mother and Father:
for taking us kids to parks and beaches,
for living by the Woods,
and for their love.

Acknowledgments

I would like to thank the many park managers, interpreters, and other personnel who gave freely of their knowledge of the areas under their care. Thanks are also due to the many town and city librarians, local historians, and conservationists who helped dig up a mountain of facts.

Thanks are due to the following individuals who not only shared information but also read portions of the manuscript: David Beall of Great Meadows National Wildlife Refuge; Ralph Scott, Dave Clapp, Mike Shannon, and Cynthia Thomas of the Massachusetts Audubon Society; Philip Causer of the North and South Rivers Watershed Association; Wayne Mitton of the Trustees of Reservations; Dave Hodgdon of the Friends of the Blue Hills; Rob Burkhart of the Museum of Transportation; Katy Nixon of Arnold Arboretum; Charles Shurcliff of the Metropolitan District Commission (MDC); and Richard Heath of the Franklin Park Coalition.

Special thanks are due to these individuals who gave generously of their time in innumerable ways: Gary Van Wart, Assistant Director of the Trustees of Reservations; Captain Albert Swanson, Archivist at the MDC; Andrea Lukens, Supervisor of Interpretive Services; and Tod Lafleur, Supervisor of Recreation at the Division of Forests and Parks.

Thanks are also due to my professors at U. Mass.-Boston, particularly Lori Novak for her guidance on my photographic work, and to my friends Arthur and Ellen Leventhal for their laughter and support.

Most of all I would like to thank my mother Shirley P. Primack for her typing and editing assistance, and my brother Richard Primack for making many valuable suggestions on the organization and content.

Naturally all errors are my own.

Mark L. Primack
Newton 1983

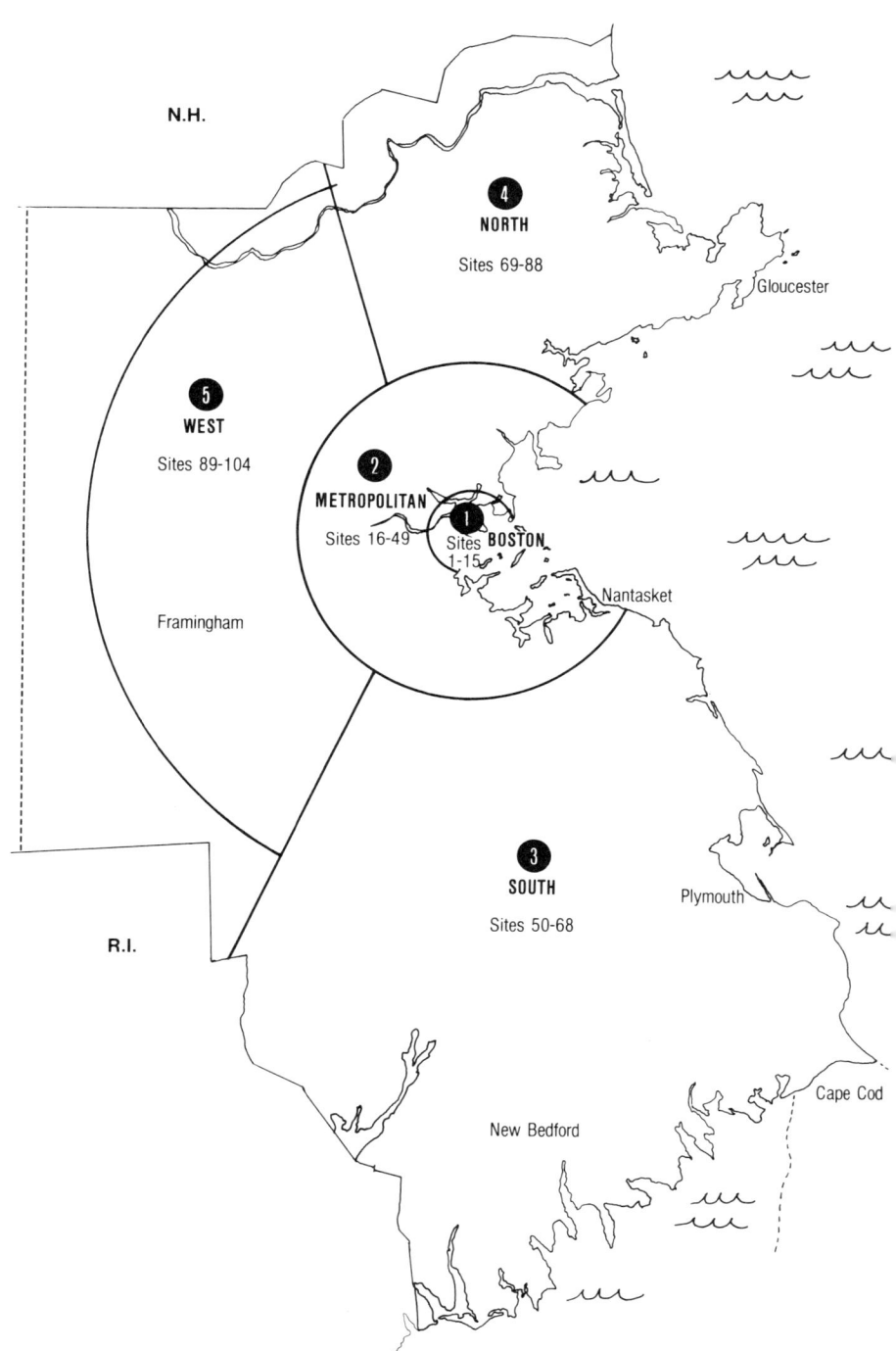

N.H.

4
NORTH
Sites 69-88

Gloucester

5
WEST
Sites 89-104

2
METROPOLITAN
Sites 16-49

1
Sites
1-15
BOSTON

Nantasket

Framingham

3
SOUTH
Sites 50-68

Plymouth

R.I.

Cape Cod

New Bedford

Contents

WEST PARKS

RECREATION APPENDIX

Introduction

Boston is famous among American cities for the beauty of its environing landscape. No one can be said really to know Boston who is not familiar with this important aspect of the city, and as the charms of the most characteristic scenery about the New England metropolis have best been preserved in ideal form in the public parks and recreative open spaces, this guide has been prepared, that both strangers and residents may obtain in compact and comprehensive shape, the information necessary for convenient access to and proper enjoyment of their various features.

In beauty of location, in artistic design, in thoughtful adaptation to peculiarities of site, in development in a way to meet the widest possible requirements on the part of the public, as well as in variety and extent, the park system of Boston and its metropolitan vicinage, existing and projected, surpasses that of any other city in the world.

Sylvester Baxter
Boston Park Guide *1896*

Herein lie the citizens' jewels, emerald green parks, dark sapphire rivers, gold-encrusted beaches, precious assets all. These are heirlooms passed on to us by our ancestors and purchased by us for our children. They are a legacy, a way for us to tell our grandchildren that we cared for them and the future. It is up to us to enjoy these jewels thoughtfully and protect them, for if we forget our charge, they will lose their sparkle and those who come after us will lose their delight.

Parks, beaches, rivers, reservations, sanctuaries, refuges, and natural areas from one acre to ten thousand acres: not one square inch just happened. Every area was bought with tax dollars and donations, lobbying efforts and petition drives, individual devotions and legislative mandate. We must not allow that investment to be wasted.

Please treat these properties tenderly, they are our common backyards.

The idea of public parks is a relatively recent addition to the human condition. Just over a hundred years ago there were only a few remnant commons and squares in the region, but not a park, a beach, a hill, or a riverbank was owned by the public. This book is written as a guide to public lands and private lands open to the public. Each chapter describes the features of a park and the origins of that park. These parks tell us many stories about the history, changing economy, and people of Massachusetts.

The people of Boston and Massachusetts have much to be proud of: no metropolitan area in the United States has done more to protect its natural resources. In 1626 Plymouth Colony passed the first forest protection laws in the New World. Massachusetts Bay Colony in 1641 decreed that the public had an inalienable right to access to the colony's great ponds, rivers, and ocean shore. In 1670 tree wardens were appointed to patrol the forests and a few years later towns began to forbid the cutting of shade trees. These early regulations, though not formally dealing with recreation, nonetheless stressed the management of natural resources for the common good.

The idea of nature as something to be enjoyed as well as exploited received a major impetus with the publication of *Nature* in 1835 by Concord philosopher Ralph Waldo Emerson. At that time Massachusetts was already the site of the first scenic rural burial ground in America, Mount Auburn Cemetery. Asa Gray and Louis Agassiz at Harvard were laying the groundwork for the future evolution of the natural sciences. In 1856 Massachusetts became the first state to stock its public waters with game fish. The latter part of the nineteenth century saw the first urban park system, the first conservation land trust, the first Audubon Society, and the first metropolitan park system in America founded in Massachusetts.

During the twentieth century Massachusetts was the first state to establish town forests, a Clean Waters Act, conservation commissions, and laws to protect wetlands and barrier beaches. Other forces have sought to develop and exploit the land for short-term goals, yet on the whole, the people of the state have maintained a feeling for land and water, the environment, and outdoor recreation that has protected public lands.

What's Here and What Isn't?

Included in this book are most of the major outdoor spaces in the Greater Boston region that are open to the public. A few sanctuaries and natural areas have been left out at the specific request of their managers because any increase in the number of visitors could harm the natural environment that the parks were set up to protect. This book omits numerous smaller and less spectacular areas, such as town and city parks, tracts of cut-over forest land, and places with limited public access. Nonetheless enough territory is here to provide many years of pleasure.

For information on other outdoor spaces in the region contact local park departments and conservation commissions.

Format for the Park Listings

1 **17.**   2 **STONY BROOK RESERVATION**
3 *Turtle Pond Parkway, West Roxbury*
4 **600 acres**   5 ***MDC**   6 **1894**

7 **Activities:**
8 **Map:**
9 **Hours:**
10 **Admission:**

11

12 **Activities:**
13 **Reading:**
14 **Directions:**
15 **Telephone:**

1. Section of the book.

2. Name of area.

3. Address. An asterisk (*) indicates that this is also the mailing address to contact for more information.

4. Number of acres in the property.

5. Agency or organization that owns or manages the area. An asterisk indicates this is the source to contact for more information. Agencies and organizations with their addresses and telephone numbers are listed at the back of this book.

6. Date of acquisition.

7. Brief listing of the recreational opportunities at the area: what to do at a glance.

8. For most of the areas listed in this book, free maps are available at the entrance (see "Maps" directly below).

9. Hours are listed according to currently available information; opening and closing times are subject to change.

10. Entry fees are listed according to information current at the time of publication and may change.

11. Each section has a general description of an area with an

overview of its history and natural history.

12. In this Activities portion the recreational opportunities of the area are given in more detail, though nature study and birdwatching are usually included in the general description.

13. Most of the books suggested in the reading section may be found in any good bookstore or library. The Massachusetts Audubon bookstore at Drumlin Farm in Lincoln has the best selection of books on the outdoors.

14. An ordinary road map or the regional map suggested immediately below will be very useful in finding each site. If you primarily use public transportation for your travels, be sure to pick up *Car-Free in Boston and All Massachusetts*, available at most bookstores.

15. Telephone number.

About Maps

Free trail maps are available for nearly all the larger areas included in this book; smaller areas do not require maps. Usually you can pick up a map at the entrance, visitor center, or headquarters on your way into a site. If you plan to visit in the off-season, it is usually best to send a self-addressed stamped envelope (SASE) to the site or agency several weeks in advance.

For free maps of State Parks, Forests, and Reservations send SASE for up to three site maps to: Interpretive Service, Division of Forests and Parks, 100 Cambridge Street, Boston, MA 02202.

Pick up or send for the free map of Metropolitan District Commission (MDC) reservations: MDC, 20 Somerset St., Boston, MA 02108. Telephone: (617) 727-5215.

The one map you should purchase is the *Explorer's Recreation Map of Metropolitan Boston*. This map will make it easier to find most of the sites in this book. It includes trails, but not always accurately. Available at most bookstores and newsstands or from Thurman Smith, Box 385, Boston, MA 02117. Telephone: 536-3583.

Topographic maps published by the U.S. Geological Survey provide detailed information about the face of the land. They not only give direction but are also fun to "read," ponder, and decipher at home. A free index to the topographic maps of the region is available at most stores that sell the maps. Topographic maps are sold at: Hammett's, 48 Canal Street, Boston, telephone 523-5778; Eastern Mountain Sports, 1041 Commonwealth Avenue, Brighton, telephone 254-4250; and Harvard Square Map Company, 99 Mt.

Auburn Street, Cambridge, 02138, telephone 497-MAPS. They also may be ordered direct from Branch of Distribution, U.S.G.S., Box 25286, Federal Center, Denver, CO 80225.

Cautionary Notes

1. *Poison Ivy:* There's a lot of poison ivy out there. The best defense against getting a rash is knowing what poison ivy looks like. It is a vine or rarely a low shrub that forms a ground cover or climbs trees. The plant has compound leaves divided into three shiny leaflets, often with a reddish tint. In late summer and winter the plants have white berries. Teach your children to avoid it. You will not get poison ivy unless you touch the leaves or stems of the plant. Long pants and socks are another good defense.

2. *Mosquitos, blackflies, etc.:* From mid-May until the end of August make sure you have insect repellent in your pocket or pack. Wear long pants and a long-sleeved cotton shirt when you explore the woods during the summer; otherwise be stoical.

3. *Ticks:* Ticks are small, flat, dark-brown insects about one quarter of an inch long, with eight legs. They are most common in tall-grass fields. Insect repellent will keep ticks off if sprayed around your socks. Also try tucking the bottom of your pants into your socks. Usually ticks will crawl around for an hour or two before digging in, so that you can just pick them off. If you find one on yourself, you may want to strip-search for any others, because they can carry human diseases such as Rocky Mountain spotted fever.

4. *Hunting season:* Deer season is the first week of December, a good time to visit a museum or library. No hunting is permitted on Sundays. Bright red clothing is advisable for forest walks during this period.

5. *Poison sumac:* This shrub is far less common than poison ivy, but if you are an explorer, learn to identify it. Poison sumac should not be confused with other very common sumacs. It occurs in swamps and has alternate compound leaves and white berries.

6. *Poisonous snakes:* Rattlesnakes and copperheads inhabit a few isolated corners of the region south of Boston. The chances of encountering one of these snakes are extremely slim; the chances of your being bitten on a walk through the woods are about one in a million. If that rare off-chance does occur, roads and civilization are never far away: go immediately to the nearest hospital.

7. *Broken glass:* Be careful of broken glass, particularly on the

most heavily used hill summits. With the Bottle Bill passed, we can hope this problem will come under control.

8. *Hiking alone:* Use your discretion. If you feel nervous, ask a companion to come along. The parks inside of Route 128 are particularly to be avoided after dark.

9. *Complaints:* If you find that an area is not maintained in the way you think it should be, complain. Call the managing agency, talk to the superintendent, write to your state senator or representative. Demand a reply. Join a local conservation organization. Don't give up.

Rules and Regulations

The entire region covered by this book is densely populated. Each tract listed here is an isolated green spot in a matrix of roads, houses, factories, and private property. These natural areas must be treated with respect to survive intact for coming generations. To ensure this protection, laws have been passed to protect public lands.

All the rules that follow could be summed up in a few phrases: Tread lightly. Leave only your cares, take only your memories. Don't litter. Leave the land exactly as you found it. Please remember that any thoughtlessness could damage the quality of experience for thousands of other people.

1. *No fires except at designated areas.* Fires are extremely dangerous in these woodlands and may cause permanent damage.

2. *Picking wildflowers or removing vegetation is prohibited.* Many flowers have become extinct or been pushed to the verge of extinction by picking. Trillium, magnolia, and lady's slipper particularly are plants that have been damaged in the past by excessive picking. There are state laws against picking cardinal flowers and orchids, including lady's slippers. There are regulations with the force of law forbidding damage to vegetation for all the properties listed in this book. The only exception is berry-picking, which is permitted at most sites; just be sure to leave some for the birds. Trees, flowers, and shrubs are of scientific interest—all are part of the irreplaceable beauty of the landscape.

3. *Disturbing, removing, or otherwise damaging a natural feature, sign, barrier, or building is prohibited.*

4. *No camping except at designated areas.* Camping in nondesignated areas may cause damage to both public health and the environment.

5. *Firearms are prohibited unless specifically permitted.*

6. *Alcoholic beverages* are prohibited at nearly every property listed in this book.

7. *Respect the right of other users to tranquility and peace of mind.*

8. *Motorized vehicles, including dirt bikes and snowmobiles, are prohibited unless specifically permitted.*

9. *Don't litter.* Dispose of your trash in a proper receptacle. The best rule of thumb is "Pack-it-in/pack-it-out."

10. State fishing license required for freshwater fishing.

Thank you.

(Rules adapted from those of the Trustees of Reservations)

BOSTON PARKS

Boston Parks
Quick Guide to Outdoor Activities

	WALKING	PICNICKING	SWIMMING	JOGGING	NATURE STUDY	SKI TOURING	FISHING	BIRDWATCHING	HIKING	CANOEING & BOATING	ICE-SKATING	PROGRAMS	CAMPING	HORSEBACK RIDING	TOWERS, ZOOS, ETC.	HISTORIC SITES	BALLFIELDS	TOT-LOTS	BIKE TRAILS	TENNIS
1. Boston Common	●	●		●							●					●	●	●		●
2. Boston Public Gardens	●	●		●												●				
3. Commonwealth Avenue Mall	●															●				
4. Back Bay Fens	●		●	●	●			●								●	●	●	●	
5. Charlesbank	●	●	●	●													●		●	
6. Olmsted Park and Riverway	●	●		●	●						●						●		●	
7. Jamaica Pond	●	●		●	●		●	●		●						●	●		●	
8. Arnold Arboretum	●			●	●			●						●						
9. Franklin Park	●	●		●	●	●	●	●						●	●	●	●	●	●	●
10. Forest Hills Cemetery	●				●			●								●				
11. Castle Island	●	●	●	●			●	●		●						●	●	●	●	●
12. Boston Beaches	●																			
12A. South Boston Beaches	●	●	●					●									●	●		
12B. Orient Heights Beach	●	●	●					●						●				●		●
13. Waterfront Park	●	●																		
14. Copps Hill Terraces	●	●														●				
15. Paul Revere Park	●	●														●				

1. BOSTON COMMON
Bounded by Beacon, Park, Tremont, Boylston, and Charles streets
48 acres   *Boston Park Department   1634

Activities: strolling, sitting, picnicking, historic sites

. . . There is a small, but pleasant Common where the Gallants a little before Sun-set walk with their Marmalet-Madams. . . .
                    John Josslyn 1674
                    An Account of Two Voyages to New England

Few downtown open spaces in the world are as beautiful or historically illustrious as Boston's sacred Common. For more than three hundred and fifty years rabblerousers and lovers, religious and social evangelists, poets and presidents, and generations of "common" Bostonians have retired here for a few moments' relief from the hurly-burly of New England's biggest village and city.

William Blaxton (Blackstone), the first white resident of what became Boston, had moved to the hilly Shawmut peninsula from the failed settlement at Wessagusset (Weymouth) in 1625. Although the peninsula had been at least seasonally occupied by Indians, the local people had been decimated by plague and attacks by the northern Micmacs. Over many years of Indian occupation the land had been cleared of all but a handful of small trees. When he settled by a clear spring, Blaxton's neighbors for the next five years were woodchuck, deer, and bittern.

The Puritans, led by John Winthrop, first settled in Charlestown, but when the poor quality of the water there became apparent, Blaxton invited them over to the Shawmut peninsula. Four years later, in 1634, several hundred residents were living in the new town of Boston. Blaxton, feeling hemmed in, sold his land to the town for thirty pounds, bought some cows, and set off for the wilderness of Providence, "to be as free of the Governence of the Puritans as that of the King." Each householder in the town was assessed six shillings to pay for the land, which was to be used as a common pasture. It was known initially as "The Commonage," but in a short time people referred to the tract simply as "The Common." To ensure that their title to the tract would not be disputed, they also paid Indian Sachems Chickatawbut and Wampatuck for the entire peninsula. An ordinance was passed in that same year forbidding the cutting down of the Common's trees.

In 1640, after talk of subdividing the Common was heard in the town, the freemen of the little community voted that the Common could not be leased or sold without a ballot of the citizenry and that nobody could build a house or even a garden there. (Even today, only the Common and Faneuil Hall are excluded from those broad powers of superintendence which the Mayor and City Council have over city property.) Six years later another ordinance was passed limiting grazing to "seventy milch kine [milk cows], no dry cattel, yonge cattel or horse," though four sheep could be substituted for a cow. This privilege was not granted to everyone, but only to seventy prominent householders and their descendants. A keeper of kine was designated and a fee system was instituted.

While the upper Common provided milk to the town's babes, the great field overlooking the Back Bay marshes served as a "trayning" ground for the militia. Infantry, light horse brigades, and artillery formed and marched here. On the little hill above the Frog Pond a powderhouse was built to store the militia's ordnance. In 1643 joint exercises were held on the Common with a visiting French troop.

As the Common became a public gathering place, few events attracted as many people as the public hangings and punishments in the stocks. Criminals, pirates, and other malefactors were dispatched from a branch of an elm tree. In 1660, during one of the town's most ignoble displays of intolerance, four Quakers were hung here—one of them, Mary Dyer, is now honored with a statue by the State House steps. If the Quakers felt oppressed on the Common, they also felt redeemed there. General Atherton, one of their most "daring and hardened persecutors," was riding home from militia training one day when his horse was scared by a cow. The steed bucked, throwing him to the ground, causing a concussion that resulted in his death. The Quakers felt that this was a "shocking instance of divine vengence."

Hangings continued from a limb of the tree that became known as the Great Elm until 1769 when a gallows was built. The gallows stood warningly on the Common until 1812, when it was moved to South Boston.

In 1675 the first walkway was laid out on the Common, providing a retreat for those not-quite-Puritans who would rather enjoy nature than subdue it. In 1728 the first mall was laid out and lined with tree plantings along the edge of the road that would become Tremont Street. Smoking, now allowed in public, was tolerated around the Great Elm, and so that was where the town's most conversational and rebellious types congregated.

In the seventeenth and eighteenth centuries the Common became the site of several public buildings. An almshouse was built in 1662 for the town's poor and chronically ill, a later version of which also held the insane and criminal. The South Burying Ground was laid out along Frog Lane (Boylston Street) and next to it a granary was built in 1737 to supply the town with corn and wheat in bad crop years. In 1738 a workhouse was built on the Common to forcibly ensure the labor of those supposed too lazy or not enterprising enough to find a steady job.

As the oppressive domination of the British became more and more difficult for Bostonians to bear, the Sons of Liberty began to hold meetings beneath the boughs of the Great Elm. With the Repeal of the Stamp Act in 1766, the Sons of Liberty held a great celebration on the Common with bonfires, fireworks, and a huge pyramid illuminated by 280 lamps. The arrival of General Gage in the 1770s and the semi-abandonment of the town saw the Common become a bivouac for the hated Redcoats. In spite of ever-growing antagonisms, the Boston boys successfully forced Gage to concede their right to play football on the Common. From the foot of the Common the Redcoats set out on their ill-fated expedition to Lexington and Concord.

Once hostilities began in earnest, the British dug into the Common, constructing trenches and earthen barricades. Forced to flee the town in 1776, when Washington placed cannon on Dorchester Heights, as a last act of vengeance the Redcoats, forbidden by General Howe to torch the town, cut down all the trees along Tremont Mall that they hadn't already cut for firewood.

After the Revolution, in 1789, Washington returned to Boston for a joyous celebration on the Common. Two years later, architect Charles Bulfinch began to develop Beacon Street, where his State House was built; Park Row, where residences were constructed; and Tremont Street, where Colonnade Row was erected. As exclusive dwellings went up around the Common, all the buildings on the Common were torn down to enhance the value of the new district.

In 1815 Beacon Street Mall was laid out, followed eight years later by Charles Mall along the newly filled Charles Street. In 1824 Tremont Mall was rechristened Lafayette Mall on the occasion of Lafayette's memorable visit to the city. That same year a cast-iron fence was placed around the Common, the remnants of which still run along Beacon Street. Cows were finally prohibited from grazing on the Common in 1830.

When Charles Dickens visited Boston in 1824, he found the Common ". . . beautiful; and from the top there is a charming panoramic view of the whole town and neighborhood." The elms of the Common were favorably compared to those of Windsor Castle by William Thackeray, author of *Vanity Fair.* On the Long Path, which runs between Joy Street and Boylston Street, Oliver Wendell Holmes proposed to his wife. Along Beacon Mall, where earlier he had walked the family cow, Ralph Waldo Emerson

argued with Walt Whitman, the old philosopher urging the young poet to clean up the lusty innocence of his *Leaves of Grass.* Whitman wouldn't budge and eventually his book was "banned in Boston."

The Great Elm had grown and grown over the years and when the City Engineer measured it a foot above the ground in 1855, it was twenty-two and a half feet in diameter. In 1869 the huge spreading tree was rent asunder by a storm; seven years later it blew completely down. The spot where it once stood, at the base of Flagstaff Hill, the little hill above the Frog Pond, is the converging place of many of the Common's paths. In 1877 the city erected a Civil War monument on the summit of Flagstaff Hill. Designed by Martin Millmore, it depicts, among other things, the U.S. Sanitary Commission, predecessor of the Red Cross, whose first head was Frederick Law Olmsted.

In 1888 a memorial to the victims of the Boston Massacre was sculpted by Robert Kraus and erected on Tremont Street near Boylston. With abolitionism still fresh in their hearts, Bostonians made sure that the name of Crispus Attucks, a black killed in the massacre, was placed first on the list of victims. Attucks's sculpted hand, reaching out from the bas-relief at the base of the monument, has been burnished by generations of Bostonians reaching out to touch it for good luck.

In 1897 one of the Common's and the country's most outstanding pieces of statuary was unveiled, a memorial to Robert Gould Shaw and the 54th Massachusetts Regiment. The 54th was the first regiment whose soldiers were free blacks. Shaw, son of one of the city's notable families, agreed to serve as the regiment's commanding officer. In May 1863 the regiment marched past the future site of the memorial as Governor Andrew stood reviewing them. That July, Gould and many of the regiment's men were killed at the battle of Fort Wagner, South Carolina. Across Beacon Street from the State House, the Shaw Memorial was designed and sculpted by Augustus Saint-Gaudens.

The year 1897 also saw the Lafayette Mall and the rest of the Common along Tremont Street excavated to build entrances for the nation's first underground trolley. In 1907 the ornate "Ft. Noble" was opened as a public toilet.

Between 1910 and 1913 the Common was almost completely renovated by the Olmsted firm under the direction of F. L. Olmsted, Jr. It was dug up to a depth of four feet and the worn-out soil was replenished by adding humus, manure, ground bone, and lime. Many of the mature trees, weighing as much as fifteen tons, were hoisted onto specially constructed carts and hauled to new planting sites. Each tree was so difficult to move that it took up to six men six days to accomplish a successful replanting. The Frog Pond was rebuilt and the Common's walkways were paved and lined with "kidneystone" gutters. Turf was laid, creating the spacious, almost unbelievably resilient green lawns we find on the Common today.

Activities:

Boston Common is still a fine place for "Gallants" and "Marmalet Madams" to stroll around. Have a picnic on the grass or wander around taking the time to look at the statues and memorials. Lean back on a shady bench and watch the city go by. Listen to the crooning street musicians or the Hare Krishnas. Toss some peanuts to the squirrels or entice them to eat out of your hand. Know ye that this is ours and we have a right to be here.

Depending on the whim of the city administration and the proximity to an election year, the Frog Pond may be filled with water in the summer as a wading pool and frozen in the winter as a skating rink. During the Christmas season usually a display of the Nativity and a herd of plaster deer are placed on the Common, and many of the trees are hung with colored lights.

The back of the Common, overlooking Charles Street, is a fine and noble place to toss a Frisbee. A small tot-lot with swings and jungle gym will be found by the Frog Pond. There are also ballfields and tennis courts on the Common. The tennis courts are open to the public, but expect a wait. Contact the Boston Parks and Recreation Department for more information about the Common's ballfields and the status of the Frog Pond.

Telephone: 722-4100.

2. BOSTON PUBLIC GARDEN
Bounded by Arlington, Beacon, Charles, and Boylston streets
25 acres   *Boston Park (1852)   Laid out in 1838

Activities: strolling, picnicking, swan-boat rides, nature study, historic statues
Hours: dawn to dusk

Boston Public Garden, the first public botanic garden in the United States, is a sanctuary of shade trees and flowers surrounded by the busy city. The site that was to become the garden was once a marsh on the Back Bay. The waters of the tidal Charles River flooded all the way to the foot of the Common. The "marsh at the foot of the Common," from which the British embarked "by sea" for Lexington and Concord in 1774, became the site of several ropewalks in 1794. In that year the city gave the shallow marshes to rope manufacturers who had been burned out of the old South End by a fire. After the mill dam was constructed across Back Bay in 1821, the area became stagnant and smelly, so that three years later the city repurchased the area at a cost of $55,000 in order to improve it. Later that year the city tried to sell this portion of the marsh, but when the proposal was put to the citizens, they voted 1,632 to 176 to fill the marsh and retain it for public purposes.

The city filled and annexed the marshes, then, in 1838, gave the area to a civic group organized by Horace Grey, "Proprietors of the Botanic Garden in Boston." The Proprietors, funded by donations, planted their "public garden" with tulips, camellias, roses, dahlias, and azaleas. But financial difficulties forced them to return the Garden to the city in 1852. Again the city tried to sell the area, but Bostonians voted sixty to one in favor of keeping it a public garden with no buildings except "such as are expedient for horticultural purposes." A design competition was held for the layout of the grounds. George Meacham, a young Boston architect, won with the design for the French-style garden we have here today.

In 1868 the Ether Monument was built as a memorial to the world's first use of anesthesia a few years previously at Massachusetts General Hospital. The following year the bridge across the Lagoon (a replica of the Brooklyn Bridge) was constructed and the Equestrian statue of Washington by sculptor Thomas Ball was erected.

During the late 1870s pedal-powered swan-boats designed and operated by Robert Paget began to ply the Lagoon. The statue of orator and abolitionist Senator Charles Sumner, also by Ball, was put up. And nearly a thousand trees were planted.

Just before 1900 a portion of the Garden along Boylston Street was lost for the entrance to America's first subway. Two new statues were added to the park that was becoming Boston's sculpture as well as botanic garden: Richard Brooks's statue of Ireland native and Civil War hero Colonel Thomas Cass, and Herbert Adams's statue of the great Unitarian divine William Ellery Channing.

In 1901 flower gardens were laid out along the walkways. Four years later the Japanese Lantern was put in the Lagoon; it is a relic

from the palace of Toyatami Hedeyosi, one of the generals who unified Japan in the sixteenth century. Wendell Phillips, another great orator and abolitionist, was honored in 1915 by a statue sculpted by Daniel Chester French. In 1924 a French statue of philanthropist George White was installed (see Section 15, Paul Revere Mall). The 1913 statue of author Edward Everett Hale by sculptor Bela L. Pratt and the 1927 statue of Polish-American Revolutionary War hero General Tadeusz Kosciuszko by Mrs. Henry Hudson Hitson round out the statues of the Garden.

Activities:

Boston Public Garden remains an island of cultivated greenery in downtown Boston. The atmosphere of the Public Garden is distinct from that of the Common, more "cultivated," as it were. It's a terrific place for a picnic lunch or to feed the famous mallards that nest on the

Lagoon island. Kids appreciate feeding ducklings. Plenty of shady benches for sitting. Every spring and summer tulips, alyssums, and hundreds of other flowers from the city's Jamaica Plain greenhouses enliven and brighten the Garden's pathways.

Swan-boats: Still operated by the Paget family after more than a hundred years. A ride on these graceful man-powered boats is essential for every Bostonian and visitor. Bring some stale bread or popcorn and honking ducks will follow your passage through the Lagoon like a troop of well-heeled dogs.

Nature study: Nearly fifty species of trees from the far reaches of the world have been planted in the Garden. Many of the trees have identifying labels and among the rarities are seven species of elms, a weeping beech, a Japanese pagoda tree, and even a giant sequoia. Ornamental trees and shrubs fill the Garden with sweet-scented blossoms during the spring and the treetops shelter a surprising diversity of birdlife.

Reading: *Make Way for Ducklings* by Robert McCloskey.

Directions:

MBTA: Arlington station on the Green Line.

Parking: Under-Common Garage on Charles Street.

"PEOPLE FOR PARKS"

A park should belong to the people; so that every man, woman, and child, rich or poor, who frequents it can say, "This is my park and I have a right to be here."

> Thomas Lamb
> "Public Hearing on Parks," 1869

In 1875 Boston's population was nearly 300,000 souls, a tremendous increase from the 1790 population of 18,000. Fleeing the potato famine, waves of poverty-stricken Irish immigrants swept into the city. Yankee farmers fled from worn-out New England hillsides to the factories of the region. Horse traffic filled the narrow streets. Wood heat was being displaced by Pennsylvania coal, but only remnants remained of the virgin forest that had once mantled the region. Cities and towns poured their raw sewage directly into the Charles, creating an awful stench when the tide went out. Malaria and tuberculosis reached plague proportions in the crowded, rambling tenement districts.

At the same time, youths who had listened to Emerson expound on nature's glory were maturing. Such outdoor sports as sailing, bicycling, baseball, ice-skating, and lawn tennis were becoming popular, and Puritan prohibitions against recreational fishing were fading. Appreciation for the flora and fauna of the region was growing.

The pressures of a rapidly expanding population were laying down houses and factories on every available parcel of land. The city of Boston, with 22,288 acres of land, had set aside only 115 acres as public open space: 48 acres purchased from William Blaxton in 1634, Boston Common; the 28-acre Public Garden, established by Horace Grey on fill in 1838; and a few scattered small parks and squares. This 155 acres compared very unfavorably with other American cities: New York had 1,358 acres of parkland including Central Park; Chicago had obtained 1,897 acres; Philadelphia owned 3,074 acres of public open space; Baltimore had 771 acres of greensward; and Brooklyn owned 550 acres. Boston was behind other cities and nearly "criminal," in the words of some, in providing for its own citizens.

Boston's first major forum for public discussion of the parks issue occurred in November 1869, when two days of public hearings were held. Marshall B. Wilder led off the first hearing by saying that parks would inevitably be created in Boston because they were definitely needed and that because land values were rising, it would be cheaper to begin immediately than to wait. Appealing to the honor of Boston, he declared: "Not only should she have a park, but she should have had the first park in the country." He felt shamed by the lack of parks, saying, "I must confess to a little mortification, that we are not up to the mark" regarding parks. As to the purpose of parks, Wilder said that they should "be planted with trees and set apart for recreation, that is the proper term, and signifies the object and the purpose of a park, set apart for the recreation of that class in the community who have not the means of riding 'round the suburbs of the city,—the poor, or common class. . . ."

Edward Crane, a prominent educator and lawyer, attacked the tight-fisted attitudes that were sure to oppose any park plan: "Are we not, in New England, a little apt to hug the Almighty dollar too close ... and leave little room for recreation? Recreation! It is recreation which leads a man to work his eight hours, and from his work go forth and breathe the fresh air, and drink in a new life. ... Are we not apt to err in not taking recreation seriously enough ... ?" He felt it was "far more essential for the people to have good air than $16,000,000 in the savings bank" because parks could curtail "lounging in grog shops" and create a "vigorous and healthy population."

Educator George B. Emerson began his speech by saying that "The neighborhood of Boston is the most beautiful in the world." He favored small parks in every section of the city rather than one big park that only rich carriage owners could enjoy. He particularly wanted tree plantings in any parks and along park drives, declaring that "nothing that you can do would add so much to the happiness of the common people, of all people, as to induce the love of beautiful trees. A person who, while young, gets to have a love of vegetation, of the trees and shrubs, has a source of happiness open to him for all the rest of his life."

Feeling that parks were needed not merely for active sports and recreation but also for solitude, William Moriarty declared: "I believe with Stuart Mill that it is not well that one should always be, perforce, in the presence of his fellows; that forced communion is not favorable to the development of character. When we roam in the woods, walk by the river, or stroll the seashore, we have scope for that silent meditation which constitutes a man."

It wasn't until April 5, 1875, after five years of political wrangling and public hearings, that the mayor was authorized to seek land-taking power from the General Court (the Legislature) providing that a simple majority of city voters agreed. The Legislature passed an act creating the first park commission in the state, giving it land-taking power. On June 9 it was accepted by Boston voters; 3,706 for, 2,311 against. In July the Mayor appointed a Park Commission.

On January 10, 1876, the Park Commission made its first report, briefly indicating that it had begun to look at specific sites and hold hearings of its own. On March 20 the City Council received a petition from 720 businesses and individuals "praying for early action on the matter of drainage and public parks." On April 24, after consulting with Frederick Law Olmsted, the Commission report set forth a comprehensive plan for the creation of a park system.

The "Second Report of the Boston Park Commissioners" was a detailed and well-argued plan for creating a park system. Four "guiding considerations" were developed for choosing park sites: "First—Accessibility, for classes of citizen by walking, driving, riding, or by means of horse or steam cars. Second—Economy, or the selection so far as is practicable, of such lands as are not at present income producing property, and which could least hamper the natural growth of the city in its business and domestic life, and those which would become relatively nearer to the center of population in future years. Third—Adaptability, of the selection of lands possessing in the greatest degree the natural physical characteristics necessary for park purposes, and requiring the least expenditure for subsequent development. Fourth—Sanitary advantage, or the selection of such lands as would probably become unhealthy if built upon."

With those considerations in mind, the Commission recommended parks along the Charles, and at Back Bay, Parker Hill, South Bay, Savin Hill, City Point, East Boston, Chestnut Hill, Jamaica Pond, and West Roxbury.

In the first week of June 1876, a large number of Boston's most prominent citizens joined to place ads in the city's newspapers calling a public meeting to endorse the report of the Park Commission. The "Parks for People" meeting was held at Faneuil Hall on June 7. It was chaired by merchant and State Representative Joseph S. Ropes.

Ropes was the state representative who had reported the Park Act in the Legislature and so he well knew the opposing arguments, and stated them and his rejoinders for the meeting. To the argument based on the beauty of the suburbs, Ropes replied: "But what application has this, my friends, to the working man, to the masses of our population, whose idea of the suburbs consists in an hour's rattling drive in a crowded street car, and an hour's seat by the side of a dusty thoroughfare?" To the argument that Boston could ill afford the luxury of parks, he responded: "So long as the city of Boston could afford prisons and jails, and any number of millions spent for liquor and for hurtful indulgences, and for the repression of vice and crime, it could afford to spend money for this peaceful and healthful and elevating enjoyment for the people."

Making at least his third appearance at a public meeting for parks, Richard Henry Dana, Jr., declared that the entire Boston region had declined in natural beauty as the population had grown.

Fresh Pond and Jamaica Pond were being fouled by abutting manufactories and tanneries. The "Athens of America" had "Allowed every city in the United States to get in advance of it." Dana was particularly pleased that the Commission had consulted on their plan with Olmsted, "who had laid out Central Park, and he is the highest authority on the construction of parks in the country; and he has been all over the neighborhood, viewing the localities. . . . What is the result? Rather than merely a water park or a country park, a system [of parks] based on the natural characteristics of the neighborhood of Boston."

Like so many others, Oliver Wendell Holmes urged immediate action. He thought that the highest priority should be a park along the lower Charles to relieve the crowded tenement district spilling off the north slope of Beacon Hill. He said a park nearby would become a "priceless sanitorium" for the district. But more, Holmes wanted "a chain of pleasure grounds" that took in the entire city. "We must provide ourselves with the equipment, not of a village community, not of a thriving town, but of a true metropolis. . . ."

The Reverend Neale, oldest settled pastor in the city, declared: "We are all of us, I suppose, more or less subject to the blues, businessmen, clergymen, and even politicians. The best remedy is a walk, a good long stretch into the country, fresh air, a hearty laugh with a friend. . . ." Though he hoped that parks wouldn't "supersede the sanctuary and the sermon" on Sundays, he asserted that "a ramble through green fields at any time, and along sparkling streams, is better than the sick-bed, or the apothecary's drugs and doses."

As a spiritual balance to Neale, Reverend J. P. Bodfish, Rector of the Catholic Cathedral of the Holy Cross, also spoke. Bodfish was concerned about the mean condition of the lower classes and felt that parks would be a great help in their moral salvation. "When I think of the conditions under which a great many of our poor people live, I am not very much surprised that they are goaded into desperation to commit some fearful crime, because we know that where a person lives in the country . . . he is removed from temptations that are common to a large city . . . therefore everyone who wishes well for the religious welfare of the people would be glad to have these parks established as a real moral agent in the community and to the people."

On June 26, 1876, the city's Committee on Common and Public Grounds favorably recommended the park commissioner's plan and urged the city to appropriate nearly five million dollars to begin the actual work. Petitions signed by more than a thousand people were submitted to the aldermen requesting immediate action on the parks issue. The park commissioners were ordered to bond the lands they had selected so that the Council and aldermen would have a more exact picture of the actual costs.

A Joint Special Committee was formed to work out the problems. In November the Committee recommended that the loan be authorized, but the Common Council refused. Finally in 1877 the City Council and the aldermen agreed to appropriate $900,000 and the work of acquiring land for Boston's park system was finally begun.

Reading:

The transcripts of the park hearings and "People for Parks" meeting are outstanding documents in the history of Boston and fascinating as well. The 1869 hearing will be found in *Boston City Documents* for that year as No. 123. The record of the "People for Parks" meeting will be found in *Public Parks* (Boston: Rockwell and Churchill, 1877). Both are available in the Reference Library of the Boston Public Library.

FREDERICK LAW OLMSTED: THE MASTER

What artist is so noble . . . as he who, with far-reaching conception of beauty and designing power, sketches the outlines, writes the colors, and directs the shadows of a picture so great that Nature shall be employed upon it for generations, before the work he has arranged for her shall realize his intentions.

Frederick Law Olmsted

Landscape architect Frederick Law Olmsted is the individual most responsible for the excellence of the park system in greater Boston, and the resulting quality of life. Working with polluted tidal basins, wasted urban streams, and cut-over hills, he and his Brookline associates changed the shape of our landscape by creating some of the most outstanding parks in the world within the Boston and Metropolitan Park Systems.

Olmsted and Calvert Vaux, an associate, designed New York City's Central Park, the first significant public park in America. Olmsted and his firm also designed Mount Royal Park in Montreal, Prospect Park in Brooklyn, Fairmount Park in Philadelphia, and parks for Louisville, Hartford, Buffalo, and other American cities. He laid out the grounds for Amherst College, Stanford University, the University of California at Berkeley, and Princeton University, the World Columbian Exhibition of 1893 in Chicago, Commodore Vanderbilt's Biltmore Estate, and hundreds of other private estates. His efforts to preserve Yosemite and Niagara Falls for the public's enjoyment were the beginnings of our national and state park systems. His landscaped suburban subdivisions, Sudbrook in Maryland and Riverside in Chicago, have long been the models for enlightened developers, regional planners, and happy residents. The list of Olmsted's accomplishments just seems to go on, yet he came to his profession late, at the age of thirty-five.

The idea of public parks was in its infancy when Olmsted began his work, only two public parks having been created earlier in Europe, Birkenhead and Victoria parks in England. Central Park had first been proposed in 1844 by poet and newspaper editor William Cullen Bryant, and land takings had begun in 1853. But the design for the park and its construction were held up by disputes between the city and the state until 1857. Horace Greeley, Asa Gray, and Bryant all urged Olmsted, who had achieved modest success as an experimental farmer and progressive writer, to apply for the position of park superintendent. In September 1857 he was appointed superintendent of Central Park.

Olmsted and English architect Calvert Vaux created a plan for the park, "Greensward," and together they worked on it for the next fourteen years, overseeing a workforce of thousands. In this project Olmsted tested the theories and themes he would use in hundreds of later works, including the Boston Park System. Olmsted's designs were derived in principle from the landscape aesthetics of William Gilpin, proponent of the idea of the picturesque. The picturesque theory of design sought natural-seeming landscapes as opposed to the formal gardens of the Italian or French style. Olmsted's works derived from and expanded upon the works of English Romantic landscape gardeners Humphrey Repton and Capability Brown. Olmsted believed that the beauty of nature was a necessary corrective to the constrictive urban environment of post-Industrial Revolution cities. He was sure that pleasing views would not only soothe the harried minds of cityfolk, but also that

parks would elevate their morality. Although he thought that rich and cultured people were best prepared to enjoy parks, it was particularly the poor and working classes whom he wanted his works to benefit. He and others felt that parks would become "the lungs of the city," helping stamp out the rampant spread of disease. Thus a park would be art for the upper classes and exercise, air, and moral uplift for the masses.

In 1861 Olmsted left his duties at Central Park, tired of the political wranglings of the city administration. He joined the Northern Civil War effort as executive secretary of the U.S. Sanitary Commission, predecessor of the Army Medical Corps and the Red Cross. In 1863 after two exhausting years, he left Washington for California to become superintendent of the Mariposa Mining Estates. While in California he became a leader in the fight to preserve the Yosemite Valley, serving as commissioner of Yosemite and Mariposa Big Tree Grove and writing the legislation that made Yosemite the first state park in America.

In 1865 Olmsted resumed work on Central Park, though the political difficulties remained. As work haltingly progressed on the park, Olmsted also designed Prospect and Mount Royal parks and led the campaign to preserve Niagara Falls.

Olmsted came to Boston in 1870 to deliver a lecture titled "Public Parks and the Enlargement of Towns" at a meeting of the American Social Science Association, of which he was a founding member. While in Boston, he met with Arboretum Director Charles Sprague Sargent to discuss the prospect of laying out Harvard's planned arboretum. Six years later, Olmsted was called in by the recently constituted Boston Park Commission for advice on their plans for a Boston park system. In 1878 Olmsted was called in again to review plans submitted for the design of the proposed filling in of Boston's Back Bay. Olmsted found none of the designs to be really suitable, and so the Park Commission asked him to submit a design of his own. The Commission was so impressed with Olmsted's design that they appointed him landscape architect for the whole park system.

Olmsted was challenged by the scale and diversity of his work in Boston and also found the city a congenial place that respected both his genius and civic virtue, in contrast to the political corruption he found in so many other cities where he worked. In 1883 he purchased a house to serve as home and office in Brookline, a town whose tree-lined streets impressed him. His friends, architects H. H. Richardson and Robert Peabody, and Sargent all lived in the same neighborhood. From that house, which he named Fairsted, Olmsted and his apprentices worked on his projects around the country, at the same time giving special attention to the Boston parks.

In 1895 Olmsted retired, leaving his son, stepson, and a former apprentice, Charles Eliot, to carry on the work of landscaping America's cities. In December of that year his mind snapped and he was admitted to McLean Asylum, where he had laid out the grounds just a few years earlier. He died there eight years later. Though his body withered away, his spirit still flowers in the many parks he designed throughout the Boston area.

Reading:

The best (and most reasonably priced) introduction to Olmsted and his works is *Frederick Law Olmsted, Sr.,* by Fabos, Milde, and Weinmayr. An excellent discussion of Olmsted's theories and aims is *Art of the Olmsted Landscape* by Kelly, Guillet, and Hern. Two fine biographies are *FLO* by Roper and *Parkmaker* by Stevenson. These and other books on Olmsted are available at Olmsted National Historic Site in Brookline.

The recently released *Frederick Law Olmsted and the Boston Park System* by Cynthia Ziatvevsky is an excellent, lavishly illustrated, thoroughly researched account of Olmsted's work in Boston.

Massachusetts Association for Olmsted Parks:

This organization seeks to increase public understanding of the value of Olmsted's parks and to protect the parks themselves. For more information, write: Massachusetts Association of Olmsted Parks, 25 Edgehill Road, Brookline, MA 02146.

FREDERICK LAW OLMSTED NATIONAL HISTORIC SITE
99 Warren Street, Brookline, MA 02146

Hours: Friday, Saturday, and Sunday—noon to 4:30 P.M.
Admission: no charge

Fairsted, Olmsted's house and office in Brookline, remained the site of the firm he founded from the time of his retirement until 1979, when the house and landscaped grounds were designated a National Historic Site. Olmsted and the firm that carried on his work have been an incredible force for the beautification and preservation of the American landscape. Birmingham, Denver, Bridgeport, Hartford, New Haven, Atlanta, Chicago, Louisville, Lexington (Kentucky), Baltimore, Brookline, Cambridge, Lowell, Buffalo, New York City, Rochester, Seattle, Philadelphia, Memphis, and Milwaukee: each of these cities has at least six parks designed by Olmsted and his successors. In all, some five thousand parcels have been designed at Fairsted, ranging from private estates and gardens to such national parks as Grand Canyon, Everglades, and Arcadia.

As the firm grew, beginning during Olmsted's active practice, the house was expanded with additions. Each addition used only half-stairways so that the building would conform to its site and residential neighborhood. At its peak in the 1920s, the firm employed sixty landscape architects, draughtsmen, secretaries, arborists, and other personnel. More than a hundred thousand plans and drawings were made here, and a copy of each was stored in three great document vaults. These plans and maps are still in the house and they provide a graphic record of Olmsted and his legacy from 1860 to 1979.

Frederick Law Olmsted National Historic Site is a place that anyone who loves parks must visit. The walls are hung with maps, photographs, and other exhibits of the Olmsted legacy. A bookstore features works by and about Olmsted.

Directions:

MBTA: Riverside Green Line to Brookline Hills. Walk down Cypress Street to Boylston Street (Route 9), turn right at the lights, then left at the lights at the top of the hill to Warren Street.

Auto or bike: Boylston Street (Route 9) west from Boston, through Brookline Village. Turn left at lights at top of hill to Warren Street.

Telephone: 566-1689

3. COMMONWEALTH AVENUE MALL
Commonwealth Avenue, Arlington Street to Charlesgate Park
12 acres   *Boston Park System   1894

Activities: strolling, historic sites

Back Bay was once a tidal marsh and mudflat, flooded twice a day by the Atlantic pouring up the Charles River. The waters of the bay were bounded by the foot of Boston Common, Washington

Street in Roxbury, and Sewell's Point, now Kenmore Square. In 1821 a stone, rubble, and earthen dam was built from the foot of the Common to Kenmore Square by the Roxbury and Boston Mill Company. They hoped to use tidal power to run mills to grind grain, cut lumber, and manufacture cotton goods, woolens, paint, and other commodities. A toll road was laid out across the crest of the dam, now Beacon Street. The dam was not financially successful, but drastically altered the area's fragile estuarine ecology.

The dam cut off cleansing tidal currents, a situation made worse by two railroad embankments built across the "dammed" Bay. Sewage flowing into the Back Bay from local communities began to accumulate. In 1849 the Boston City Council described the Back Bay as "nothing less than a cesspool"; citizens' complaints about the stench often appeared in the newspapers (see Section 42, Charles River Basin).

Finally in 1858, after a long battle with the City of Boston, the Commonwealth of Massachusetts took control of the Bay and began to fill it with trainloads of gravel from Needham. In 1860 Arlington Street was still a "muddy beach," yet only a few years later, the state was selling land there at three times the cost of filling. Many of Boston's wealthiest citizens flocked to the Back Bay from their crowded quarters on Beacon Hill, building brownstone houses for themselves. To enhance the value of the new district, the state decided to make the central street of the district, which it had named Commonwealth Avenue after itself, into a pleasure drive. A contest was held for a design. Architect Arthur Gilman won with a plan for a Parisian-style boulevard that included a central promenade and setbacks from the street, so that gardens and trees could be planted between each house and the sidewalk.

In the late 1880s, as the Boston Park System was nearing completion, Olmsted and the park commissioners refined Gilman's idea so that Commonwealth Avenue would be a green link between Boston Common and the Public Garden and the rest of the park system. Numerous elm trees were planted and the promenade was landscaped—thus a pleasant stroll or carriage ride could be had all the way from the State House to Franklin Park.

When the mall was laid out only horse traffic filled the street. Fashionable patricians, whose architect-designed homes lined the boulevard, came out to promenade on Sunday afternoons. The elms grew tall, their branches spreading over the road, creating a cool, cavernlike effect from Boston Garden to Charlesgate Park.

Statues:

Alexander Hamilton, statesman and first U.S. Secretary of the Treasury, by William, 1865.

William Lloyd Garrison, abolitionist and publisher of *The Liberator*, by Olin Levi Warner, 1886.

Patrick Andrew Collins, second Irish mayor of Boston, by Henry H. and Theo Alice Kitson, 1906.

John Glover, Revolutionary general from Marblehead, by Martin Milmore, 1875.

Leif Eriksson, Norse explorer, by Anne Whitney, 1887.

Samuel Eliot Morison, author and historian, 1982.

Activities:

Although all the old elms have died and carriages have been replaced by automobiles, Commonwealth Avenue is still among Boston's loveliest streets. The promenade has been replanted and is a pleasant place to stroll or sit. If you have an active imagination, try to picture the folks who lived in the houses up and down the boulevard.

Reading:

Houses of Boston's Back Bay by Bainbridge Bunting describes almost every house along Commonwealth Avenue, its detail, architect, and original owner. *Boston: A Topographical History* by Walter Muir Whitehill describes the filling of Back Bay, with many maps.

Directions:

Commonwealth Avenue from Arlington Street to Kenmore Square.

MBTA: Arlington Street station, then two short blocks to Commonwealth Avenue.

4. BACK BAY FENS (THE FENWAY)
Bounded by the Fenway and Park Drive
150 acres   *Boston Park Department   1879

Activities: strolling, picnicking, playing fields, jogging, totlot, rose garden, birdwatching

Hours: dawn to dusk

As the receiving basin of the Back Bay mill dam was being filled to create the Back Bay district (see Section 3, Commonwealth Avenue Mall) in the 1860s, two simultaneous issues were galvanizing the citizens of Boston: the need for public parks and the need to do something about the mill dam's basin. A continuous clamor of complaints came from the upper-class residents of the newly filled area along Commonwealth Avenue about the stench coming from the basin mudflats every time the tide went out. Raw sewage was pouring down the Stony Brook and the Muddy River and settling on the flats of the basin. Typhoid and malaria were increasing at an alarming rate among the poor who had erected shacks on the wastelands around the basin. The newspapers of the city, reflecting the worries of the people, demanded that something be done about "the pestilential vapors flowing out of the Back Bay and covering the city."

One hundred acres of the basin was purchased by the Park Commission at ten cents a square foot as their first land acquisition in the city. A design competition offering a five-hundred-dollar prize was held for the "Back Bay Sanitary Improvements" early in 1877. Nearly two dozen plans were offered to the Commission and the prize was awarded to Herman Grundel. But when his plan was submitted to Frederick Law Olmsted for review—Olmsted already having consulted with the Commission on their 1876 preliminary park proposal—the plan was shown to leave unsolved the huge sanitary problem. Olmsted formulated a new plan that was enthusiastically accepted by the commissioners. They found Olmsted's plan so exemplary that they retained him as landscape architect for the entire Boston Park System.

Olmsted's plan called for a tidal gate across the mouth of the Charles River to control the water level in the Back Bay, preventing the incoming high tide from flooding the South End. The bay was to be excavated as a holding basin for floodwaters pouring out of the Stony Brook culvert; these floodwaters could be released through the tidal gate into the Charles at low tide. The mud dredged from the holding basin was to be piled on the shore to make firm ground for the surrounding parkland. About the park itself Olmsted wrote: "The scenery of a winding brackish creek, within wooded banks; gaining interest from the meandering course of the water; numerous points and coves softened in their outlines by thickets and with much delicate variety in tone and color through varied, and, in landscape art, novel forms of perennial and herbaceous growths, the picturesque elements emphasized

by a few necessary structures strong but unobtrusive." Olmsted's overall image of the park was of "a fenny verdure, meandering water, and blooming islets." The area was named the Back Bay Fens after the marshlands or fens of eastern England.

From 1880 to 1890 the old millpond was dredged from two to five feet deep and the shore built up with the spoils. The Fens appears to be a lucky accident of preservation, but in fact, "the landscape was entirely created from foul tidal flats." Salt water entered the Fens at each high tide until 1910 when the Charles River Dam was built.

When the Back Bay Fens was completed in the early 1890s, it immediately attracted thousands of horseback riders, carriage drivers, and promenaders, at the same time encouraging residential and institutional development in the surrounding district. Over the next twenty years the Museum of Fine Arts, Mrs. Gardner's "Palace," several colleges, and many apartment houses were built around the park.

Once the landscaping was accomplished, the Fens was regularly embellished. In 1894 a statue by Daniel Chester French memorializing John Boyle O'Reilly, editor of the Catholic daily *The Pilot* and vocal proponent of public parks, was erected across from Westland Avenue. A few years later the entrance gates at Westland Avenue were put up, designed by Guy Lowell, architect of the Museum of

Fine Arts. The city's Scots, not to be outdone by their Irish brethren, contributed funds for a statue of the poet Robert Burns by Henry Kitson in 1920. In 1937 a statue of John Endicott, first governor of Massachusetts Bay Colony, by sculptor C. P. Jennewan, was placed across from the Museum of Fine Arts in a small patch of greensward.

Playing fields were laid out in the Fens in 1912 and surrounded by a stadium in 1925; the fieldhouse followed three years later. In 1927 the Fire Department built its beaux arts-style Fire Control Center on the eastern shore to receive all fire alarms in the city. The Rose Garden was laid out and planted on designs by landscape architects Shurtleff and Merrill in 1930. During World War II a marshy portion of the Fens was converted into a Victory Garden, that area still being used today as perhaps the largest urban community garden in New England.

While the trees grew taller and the shrub plantings filled out, the postwar period witnessed the rather needless devastation of two parts of Olmsted's design. Much of the little park around the Charlesgate floodbasins, which connected the Fens and Charles River parklands, was obliterated by the Park Drive overpass from Storrow Drive. At the other end of the Fens the connecting link between the Fens and the Riverway was buried beneath Sears, Roebuck's parking lot, a misuse of a work of landscape art. Nonetheless the many willows, dogwoods, lindens, hawthornes, and red oaks planted under Olmsted's direction form some of the most beautiful landscape scenery found in any urban park in the world.

Activities:
This is a sanctuary of tranquility in the midst of the city, fine for a small picnic, a romantic rendezvous, or a simple stroll. A jogging circuit is slowly edging toward completion. Ballfields must be reserved with the Boston Park Department. Toilets at field house. The birding here can be amazing for the city: on a typical summer afternoon you may see a purple finch, kingfisher, snowy egret, green heron, or Baltimore oriole here.

Directions:
MBTA: The Fens is a short walk from the Museum of Fine Arts stop on the Arborway Green Line subway.
Bike or auto: Commonwealth Avenue or Beacon Street to Charlesgate Park to Park Drive.
Or: Boylston Street (near the Prudential Center) to the Fenway.

5. CHARLESBANK PARK
Across Storrow Drive from Massachusetts General Hospital and Charles River Park apartments
17 acres   *MDC   1891 (Boston Park)

Activities: picnicking, ballfields, tennis, swimming pool, jogging, bicycling
Hours: 8:00 A.M. to dusk

In 1879 the West End (or West Boston) was the largest of Boston's crowded tenement neighborhoods. Poor Irish and Italian immigrants, packed into the run-down buildings of the district, had the highest infant mortality rates in the city. Therefore, the park commissioners decided to build nearby the first park in the city constructed solely as a park. They chose a site along the Charles River that was occupied by cheap wooden tenements and fishing shacks. The buildings were bought and demolished, a seawall was built, and the land was filled and leveled, creating the first embankment park along the Boston side of the Charles.

Charlesbank Park, designed by Olmsted, included the first free outdoor gymnasiums in the country. Olmsted's object was to provide "rational outdoor education." The two gyms themselves, one for men and one for women and children, were designed and furnished by D. A. Sargent, professor of physical culture at Harvard.

The women's track, screened by a wall of shrub plantings, enclosed one of the first children's playgrounds in the city. It had newfangled swings, seesaws, slides, sandboxes, ladders, and poles, all equipment just recently invented by Boston's Joseph Lee. Free day-care was provided to working mothers.

When Charlesbank opened in 1891, after twelve years of delay, it was an immediate success. Four years later, a local reporter declared that the park "had already saved hundreds of infants from cholera."

Except for a big old maple or two, little remains of the original Charlesbank. In 1947 the park was transferred to the MDC, and soon after this much of it was buried underneath Storrow Drive. Yet it remains the vital first link in the chain of parkland that lines the Charles today (see Section 42, Charles River Basin).

Activities:

Picnicking: Under a few shady trees along the river. Some benches.

Jogging, walking, bicycling: The path along the Charles begins here, just below the dam, and runs all the way to Watertown and Cambridge.

Tennis: Four asphalt courts. First come, first served.

Athletic fields: Two softball, one soccer. Contact MDC, telephone 727-5118.

Swimming pool: Open 9:30 A.M. until dusk, summers. Information, telephone 523-9746.

Directions:

Cross the street by the pedestrian overpass at the end of Charles Street, turn right.

MBTA: Science Museum station on Green Line subway or Charles Street station on Red Line.

Auto: End of Storrow Drive. No parking at Charlesbank Park.

Bicycle: Dam end of Charles River bicycle trail.

6. OLMSTED PARK AND THE RIVERWAY
Riverway and Jamaicaway, Boston and Brookline
*Boston and Brookline Park Departments   1881

Activities: walking, bicycling, nature study, jogging

A chain of picturesque fresh-water ponds, alternating with attractive natural groves and meadows. . . .

Frederick Law Olmsted

Muddy River was the boundary between Muddy River Hamlet (renamed Brookline in 1705) and Boston. Originally the little brook was surrounded by farmsteads and pastures; by the 1870s it had become a waste place, filled with pollution, abutted by dumps, and lined with squalid shacks. The tracks of the Boston and Albany Railroad ran along the west bank. Yet in Olmsted's eyes the Muddy River had the potential to be a linear greensward connecting the Fens with Jamaica Pond, Franklin Park, and the Arboretum. His 1879 Boston park plan included this link and in the following year he submitted a formal plan for rehabilitating the Muddy River.

Between 1885 and 1895 Boston and Brookline bought the property along their respective riverbanks and constructed the park according to Olmsted's design. More than any other site in the Park System, today's Muddy River appears to be a remnant natural area, yet, like the Fens, it is almost completely man-made. The brook channel was excavated and the banks sculpted and molded with gravel and many tons of earth. A planted embankment was constructed between the narrow park and the Boston and Albany tracks (now the Massachusetts Bay Transportation Authority, or MBTA) to screen the sight and sound of the railroad out of the pastoral scene. The Riverway and Jamaicaway were laid out alongside the park as carriage drives. To protect the park from any bustle associated with the carriage roads, these were designed not to be seen from within the park. Inside the park, bridle trails and walking paths were built.

A number of structures were constructed to complete the linear park, including a great Olmsted-designed bulkhead above Ward's Pond at the head of the valley. Several small bridges around Leverett Pond and over the little river valley, and a shelter near Longwood Avenue were designed jointly by Olmsted and the firm of Shepley, Rutan, and Coolidge. At the foot of the park, maintenance buildings were put up.

The final problem Olmsted dealt with was the polluted waters of the brook. Though the Muddy River appears to enter the Fens near the Sears, Roebuck building, in fact, a conduit was built directly from the foot of the river to the Charles, excluding the stinking water from the Fens.

Olmsted Park, allowed to decline over the years, now is one of the few places in the city that feels like a real wilderness. Great oaks, among the biggest in the region, tower over the hills and ponds. The upper reaches of the Muddy River are lined with goatsbeard, forget-me-not, iris, violet, and sensitive fern. The little ponds are crowded by purple loosestrife and waving groves of reeds. Viburnum, flowering dogwood, and other ornamental trees and shrubs enliven the Brookline side of Leverett Pond, where ducks ripple the water of a quiet afternoon.

The lower portion of the Muddy River parkland, the Riverway, is lined with great oaks, silver maples, and birches. Buttonbush, blue and yellow iris, sweet pepperbush, and flowering dogwood hang over the water's edge. Raspberry and elderberry bushes alternate with little groves of tupelo and beech just back from the water. It is not unusual to see a green heron, a kingfisher, or a snowy egret standing in the turbid shallows, looking for a sunfish or goldfish hiding beneath the overhanging boughs.

Activities:

Despite some litter and facilities that have been allowed to become a bit decrepit, the "Muddy River Improvement" has been somewhat rehabilitated in recent years. It is a beautiful green ribbon running through the metropolis.

Walk on either side of the river from the front of Sears, Roebuck to Jamaica Pond, a round-trip distance of about four miles. This can be one of the most tranquilizing walks in Boston. Lots of benches for relaxing in the deep shade along the slow-moving river.

Bicycling and jogging: Part of the continuous route from the Charles, through the Fens, to Jamaica Pond, the Arboretum, and Franklin Park. Delightful, but use caution crossing the intervening streets.

Ballfields: Two fine softball and baseball fields surrounded by shade trees. Illuminated at night. Boston Park Department reservations required.

Directions:

MBTA: Fenway or Longwood stations on the Riverside

Green Line.
Auto: Boylston Street to Leverett Pond near the Jamaicaway.
Parking: Alongside Leverett Pond or at ballfields.

7. JAMAICA POND
Jamaicaway, Jamaica Plain
122 acres   *Boston Park Department   1890

Activities: boating, walking, jogging, ballfields, bicycling, fishing, picnicking
Hours: dawn to dusk
Admission: free

Jamaica Pond is the largest and purest body of water naturally occurring in Boston. This kettlehole pond formed when a massive chunk of ice broke off the retreating glacier twelve to fifteen thousand years ago. The chunk was surrounded by dirt and rock tumbling in meltwater streams from the face of the glacier. When the ice block finally melted, there was a big hole where it had been, surrounded by walls of gravel, sand, and rock dust. Walden Pond, the Mystic Lakes, and many Cape Cod ponds were formed in a similar manner. Natural groundwater springs then filled the abyss. Jamaica Pond is sixty-two acres in extent and fifty-three feet deep at its deepest point.

In 1795 the pond was ringed by the large farms of Jamaica Plain. At that time a group of businessmen formed the Jamaica Pond Aqueduct Company as a water-supply business in Boston with wholly inadequate supplies of the vital fluid, supplying 1,500 households out of 8,000 in the city irregularly by 1825. After the Cochituate Aqueduct was put into operation in 1848, the private water business rapidly declined and eventually the city bought out the company.

Back at the end of the eighteenth century many of the farms around the pond were being converted into summer estates by wealthy Brahmin families. In those days going to Jamaica Plain from downtown could be a two-hour journey, and so it was really "country." Concurrently, and somewhat ironically, the pond also became industrialized at that time—the same clear water that had attracted the water jobbers now put a gleam in the eye of the ice merchants. Boston was the center of the international ice trade and the people of Boston themselves had developed a penchant for this newfangled product in their summer drinks and food coolers. Cheap housing for the ice cutters was built on the shore, as were stables for the horses that dragged the ice off the pond, down to the piers, and later into the iceboxes of sweltering Boston.

After Jamaica Pond was again proposed as a park in 1882, the city finally purchased the pond and its shores in 1890. Olmsted described the pond and his design for it: "a natural sheet of water, with quiet, graceful shores, rear banks of varied elevation and contour, for the most part shaded by a fine natural forest growth to be brought out overhangingly, darkening the water's edge and favoring great beauty in reflections and flickering half-lights. At conspicuous points numerous well-grown pines, happily massed, and picturesquely disposed."

Following Olmsted's plan, the shores of the pond were completely rebuilt and graded with granite, gravel, and loam. A variety of tree and shrub species were artistically planted to frame the pond and unconsciously soothe hurried city people; irregular rows were also planted to screen out the bustle of nearby roads. Edmund Wheelwright designed the gazebo and combination boathouse and concession stand in the German Gothic style.

Across the street from the pond a monument was erected to historian Francis Parkman. The monument's Indian portrait, carved by Daniel Chester French out of an immense block of native granite, remains one of the most noble anywhere of the race that drank these clear waters long ago. Cucumber, tulip, magnolia, and walnut trees now in their prime form a green frame around the memorial. The trees planted around the pond have grown well since Olmsted's day, and the big sugar and silver maples, oak, beech, white pine, and sycamore attest to the foresight required for landscape architecture.

Activities:

Jamaica Pond is still an egalitarian stomping ground. Bicyclists of every age and complexion fly by. Mothers and fathers from Honduras and Cambridge are pushing carriages. Joggers of every shape and size weave in and out of the amblers. The many benches are a United Nations. The atmosphere here is open yet soothing, busy but not outrageous, and just about everybody seems relaxed.

A bathroom is open at the concession stand in the

summer during the day. A bubbler provides water on summer days and a small snack bar sells cold drinks, candy bars, potato chips, and ice cream.

Jogging or bicycling: The one-and-a-half-mile asphalt and synthetic path around the pond is mostly level; with a few gentle grades it follows the banks and enters little shaded woods. Bubblers at boathouse. The track is often crowded, so that courtesy is always in order. This is a place to work out, not go "all out."

Boating: Rowboat rentals on summer days, two dollars an hour at boathouse; a real bargain. Room for four or five people in a boat. No private boats.

Fishing: The pond has been stocked with trout for many years. Mayor Curley, who lived across the street, was traditionally the first to cast his line in every year when the season opened. Several years ago the pond was reclaimed: too many fishermen and children had set sunfish and perch caught elsewhere free in the pond and they had prospered, eliminating trout habitat.

The pond is stocked with trout usually twice a year. Pickerel, largemouth bass, hornpout, and perch thrive in the pond as well. The cool waters of the deep pond produce some good-sized fish. In addition to a state fishing license, a special permit is required to fish Jamaica Pond—it is freely granted to anyone who writes or goes in person to the Parks and Recreation Department, Room 802, City Hall, Boston, MA 02201. For free depth chart see Fishing Section at the back of this book.

Walking: Excellent strolling around the pond, including Pine Bank Hill and the Parkman Memorial. Lots of benches. Exercise course with twenty-four stations if you want to work out.

Picnicking: Grassy knolls and plenty of park benches; toss a blanket down. Bubbler, bathrooms, and snack bar at boathouse. Please don't litter. Big timber jungle gym and space to run around or play catch on far side of Pine Bank Hill.

Ballfields: Reasonably well-maintained baseball and softball diamond on hill.

The Open Door Theater: The park presents plays by Shakespeare, Genêt, and contemporary playwrights as well as concerts, all under the stars in the park's outdoor amphitheater. Call Park Department or consult newspaper listings.

Directions:
MBTA: Arborway Green Line to Center Street. Get out at Pond Street and walk up that street four minutes to the pond.
Bicycling: Trail begins in front of Kenmore Square Sears, Roebuck, then runs through Riverway and Olmsted Park to Jamaica Pond. A terrific urban bike path, but use caution crossing the highways.
Auto: On the Jamaicaway a mile south of Boylston Street.
Parking: Around pond.

8. ARNOLD ARBORETUM
The Arborway, Jamaica Plain, MA 02130
265 acres   1872   Harvard University
1882   Boston Park System

Activities: nature study, walking, jogging, birdwatching, and scenic, historic, interpretive programs and lectures
Map: map of trails and plantings available from Visitor Center for twenty-five cents or send SASE and a quarter
Hours: dawn to dusk
Admission: free

"America's Greatest Garden"

In 1863 James Arnold, a wealthy New Bedford businessman and amateur gardener, left a portion of his estate in trust to Harvard University "for the promoting of Agricultural or horticultural improvements. . . ." Arnold's trustees moved slowly until Harvard botanist Asa Gray proposed that the Harvard Corporation use the money to create an arboretum, a living museum of trees, near the university's herbarium (dried plant collection) in Cambridge. The nation's leading plant scientist, defender of Darwin's theories, and author of *Trees of North America,* Gray wanted his students to have the opportunity to examine living specimens rather than relying solely on textbook pictures and dried plants for their education.

Harvard and Arnold's trustees were enthusiastic about this novel idea. But both feared the annual interest on the trust would not be enough for land acquisition, never mind plantings and management.

Out in the Jamaica Plain section of West Roxbury, Harvard had recently opened the Bussey Institution of Agriculture and Horticulture on land left to the university by Benjamin Bussey in 1842 for that purpose. Because the school took up only seven acres of the 394-acre estate, President Charles W. Eliot of Harvard suggested that this would make a better site for the proposed arboretum than the increasingly congested Harvard campus. After two years of negotiation Harvard and the Arnold trustees agreed to create an Arnold Arboretum on 137 acres of the Bussey estate. Harvard was to raise "as far as is practicable, all the trees, shrubs, herbaceous plants, either indigenous or exotic, which can be raised in the open air of said West Roxbury. . . ." With the annual income of $3,000 from the trust, Harvard was to hire a professor to superintend the project. A few months later Charles Sprague Sargent was hired as Arnold Professor.

Sargent was initially hampered by lack of funds to hire staff, lay out grounds, or even purchase trees. As a result, work progressed slowly at first. In the summer of 1878 Sargent and Olmsted met to discuss the possible inclusion of the Arboretum in the proposed Boston Park System. The two men decided to suggest to Harvard and the City of Boston that the Arboretum somehow be included in the Park System. After four years of contentious negotiations— the city was resistant to helping the private university and Harvard was afraid of the city's politics—an agreement was reached. In exchange for Harvard's opening the Arboretum to the public, the city would pay the cost of preparing the grounds, building roads, and providing police protection. The Bussey land was conveyed to the city and leased back to Harvard for a thousand years at a dollar a year. The Arboretum was to serve as a "museum of living plants, scientific station, school of forestry, and popular educator." In 1883 work on the Arboretum finally began.

By August 1886 seventy thousand native and exotic trees and shrubs were in the ground; in another year the total reached one hundred and twenty thousand. Each plant was individually sited by Sargent and his assistants according to his scientific plan. Olmsted and his young apprentice Charles Eliot ensured that the plantings would please the eye as well as the intellect of the beholder.

Sargent had made expeditions to study trees through much of North America, and so he was satisfied that the Arboretum's collection included nearly every tree or shrub on the continent that would grow in West Roxbury. But the task of the Arboretum was broader—it was to have *all* trees that would grow there no matter where in the world they originated. Cuttings arrived from England's Kew Gardens and horticulturalists in Europe, but Sargent grew more fascinated by the relationship of American species to those of East Asia, particularly Japan and China. After soliciting cuttings from English plant collectors in Asia, Sargent began sending out collectors of his own.

The Arboretum's greatest East Asian collector was a young Englishman, Ernest H. "China" Wilson. Wilson toured the unexplored interior of China during the dangerous days of the Boxer Rebellion. Climbing steep mountain ranges, trekking across barren plateaus, he searched for new plant species all the way to the forbidden steppes of Tibet. Thousands of small cuttings, dried seeds, and pressed plants resulted from his investigations.

Once the cuttings and seeds had completed their ten-thousand-mile journey to Jamaica Plain, the principal Arboretum propagator, Jackson Dawson, nursed them into life. Dawson's prowess was legendary: it was said that he was "capable almost of resurrecting a dead stick and certainly of coaxing into vigorous growth a twig found in the pocket of a shooting-jacket weeks after this had been laid aside."

Before he retired in 1927, Sargent set the Arboretum's future priorities: "The exploration of the tropical forests of the world will require perhaps a century and a large expenditure of money to accomplish. It is this work that the Arboretum should begin and steadily push forward." Today the Arboretum sends out botanical researchers to the outback of China, the rain forests of Costa Rica, and the jungles of Borneo. This facet of the Arboretum's work, nearly invisible to us, has become increasingly important: the tropical forests of the world are being logged off at a rapid rate just as we are beginning to understand their incredible diversity of species and their importance in sustaining the world's supply of oxygen.

Activities:

Arnold Arboretum is among the most beautiful and comprehensive arboreta in the world. From April through November it is a changing panorama of bright natural colors. The little surprises that Olmsted and Sargent planned for our education and delight increase with each passing year as seeds and cuttings planted a hundred years ago reach maturity.

Blossom time: The map prepared by the Arboretum, available at the administration building or by sending twenty-five cents and a SASE, gives a month-by-month breakdown of what is in bloom. Call 524-1717 for a tape-recorded what's-in-bloom message.

Walking: The Arboretum is an exceedingly lovely place to wander around. The easy grade of most roads and trails makes it a fine place for families with young children or oldsters, yet there is enough territory to give the most energetic legs a good stretching. Guided walks are available by contacting the administration building. Be sure to pick up a map of the Arboretum, which includes not only roads and trails but also major planting groups.

Birdwatching: Nearly a hundred and fifty species of birds have been sighted here. For guided birdwalks call 325-1483.

Jogging: Permitted, but try not to disturb other visitors.

Not permitted: Picnicking, bicycling, or picking, removing, or damaging any plant materials or labels.

Special activities: The Arboretum offers an extensive series of lectures and courses ranging from wild edible plants to pruning roses. Guided walks are offered during the warmer months. Call 524-1718 for more information on Arboretum events.

The Hunnewell Visitor Center: Now open to the public, has an art gallery with changing, well-thought-out exhibits and a gift shop filled with prints, cards, and books of interest to the plant or landscape fancier.

Directions:

Green Line Arborway car up Center Street to Civil War monument at South Street. Walk one block to the Arborway, cross to Arboretum entrance.

Bike: Bicycle path from Fenway to Riverway, through Olmsted Park and around Jamaica Pond to the Arborway and entrance.

Auto: Jamaicaway to Arborway.

Parking: At entrance and along Arborway.

Telephone: 524-1717

9. FRANKLIN PARK
Morton Street and Blue Hill Avenue, Jamaica Plain, Roxbury, Dorchester
500 acres (originally 527)   *Boston Park Department
   1885–1898

Activities: picnicking, jogging, walking, bicycling, horse-back riding, ballfields, tennis, scenic viewing, nature study, ski touring
Map: free from Franklin Park Coalition (see explanation below)
Hours: dawn to dusk
Admission: free

The prime object will be to present favorably to public enjoyment a body of rural and sylvan scenery, large in scale, simple and tranquil in character; and, in contrast and as a foil to this, passages of a wild, rugged, picturesque and forest-like aspect.
Frederick Law Olmsted
"Report on West Roxbury Park," 1884

The Hope Diamond dangling at the end of the Emerald Necklace, Franklin Park is not only the largest park in Boston, but it is also considered one of the three finest Olmsted park designs of several hundred around the country. Standing on the crest of Scarboro Hill we have the illusion of being in Eden-like Vermont dairy country, waiting for a herd of cows or a soaring hawk to pass. For many years the park has been seen as Roxbury's and Dorchester's turf, but, in fact, the park belongs to all the people of the city: because of its beauty it deserves to be frequented more by all Boston-area citizens.

During the great park debates from 1869 to 1876 no site, with the possible exception of the Back Bay, received more endorsements as a potential park than the rocky pasturelands of West Roxbury. As Frederick Law Olmsted would say in 1886: "What can be said for the property as a whole is this: That there is not within or near the city any other equal extent of ground of as simple, and pleasingly simple, rural aspect."

Olmsted had supported the idea of a West Roxbury park since at least 1876 when he helped the Park Commission in their initial planning of Boston's green spaces. In 1884, the year after he moved his office to Boston, Olmsted, assisted by his son John Charles Olmsted, began to work up plans for the park. His first general plan was presented to the park commissioners a year later, only the name had been changed from West Roxbury Park to Franklin Park. Benjamin Franklin had left a thousand pounds in his will as a bequest to the city of Boston with the stipulation that it be invested for a hundred years before the city gained its use. Someone realized the fund would come due in 1891 and that it would be sufficient to cover the million-dollar-plus cost of acquiring the proposed parkland. In hopes that the fund would be used to pay the park debt, the name was changed to Franklin Park, though ultimately the money was used for other purposes.

In 1885 Boston was virtually the only major American city without a large "country park." New York had its Central Park; Philadelphia, Fairmount Park; and even such smaller cities as Detroit and Buffalo had country parks. A feeling had swept America's cities that everyone needed regular doses of rural scenery as much as vitamins to prevent restlessness and violence, depression, even physical illness. As a social scientist and humanist Olmsted promoted parks as a necessary reform; as a landscape architect he carried the idea to fulfillment. And his plan for Franklin Park realized the ideal: providing rural and wild scenery for the people of Boston.

Olmsted's design, fleshed out in 1886, devoted two thirds of the tract to a Country Park to be used "exclusively with reference to the enjoyment of rural scenery." In this section Olmsted proposed that "nothing be built, nothing set up, nothing planted as a decorative feature; nothing for the gratification of curiosity, nothing for the advancement or popularization of science. These objects are provided for suitably in the Public Garden and the Arboretum. . . ." The lay of the land was felt to be too rocky and rolling for playing fields, though grass tennis courts, croquet grounds, archery ranges, and small children's lawns were all included in the area. In 1891, the plan of the Country Park was altered to include Scarboro Pond, for many people felt that a water scene was imperative in such a large park. This man-made pond was excavated alongside Rock Milton, a sleeping puddingstone (Roxbury conglomerate) leviathan, and was crossed by carriage and footbridges designed by Shepley, Rutan, and Coolidge, successors to H. H. Richardson.

Franklin Park's second major division was the hundred-acre "Wilderness," a woodland intended to remind Bostonians of the face of the land in 1630. John Charles Olmsted designed a massive arch to connect the Wilderness to Ellicottdale. "Ninety-nine Steps" were built of native puddingstone in 1892, leading from the park's circuit road to the summit of Hagbourne Hill, in the center of the "Wilderness," where a lookout and picnic area were laid out.

The third major division of Franklin Park was the "Playstead," a play area for schoolchildren and site for their public ceremonies. The land was leveled and thousands of rocks were removed to make it suitable for playing, then turf was planted. So that children would have a place to shower and change, and their parents could watch them at play, a vast eight-hundred-foot-long Overlook was constructed of boulders cleared from the fields. A shelter building, personally designed by Olmsted to blend into its surroundings, was sited on the Overlook terrace.

The last portion of Franklin Park was to be the "Greeting," the formal entrance to the park and promenade. But the linear plantings, music court, and deer park of the Greeting were never carried out.

In 1894, to ensure that active sports would not disturb the tranquility of Franklin Park or dig up the thin soil, a hundred-acre former muster field was purchased down Blue Hill Avenue and laid out as football and baseball fields. Named Franklin Field, it gave the children of Dorchester a place to let off the steam of youth.

Unlike other sections of the Boston Park System, Franklin Park was not an immediate success. The public seemed more desirous of "doing something" than of passively receiving the beauty of nature, though picnicking, lawn tennis, and horseback riding all became popular. Golfers had begun to use the park in 1896 and from 1915 to 1922 the great meadow of the Country Park was laid out as a golf course.

To attract more people to the park, in 1910 Park Commissioner Robert Peabody, an architect and a friend of Olmsted, proposed a zoo for the undeveloped Greeting space. Arthur Shurcliff, landscape architect and former Olmsted apprentice, was hired as the master planner and designer of the new zoo. In 1911, work began on the flying cage and bear's dens. The dens, which opened in 1913, were stocked with elk, bear, and cougar brought in from Yellowstone Park. In 1914 work began on the elephant house, an ornate building still vivid in the memories of many Bostonians. The fluted granite columns installed at the zoo's entrance in 1917 held up the original dome of Ammi Young's Boston Custom House until removed when the present tower was built by the firm of Peabody and Stearns. In 1929 a pair of statues, "Commerce and

Industry," were placed at the far end of the zoo. These statues, sculpted by Daniel Chester French, had once stood high on the late post office and subtreasury building in Post Office Square.

With staff and maintenance cuts during the Depression, the zoo began to decline: because the zoo had no fence around it both the animals and buildings were repeatedly vandalized. In 1957 the tattered zoo was transferred to the MDC, the feeling being that it was more the region's zoo than just Boston's and so the region should share the bill. The MDC did build a fence around it, but they did not know how to manage a zoo. In 1969 the zoo's direction was turned over to the Boston Zoological Society, a group formed in 1952 to "make Franklin Park Zoo a great place." Soon money began to be allocated to the zoo and improvements began, if slowly. Both the zoo and Franklin Park itself have dramatically improved since 1975. Cars have finally been gotten off the grass by lining the park roads with boulders, many of them from railway embankments being torn up for the Southwest Corridor project. New pathways have been laid out and other improvements have been undertaken. The park is cleaned regularly and is becoming a delightful place once again.

Franklin Park has gotten a reputation as a high crime area in recent years. In fact, the park and the zoo have a much lower crime rate than the surrounding districts. Although walking around after dark can be unsafe here as in any park, during the day people are friendly and the atmosphere is very pleasant. Folks are out jogging around or having picnics, sunning themselves in Ellicottdale or playing softball in the Playstead. Visit one of America's most beautiful country parks if only to stroll around and enjoy the scenery.

Activities:

Picnicking: A small developed picnic area occupies a part of the Wilderness. Scarboro Hill, Schoolmaster Hill, Ellicottdale, and the shady areas around the ballfields are all good places to toss down a blanket.

Jogging and bicycling: A paved pathway leads around the Country Park, providing some of the best runner's scenery in the city. It is approximately 1.5 miles in length and gently graded. A spur ascends Scarboro Hill. The closed-to-traffic roads around the Playstead are also good for jogging or family bicycling.

Fishing: Carp and sunfish in Scarboro Pond.

Horseback riding: The only bridle trail in Boston is here. The trail is a good hour's ride for most people. Stable: Forest Hills Stable, 19 Lotus Street, Jamaica Plain, MA 02130 (behind the MBTA Service Center on Forest Hills Street).

Ballfields: Four softball and baseball fields on the Playstead, one on Ellicottdale. All fields have shade trees suitable for picnics. Ellicottdale has room for soccer, badminton, or volleyball games; bring your own net.

Tot-lots: Two well-equipped tot-lots; one near the corner of Seaver and Humbolt, the other near the corner of Walnut and School.

Tennis: Two new courts near Ellicottdale. Some wait on busy weekends and evenings.

Ski touring: Pleasant track laid down by local skiers or lay down your own. The meadow (golf course), Scarboro Hill, and the Wilderness make for delightful and varied skiing here.

Nature study: Franklin Park probably has the most diverse native flora and fauna of any park within Boston. Scarboro Pond is surrounded by tupelo, red maple, silky dogwood, blue spruce, and yellow and blue iris. On the hill above, flowering dogwood and a grove of European beech flourish. The Wilderness is filled with a large variety of big trees, including walnut, tulip trees, black locust, several species of oak, hickory, and hemlock. The Wilderness also supports an interesting variety of wildflowers, including an abundance of spring violets, musk mallow, and round-leaved pyrola.

"A Field Guide to the Geology of Franklin Park" by James W. Skeehan, S.J., thoroughly describes the geology of the park and gives an excellent description of the formation of the Boston Basin and our ubiquitous puddingstone. The booklet is available for two dollars and fifty cents mailing from the Franklin Park Coalition.

Franklin Park Zoo: Two major exhibits are currently open: A Bird's World and the Hoofed Animal Range. A Bird's World is an indoor walk-through exhibit with five habitats for birds from around the world; exotic birds fly around us during our stroll because no grates or glass separate them from us. Outside, a Free Flight Aviary is inhabited by flying birds in every color of the rainbow, calling and squawking in every bird language imaginable. The artfully designed Hoofed Animal Range includes zebras, antelopes, bongos, markhors, and other exotic animals.

The zoo is improving with each passing year and is already a great place to take children and an interesting spot for adults as well. Admission is free. Open 10:00 A.M. to 4:00 P.M. in the winter and 10:00 A.M. to 5:00 P.M. in the summer. Secure parking in the rear.

Franklin Park Coalition: This citizen's group has led the battle to restore Franklin Park to its glory. They sponsor nature and landscape architecture walks and a range of other activities for children and adults. The group also publishes more than a dozen booklets and brochures about the park. For more information, a list of publications, a free brochure, and a map of Franklin Park send a self-addressed stamped envelope to Franklin Park Coalition, 319 Forest Hills Street, Jamaica Plain, MA 02130.

Reading:
Two Walking Tours of Franklin Park by the Franklin Park Coalition is an excellent guide to the park.

Directions:
MBTA: Take the Orange Line to Forest Hills. Walk five minutes up Morton Street to park entrance.

To the zoo: Take "Mattapan" or "Franklin Park" bus from Egleston station.

Auto: Take Riverway to Jamaicaway to Arborway to rotary and park entrance.

Bicycle: Bike trail from Fenway to Arboretum, down past Forest Hills station, up Morton Street to park entrance.

Parking: Plenty.

10. FOREST HILLS CEMETERY
Forest Hills Avenue, Jamaica Plain, MA 02130
260 acres   *Forest Hills Cemetery Association   1848

Activities: strolling, birdwatching, historic sites, scenic viewing
Hours: 9:00 A.M. to 6:00 P.M.
Admission: free

General Henry Dearborn, first president of the Massachusetts Horticultural Association and designer of Mount Auburn Cemetery, was elected mayor of the Town of Roxbury in 1847. Disturbed about the crowded and neglected condition of that town's cemeteries, he proposed that a "country" cemetery be created similar to Mount Auburn that would not only serve the town's burial needs but also its need for public outdoor space. With the approval of the town several months later, Dearborn and his assistant Daniel Brims began to lay out America's first municipally owned rural cemetery on the site of the old Seaverns farm.

After the grounds were consecrated, the remains of John Eliot, preacher to the Indians who had died in 1690, and Joseph Warren, killed in the Battle of Bunker Hill, were reinterred at Forest Hills. When Roxbury was annexed to Boston in 1868, the cemetery became a private corporation. William Lloyd Garrison, William Ellery Channing, Eugene O'Neill, and e. e. Cummings are among the notables whose graves will be found here.

The beautifully landscaped grounds, planted with flowers, ornamental shrubs, and flowering trees, provide an exceptional show of color in the spring, summer, and fall. The highest hill provides a distant view of the Blue Hills and Dorchester. Though Dearborn's original Egyptian Revival portico is long gone, the cemetery boasts many fine examples of nineteenth-century Gothic Revival architecture: Entrance Gate (1865), Receiving Tomb (1871), Bell Tower (1876), Chapel (1884), and bridge over Greenwood Avenue (1892). Many of the gravestones and monuments are intriguing, particularly Daniel Chester French's "Death Staying the Hand of the Sculptor."

Activities:

Study the ornate gravestones and memorials, enjoy the big old trees and the flowers, stroll the scenic grounds, and look at the birds. Activities that disturb the tranquility of the cemetery are prohibited.

Directions:

Across the street from Forest Hills entrance to Franklin Park. Intersection of Arborway and Morton Street.
MBTA: Five-minute walk up Morton Street from Forest Hills station on the Orange Line or Arborway Green Line.

11. CASTLE ISLAND/CITY POINT
City Point in South Boston
34 acres   *MDC   1891
Activities: swimming, historic site, fishing, walking, picnicking
Hours: 8:00 A.M. to dusk
Admission: no charge

In 1889 Frederick Law Olmsted was given the go-ahead to design a marine park at City Point Battery facing Castle Island. By a special act of Congress and the Secretary of War the city was given the land around Fort Independence on Castle Island, subject to the needs of the military. Olmsted linked the Battery and the island with a footbridge to create Pleasure Bay. Marine Park, as the area was called, was equipped with fishing piers, gyms, beaches, a giant bathhouse (the Head House) designed by City Architect Edmund Wheelwright in the German Gothic style, and boathouses.

The first fort on Castle Island had been erected in 1634 under the authority of Governor John Winthrop as a defense for the new town of Boston. The fort, which consisted merely of a mud house and two wooden stages, was replaced by a pine and rock fort that burned down in 1674. A new fort was built of brick and stone and named Castle William after King William IV. In the years before the Revolution, the fort became the headquarters of the British forces and a refuge for Tories. The hated stamps forced on Americans by the Stamp Act were stored under guard at the fort. It was repaired and upgraded by Royal Governor Hutchinson, and all its more than two hundred cannons were put in working order. After the Battle of Lexington and Concord, the fort became the main naval garrison of the Redcoats, and their soldiers made repeated forays from the fort to harass the Americans and obtain food. But when General Washington's guns were mounted on Dorchester Heights, the British were forced to evacuate Boston and Castle William. Not willing to let the Americans make use of the fort, the British spiked the guns and destroyed the fort before departing.

In 1778 a new fort was constructed and in 1799 it was rededicated by President John Adams as Fort Independence. Beginning in 1801 the old fort was replaced by the present five-pointed star fort, designed in part by military engineer Sylvanus Thayer, and constructed of Quincy granite.

In 1827 Edgar Allen Poe served as a soldier at the fort under the assumed name of Edgar A. Perry. Poe's story, "The Cask of

Amontillado," is based on a rumor he heard recounted there. Ten years earlier two officers had fought a duel at the fort over cards and one of them was killed. The friends of the deceased officer captured the killer and sealed him alive behind a hidden brick wall. This story was considered a mere legend, until a skeleton clothed in an old military uniform was discovered behind a brick wall in 1905.

During the Civil War the fort was garrisoned and its guns were refurbished. Over the objection of President Grover Cleveland, the fort was turned over to Boston's Park Department in 1891 after three years of effort by Congressman Patrick Andrew Collins. But with the outbreak of the Spanish-American War, the army retook control of the fort, converting it into a harbor mining station. After the war the island and fort were again taken over by the town. After several attempts by the federal government to repossess the fort as a lighthouse station, they did retake it as a fort during World War I for troop training and harbor observation. In 1932 the island was connected to Marine Park by a roadway, and in the following year a monument was erected on the island to Donald McKay of East Boston, "Father of the Clipper Ship." The fort was again manned during World War II and again returned to the state in 1962.

Marine Park was very popular when it opened in 1891, and old photographs show thousands of bathers and picnickers using Pleasure Bay and the Head House. In 1912 the Aquarium in Marine Park opened the doors to its barrel-vaulted interior lined with fish tanks. Wheelwright's Head House was destroyed by fire in 1942 and the Aquarium was torn down in the mid-1950s.

Activities:

Although Castle Island and Marine Park have declined from their glory days after the turn of the century, the area is still pleasant, refreshed by sea breezes, and a fine place to look out on the harbor.

Picnicking: A few tables, but bring a blanket or chairs and spread out on the grass or one of the fish piers. Charcoal grills allowed. Nearby tot-lot, beach, ballfields, and the fort to explore.

Swimming: One mile of gravelly but clean beach around Pleasure Bay. Bathhouse, toilets, and snack bar. Lifeguards. No waves or undertow and so a good place for children.

Fishing: Two fishing piers for rod or dropline salt-water fishing for pollock, flounder, and mackerel.

Reading: The Islands of Boston Harbor by Edward Rowe Snow, available at most libraries, tells the history and legends of Castle Island in fine detail.

Directions:

MBTA: Red Line to Broadway. City Point bus to Castle Island.

Bicycle: Massachusetts Avenue to Columbia Road, to Day Boulevard.

Auto: Same as for bicycle.

Parking: Plenty.

12. BOSTON BEACHES

12A. SOUTH BOSTON BEACHES
Old Colony Division, Morrissey and Day Boulevards, South Boston and Dorchester
*MDC

Activities: swimming and picnicking
Hours: open all summer, 10:00 A.M. to 6:00 P.M. or until dusk on hot evenings
Admission: no charge

All five of these sandy or slightly gravelly beaches are along Morrissey and Day boulevards in Dorchester and South Boston. Good for swimming when the tide is high, they are mucky when the tide is out. Light surf makes these good beaches for children. Though the highway noise may be a bit irksome to some people, it is more than made up for by the convenience of these beaches. They are surrounded by the city, but the MDC monitors the water quality regularly; it has fallen to dangerous levels only twice since 1972. Each beach has lifeguards, changing rooms, and toilets, and several have snack bars.

Tenean Beach: A short stretch of beach near Neponset Circle with the Expressway hanging over it. Picnic tables and recently constructed tennis courts. Plenty of parking except on weekends. Difficult to reach by MBTA.

Malibu Beach: On a pleasant little cove between Morrissey Boulevard and the Expressway, near University of Massachusetts, Harbor Campus. Fine white sand and surprisingly clean water. Picnic tables. Kids seem to really like this beach. Take MBTA Red Line to Columbia station and free U. Mass bus; get out before turning into U. Mass., five-minute walk to beach.

Carson Beach: A long crescent of beach looking out to the harbor islands. Behind the beach is Columbia Park with a large playground, basketball courts, well-maintained tennis courts, and three ballfields. Plenty of parking. Five minutes from Columbia station.

M Street Beach: Use L Street Bathhouse for changing and toilets. Rough sand, but decent swimming.

12B. ORIENT HEIGHTS
Orient Heights, East Boston
*MDC

Activities: swimming, ballfields, tennis courts, picnicking, birdwatching
Hours: 8:00 A.M. to dusk
Admission: no charge

Formerly a Boston beach, Orient Heights Beach, also known as Constitution Beach, was taken over by the MDC and expanded when Wood Island Park was buried beneath Logan Airport. If you or your kids like to watch airplanes taking off and landing, this is a good place to do it while sitting in the water.

Activities:

Swimming: This is about the nicest beach in Boston, a half-mile swath of surprisingly clean white sand. The sandy bottom, gentle surf, and easy drop-off make this a good place for children. Water quality is routinely monitored. Lifeguards. Bathrooms, bathhouse, bubblers, snack truck.
Tennis: Two asphalt courts in fine condition. Busy in early evening. Also basketball and racquetball courts.
Ballfields: Two, suitable for softball.
Birdwatching: Good birdwatching for an urban area, particularly early in the morning and as dusk falls. Egrets, cormorants, and an occasional great blue heron. Bay ducks and shorebirds in the winter.

Directions:

MBTA: Blue Line Orient Heights station is right here.

Auto: Through Sumner Tunnel, second exit to Winthrop, out Bennington Street, to right on Saratoga Street, then right again over bridge and into park.

Parking: Plenty, but crowded on weekends.

13. WATERFRONT PARK
Atlantic Avenue near Quincy Market
4.5 acres   *Boston Park Department   1976

Activities: strolling, sitting, picnicking, tot-lot

For the first time in almost a century people now have visual and physical access to the harbor.

> *Mayor Kevin White*
> Park dedication 1976

Waterfront Park sits several hundred yards east of Boston's original shoreline: once the waters of East Cove rolled all the way to the foot of our present City Hall. When Faneuil Hall was built in 1740 on a filled mudflat, Boston's waterfront was lined with dozens of piers. By the beginning of the nineteenth century Boston had become one of the greatest ports in the world, her tall-masted merchantmen calling at ports from Liverpool to Madrid, Oregon to Canton, Bombay to the Caribbean.

In 1823 a large tract of mudflats crisscrossed by wharves and site of the Town Dock were filled in for the construction of Quincy Market. New wharves and warehouses were thrown up to handle the huge flow of goods through the port. But by 1900 Boston had been almost totally eclipsed as a seaport by New York, Baltimore, and San Francisco. The waterfront had declined physically as well as commercially. By 1960 the waterfront was virtually obliterated by abandoned wharves, decaying wooden sheds, and warehouse buildings. There was no public access to Boston's waterfront.

In 1959 Frank Christian, a prominent banker and president of the Chamber of Commerce, raised $200,000 in private funds for a major study of the waterfront's future. Christian hoped to see the entire waterfront rehabilitated and his position in the banking industry provided an opportunity to do something about his dream. Working with the Boston Redevelopment Authority (BRA), which became involved with the waterfront at his urging in 1964, Christian arranged the financing that made possible the relocation of food and produce wholesalers so that Quincy Market could be restored. He also persuaded the operators of New England Aquarium to locate their new building on the waterfront. The Waterfront Park was dedicated upon its opening to Frank Christian, who had done so much to restore this section of the city.

Originally planned as a much smaller park, Waterfront Park's size was more than doubled by the vigorous advocacy of the Sierra Club and local citizens. The park was designed for the BRA by the Watertown-based landscape architecture firm of Sasaki and Associates and built at a cost of $2,500,000. Crowned by a 340-foot trellis slowly being filled in by the twisting vines of planted wisteria, the park is built of the sort of materials that have long been characteristic of the waterfront: timber, brick, granite, and cobblestones, the last taken from nearby streets when they were repaved. A gentle slope, created with a low embankment, leads down to the water, where massive cast-iron bollards, such as sailing ships once tied up to, are linked with anchor chain along the seawall. The tree plantings include such exotic species as Japanese and Austrian pines and Norway maples; the shrubs are mostly indigenous New England coastal species such as inkberry and bayberry. Native juneberries here are laden with the sweetest, juiciest purple berries you will ever have the pleasure of popping into your mouth in the City of Boston.

Activities:

This small park at the head of the "Walkway to the Sea" has hundreds of benches, walls, and steps to rest your bones on and even a grassy patch for sunbathing. The immensely popular children's play area includes a large sandbox, a cool wading fountain, and an oversized "ship-shape" timber jungle gym. If the crowds at Quincy Market begin to get to you, take your lunch or dinner over here and relax.

Directions:

On Atlantic Avenue between Quincy Market and Boston Harbor.

14. COPPS HILL TERRACES
Between Atlantic Avenue and Charter Street in Boston's North End
*Boston Park Department   1895

Activities: strolling, historic site

Two or three times each year I am smitten with pity for the slum people—pity and horror mixed. . . . Doorsteps crowded with unclean beings, children pushing everywhere, and swarming in every street and alley. What a relief when Charlesbank is reached! The quiet open of the river, the long, long row of twinkling lights on the river wall, rows upon rows of seats all filled with people resting in the quiet air, and watching the fading golden light behind the Cambridge towers. The new terrace at the North End is to be another such resting place. It is good to be able to do something, even a little, for this battered and soiled humanity. . . .

> Charles Eliot
> Note to his wife 1895

Copps Hill Terrace is worth notice for two reasons: it was Boston's first attempt to provide its citizens with a view of the waterfront and it is the only park in the city designed by Charles Eliot (see "Charles Eliot"). The Charlesbank had given the West End a breathing space and this park was an attempt to do the same for the North End, the most densely populated neighborhood in the city.

In the landscape office of Olmsted, Olmsted, and Eliot, Charles Eliot took on the task of transforming a steep and narrow hillside lot, crowded by tenements on either side, and a waterfront that had "disappeared under a tangle of more or less ancient seawalls, fillings, and pile structures" into the "Pleasure Grounds between Copps Hill and the Harbor." Eliot designed a series of terraces with shade pavilions so that the local folks could promenade with a "commanding view of the harbor." All the buildings across the street were removed and a children's field and a bathhouse were built, providing Bostonians with their first and only downtown beach.

Activities:
Climb the puddingstone steps and look out over the mouth of the Charles to the masts of Old Ironsides. Copps Hill Burying Ground at the top of the terraces is one of the city's oldest cemeteries, begun in 1660. Three genera-

tions of Boston's leading spiritual family, the Mathers, were buried here between 1723 and 1785. Carved headstones and cryptic epitaphs make this an interesting place to wander. Treat yourself to some real Italian slush from the snack bar near the base of the terraces.

Directions:
Between Charter Street and Commercial Street in the North End, just below Copps Hill Burying Ground.

15. PAUL REVERE MALL
Hanover Street to Old North Church Boston's North End
1.5 acres   *Boston Park Department   1934

Activities: strolling, sitting, historic sites

When George R. White died in 1922 he left a $5,000,000 bequest to the city of Boston, the annual interest "to be used for creating works of public utility and beauty for the use and enjoyment of the inhabitants of Boston." This little tree-lined park in Boston's densest neighborhoods is one of those works.

The site of the mall was once a pasture owned by Christopher Stanley, a Puritan immigrant who died in 1646. The North End, Boston's first neighborhood, grew up around the pasture, attracting many of Boston's most eminent citizens. In the days before the Revolution the successful silversmith Paul Revere lived around the corner, as did the last Colonial governor, Thomas Hutchinson. The former pasture was buried beneath tightly packed houses and a narrow lane ran from Hanover Street to the Episcopal Christ Church (Old North). It was from this church that the lanterns were hung that set Revere off on his alarm to Lexington and Concord. When Revere died, years later, he was living less than a block from here at the corner of Hanover and Charter streets.

By the time the city decided to build a fit memorial to Revere, the Puritans, and for that matter nearly everyone of English descent, were long gone from the North End. Irish immigrants had swept into the district from the nearby piers in the 1840s and 1850s, only to be displaced fifty years later by successive waves of

Jewish and Italian immigrants.

The inspiration for the mall's design was the Prado, Havana's most famous park. The mall with its high walls lined with benches, was laid out by Arthur Shurcliff, a landscape architect who had apprenticed with Olmsted years before. The equestrian statue of Revere was sculpted by Cyrus E. Dallin. Across Hanover Street is Saint Stevens Church, the former New North Church, built in 1804, the last surviving Bulfinch-designed church in the city.

Activities:

Paul Revere Mall is a deeply shaded retreat and rest spot on the Freedom Trail. Benches lining the walls of the park are a favorite hangout and chess-playing area for the local Italian community. Plaques have been set into the walls commemorating the North End's earliest settlers and the historical events that swirled around the neighborhood.

Directions:

A five-minute walk up Hanover Street from Haymarket Square.

METROPOLITAN AREA PARKS

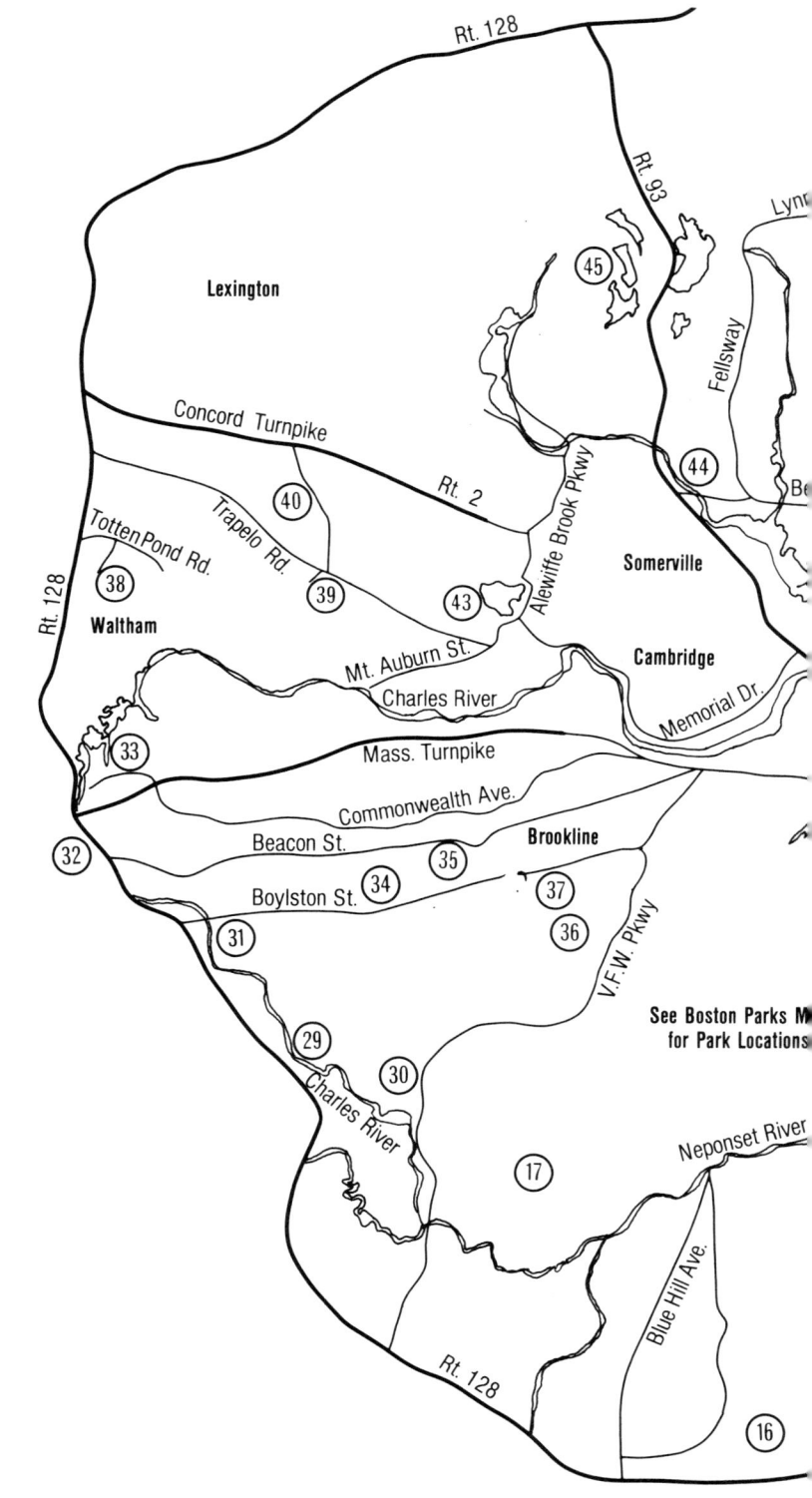

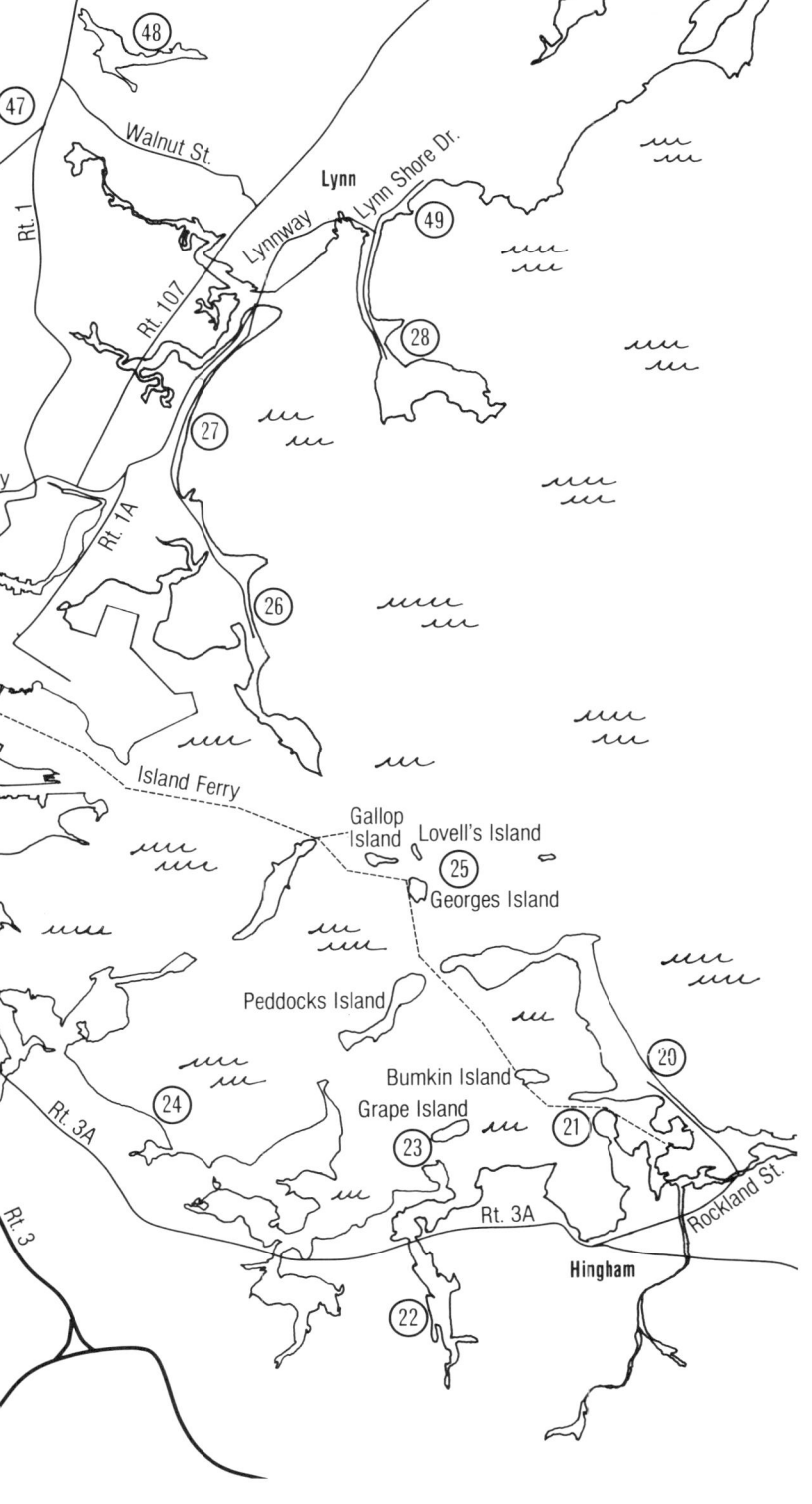

Metropolitan Area Parks
Quick Guide to Outdoor Activities

	WALKING	PICNICKING	SWIMMING	JOGGING	NATURE STUDY	SKI TOURING	FISHING	BIRDWATCHING	HIKING	CANOEING & BOATING	ICE-SKATING	PROGRAMS	CAMPING	HORSEBACK RIDING	TOWERS, ZOOS, ETC.	HISTORIC SITES	BALLFIELDS	TOT-LOTS	BIKE TRAILS	TENNIS
16. Blue Hills and Fowl Meadows	•	•	•	•	•	•	•	•	•	•	•	•	•	•	•	•	•		•	•
17. Stony Brook Reservation	•	•		•	•	•	•	•	•			•					•		•	
18. Governor Hutchinson's Field	•	•			•											•				
19. Neponset Marshes	•				•			•												
20. Nantasket Beach	•	•	•	•			•													
21. World's End Reservation	•				•	•	•	•	•											
22. Great Esker Park	•	•			•			•	•											
22A. Stodder's Neck	•	•					•													
22B. Bare Cove Park	•	•			•	•	•	•												
23. Webb State Park	•	•			•		•	•												
24. Wollaston Beach	•	•	•	•			•	•											•	
25. Boston Harbor Islands																				
25A. George's Island	•	•			•		•	•		•		•				•				
25B. Lovell's Island	•	•	•		•		•	•		•		•	•							
25C. Gallop's Island	•	•			•		•	•		•		•								
25D. Peddock's Island	•				•			•		•		•	•							
25E. Grape Island	•	•			•		•	•		•		•	•							
25F. Bumpkin Island	•	•			•		•	•		•		•	•							
25G. Great Brewster Island	•	•			•		•	•		•		•								
26. Winthrop Beach	•	•	•	•			•	•		•										
27. Revere Beach	•	•	•	•			•	•		•	•								•	
28. Nahant Beach	•	•	•	•			•	•		•							•	•	•	•
29. Cutler Park	•	•		•	•	•	•	•	•	•										
30. Brook Farm and Sawmill Marsh	•				•											•				
31. Hemlock Gorge	•	•			•	•										•				
32. Charles River Pathway	•	•			•		•	•	•	•						•				

	WALKING	PICNICKING	SWIMMING	JOGGING	NATURE STUDY	SKI TOURING	FISHING	BIRDWATCHING	HIKING	CANOEING & BOATING	ICE-SKATING	PROGRAMS	CAMPING	HORSEBACK RIDING	TOWERS, ZOOS, ETC.	HISTORIC SITES	BALLFIELDS	TOT-LOTS	BIKE TRAILS	TENNIS
33. Norumbega																				
33A. Norumbega Park	•	•			•		•													
33B. Charles River Watershed Association												•								
33C. Charles River Canoe Service										•		•								
33D. Duck Feeding Station					•			•												
33E. Norumbega Tower and Park	•	•						•	•						•	•				
33F. Commonwealth Avenue in Newton	•		•																•	
34. Hammond Woods	•	•			•	•	•	•	•	•		•								
35. Chestnut Hill Reservoir	•	•		•								•					•	•		
36. Larz Anderson Park	•	•		•	•	•	•					•					•	•		
37. Brookline Reservoir	•	•		•																
38. Prospect Hill Park	•	•			•				•										•	
39. Beaver Brook and Waverly Oaks	•	•		•	•	•	•	•				•					•	•		•
40. Rock Meadow	•				•	•		•	•											
41. Mount Auburn Cemetery	•				•			•								•				
42. Charles River Basin	•	•	•	•						•					•	•	•	•	•	•
43. Fresh Pond Park	•	•		•	•	•		•											•	•
44. Mystic River Reservation	•	•	•	•	•		•			•				•			•	•	•	•
45. Middlesex Falls Reservation	•	•	•	•	•	•	•	•	•	•		•		•						
46. Pine Banks Park	•	•			•	•			•	•				•			•	•		
47. Breakheart Reservation	•	•	•	•	•	•	•	•	•	•		•						•	•	
48. Lynn Woods	•	•			•	•	•		•	•				•						
49A. Red Rock Park	•	•		•			•	•												
49B. King's Beach		•	•																	

CHARLES ELIOT: THE BOSTON METROPOLITAN PARK SYSTEM AND THE MASSACHUSETTS TRUSTEES OF THE PUBLIC RESERVATIONS

A Lover of nature and his kind who trained himself for a new profession, practiced it happily, and through it wrought much good.
Charles W. Eliot
Charles Eliot: Landscape Architect

This summer, if you bicycle, stroll, sail, or paddle along the Charles River or attend an esplanade concert, if you climb the Blue Hills or swim at Nantasket, Revere, or Wollaston beaches, if you feed the ducks at Beaver Brook or watch birds at Fowl Meadows or the Neponset marshes, or if you jog along the Mystic River or the beach in Winthrop, or visit any of the Trustees of Reservations' sixty-seven properties, you will be enjoying the legacy of Charles Eliot.

By 1891 the population of the Boston area had grown to nearly a million inhabitants, as French-Canadians, Portuguese, Italians, Greeks, Poles, and Syrians followed the Irish, pushing many earlier immigrants and Yankees out into the suburbs. Of thirty-five cities and towns in the region, only Boston had developed parks, and the only other public lands suitable for public recreation were the causeway leading out to Nahant and the Lynn Woods. Into this breach stepped young Charles Eliot with visionary plans for protecting the region's forests, rivers, and beaches and preserving scenic natural areas all around the state for the public good.

Because Eliot was sickly as a child, his father, Harvard President Charles W. Eliot, following the wisdom of the day, urged his son to spend time outdoors. By 1875 Eliot had discovered his favorite pastime as a teenager: cross-country walking. With a friend or two, he would ride one of the seventy Boston-area horse or steam trolleys to a terminal and then walk five or ten miles through woods and fields to another trolley connection. No topographical maps existed yet, and so Eliot created little ones of his own. He took notes on the flora and fauna and the geology of the region. Having learned to draw from his mother, he sketched the landscape. In this manner, he explored every nook and cranny from Lynn to Quincy.

After graduating from Harvard in 1882, Eliot could not decide upon a profession until his uncle, architect Robert S. Peabody, told him about a new neighbor of his in Brookline, Frederick Law

Olmsted, and about the infant science of landscape architecture. Eliot knew at once that this profession would suit him. Because no formal course of study in landscape architecture was available in America, in the fall Eliot enrolled at the Bussey Institution, Harvard's Department of Agriculture and Horticulture. In the spring Eliot was introduced to Olmsted and a week later became his apprentice.

After working with the Master for two years, Eliot felt he had learned as much as he could in Olmsted's office and so terminated his apprenticeship in April 1885 with Olmsted's blessing. At Olmsted's suggestion, Eliot spent a year in Europe visiting parks and gardens. Upon his return to Boston Eliot opened his first office at the corner of Beach and Park streets in the Amory-Tichnor house. He worked mostly on the design of private estates but in 1887 he laid out Longfellow Park between Brattle Street and the Charles.

In 1888 Eliot wrote *Open Spaces for Urban Populations,* reflecting his growing distress about the lack of outdoor recreational space open to the public. Although the Europeans had preserved large tracts of land in the midst of their highly developed continent, Americans, because of their vast wilderness, had preserved little. Between Gloucester and Plymouth, the only beaches open to the public were the Nahant causeway and the new but small Marine Park at Castle Island. The only major country park for more than a million people was the new Franklin Park. And the only natural area open to the public was the Lynn Woods.

When Waverly Oaks, Lowell's Beaver Brook, was in danger of development in 1890, Eliot responded with a highly original plan for its preservation. In an article written for *Garden and Forest* magazine, he proposed "an incorporated association composed of citizens from all the Boston area towns, and empowered by the state to hold small and well-distributed parcels of land, free of taxes, just as the public library holds books and the art museum holds pictures—for the use and enjoyment of the public."

On May 24, 1890, a meeting was held under the auspices of the Appalachian Mountain Club (AMC) at the Massachusetts Institute of Technology. Presiding over the meeting was the president of the State Senate, Henry W. Sprague. In addition to AMC President Mann and Sargent of the Arboretum, the speakers included such notables as the Honorable Leverett Saltonstall, Professor Charles Eliot Norton, Judge William Shurtleff, Frederick Law Olmsted, and Eliot. More than four hundred letters of support were received, and those from Governor Brackett, Oliver Wendell

Holmes, historian Francis Parkman, and John Boyle O'Reilly, editor of *The Pilot,* were read aloud. In May, 1891, a group of these conservation-minded citizens organized themselves into the

Massachusetts Trustees of the Public Reservations, one of the first conservation land trusts in the world.

At Eliot's request, the Trustees called a meeting in December to discuss the need for a regional park plan. Every town in the region was represented. Everyone at the meeting agreed that prompt action was necessary to ensure the survival of the region's natural and scenic heritage. They were all too aware that the finest areas of the state—its rivers, beaches, and woodlands—"were in private hands, often to their destruction or the exclusion of the public." A committee of the meeting was formed, and with a committee from the Trustees, an appeal was made to the Legislature for the creation of a regional park system.

In April 1892, a legislative committee had Eliot draft an act creating a Metropolitan Park Commission on the model of the Metropolitan Sewage Commission. Included in the metropolitan area would be thirty-six cities and towns from Boston and Cambridge, north to Swampscott, west to Waltham, and south to Weymouth.

Two months later, enabling legislation was passed, officially creating the Metropolitan Park Commission. Under Eliot's knowledgeable guidance, the Commission roamed up and down the hills, watercourses, and beaches of the region, visiting every point of scenic, recreational, and natural interest within an eleven-mile radius of the State House. The following January, the Commission made its report with recommendations to the Legislature on the overall prospects for acquiring land and constructing the proposed regional park system.

The Boston Metropolitan Park Report of 1893 was the most ambitious and farsighted proposal for public open space and parkland in the United States, if not the world. The report was a concrete plan to secure for the public and future generations, for outdoor recreation and sanitary improvement, the forests, ponds, rivers, and seacoast of the Boston region. The Commission recommended the acquisition of Lynn, Revere, Nahant, Nantasket, Winthrop, Wollaston, and King's beaches; Snake Creek Valley between Revere and Chelsea; the Blue Hills, Hemlock Gorge (Echo Bridge), the Middlesex Fells, Muddy Pond (Stony Brook), and Mystic River; and the Boston Harbor islands and the shore of Boston Harbor.

Eliot declared, "for crowded populations to live in health and happiness, they must have space for air, for light, for exercise, for rest, and for the enjoyment of that peaceful beauty of nature which, because it is the opposite of the noisy ugliness of the town, is so refreshing to the tired souls of townspeople." Sylvester Baxter, journalist and secretary to the Commission, stated further that unless the Legislature acted without delay "this naturally beautiful region is in danger of becoming a vast desert of houses, factories, and stores, spreading over and overwhelming the natural features of the landscape . . . relieved by hardly an oasis."

Within six months of the report, the Massachusetts Legislature had agreed with the reasoning of the Commission and authorized creation of the Boston Metropolitan Park System. The Commission was given power of eminent domain and a substantial appropriation to begin the work of acquiring land and constructing roads and facilities.

Working as a full partner in the Olmsted firm, landscape architect Charles Eliot began to carry out the execution of his plan, a plan that had seemed a wild fantasy only a few years before. It was a great tragedy when Eliot suddenly died of spinal meningitis in 1897, at only thirty-seven years of age and in the midst of his great triumph. By 1900 his plan was virtually completed, with a few exceptions and additions, preserving 9,177 acres of reservations, 13 miles of ocean frontage, 56 miles of riverbanks, and 7 parkways.

Memorials:

Three memorials to Charles Eliot's genius have been erected around the Metropolitan region: a bridge and tower on the summit of Great Blue Hill; a granite monolith along the Charles River near Community Boathouse; and Eliot Circle at the beginning of Revere Beach.

Reading:

Charles Eliot: Landscape Architect by Charles W. Eliot is an extraordinarily sensitive portrait of Charles Eliot written by his father, including many of Charles Eliot's most important writings. *The Metropolitan Park Commission Reports* from 1893 to 1900 and the Trustees of Reservations' *Annual Reports* also make interesting reading for anyone with a taste for the history of urban design and land preservation.

Trustees of Reservations

Today the Trustees of Reservations is the largest private conservation landholding agency in Massachusetts, owning nearly 16,000 acres of land in sixty-seven properties from Monument Mountain and Bartholomew's Cobble in the Berkshires to Wasque and Cape Page on Chappaquiddick Island. Known as the "Museum of the Massachusetts Landscape," the Trustees is the oldest conservation land trust in the world. Both the beauty of its properties and the quality of its management have kept alive Charles Eliot's ideals of land preservation and public access to the joys of the natural landscape. Eighteen of the Trustees' properties are included in this book.

Membership in the Trustees not only allows one to become a part of this illustrious organization, but includes free or discounted admission to the organization's properties, a property guide that includes descriptions of the properties and directions to their locations, a newsletter about the properties, and an annual report.

Trustees of Reservations
224 Adams Street
Milton, MA 02186
Telephone: (617) 698-2066

The Metropolitan District Commission

In 1919 the Metropolitan Park Commission was merged with the Metropolitan Water and Sewage Commissions to create the Metropolitan District Commission (MDC). Unfortunately for the metropolitan parklands, open-space preservation and management were treated as perhaps the lowest priority, not only beneath water supply and sewage, but also lower than the policing and highway functions that had been mere adjuncts of the Park System. Political expediency and patronage seemed to dictate policy as park after park was divided by highways or used as free space to erect non-park related buildings. As citizens' awareness has grown in recent years, hope has renewed that the MDC will once again treat its public lands as a serious public responsibility.

The MDC publishes a free map of the MDC parks and recreational facilities, with trail maps of most of the MDC properties listed in this book. It also publishes a free booklet, *Recreational Facilities,* which details the agency's many offerings.

Metropolitan District Commission
20 Somerset Street
Boston, MA 02108
Telephone: (617) 727-5215 (Public Information Office)

16. BLUE HILLS RESERVATION AND FOWL MEADOWS
Reservation Headquarters, Hillside Street, Milton, MA 02186
6,594 acres   MDC   1893

Activities: hiking, swimming, boating, fishing, picnicking, ice-skating, ski touring, downhill skiing, athletic fields, nature study, museum, orienteering, rock climbing, bird-watching, bicycling, horseback riding, tennis, golf, camping

Map: Detailed maps of the Reservation, included in two free publications of the Friends of the Blue Hills, are available at MDC Police Headquarters, the Trailside Museum, or by mail from the Friends (see below). The Friends also publish a set of four detailed orienteering maps available for $3.50 plus fifty cents postage.

Hours: dawn to dusk

Admission: free

"The Massachusetts Forest"

The Blue Hills Reservation is the largest tract of public open space within thirty-five miles of Boston. Great Blue Hill, at 635 feet, is the highest point in easternmost Massachusetts. From the summit the view to the west takes in Mounts Wachusetts and Monadnock, Fowl Meadow, and the Neponset and Charles River valleys; to the north, the skyscrapers and harbor islands of Boston and the hills of Andover and Rockport; to the northeast, the hills and vales of the Reservation; and to the south, a rolling green near wilderness, with only church steeples, water towers, and power lines to hint at the hundreds of thousands of people who live beneath the trees.

These domelike hills of granite were once molten rock pushing up toward the earth's surface. Before reaching the air, the rock cooled and hardened. Over millions of years the softer stone that lay above and around the granite domes was eroded by wind, rain, and ice, leaving the hills as we know them. The entire range was lifted by pressures from within the earth and tilted slightly from west to east.

The Puritan settlers of Massachusetts Bay Colony expected the region they were to settle to be "a wasted and howling wilderness." But the land had already been settled by Indians for at least nine thousand years. Recent archeological findings indicate that

the Blue Hills area served as a campsite for Early Archaic hunters as early as 7,500 B.C. At some time during the Archaic period, from 7,000 to 1,000 B.C., the area appears to have been permanently occupied. We know that for much of this time the prehistoric inhabitants quarried the hills for a brown volcanic rock, Braintree hornfels, which they pounded and flaked into spearheads, arrowheads, and scrapers. It is easy to imagine the Indians surveying the surrounding territory from the highest summits.

Early explorers of Massachusetts Bay found a thriving group of Indians with numerous villages scattered about. The tribe was called the Massachuset, meaning "Place of Great Hills." These Great Hills, our Blue Hills, were the highest feature on the entire Atlantic seaboard south of Mount Agamenticus in southern Maine. The Puritans adopted the Indian name of the place as their own.

In 1630, seven hundred Puritans arrived in Boston; by 1646 another thirty thousand had disembarked there. Many settlers must have scaled the Blue Hills to scan their new home and search for new farmland. They were soon drawn back to the hills for wood to fuel their fires and supply their nascent industries—a colonial open-hearth fireplace consumed between fifteen and twenty cords of wood per year. After the immediate Boston area, including the harbor islands, had been logged off, timber merchants and ship-builders cast their eyes on the Blue Hills: large-scale logging began here in 1669.

Twenty-five years after the Puritans landed, the last natives of the area, a band of sixty "Praying Indians," was "moved" from "Neponsitt" to a six-thousand-acre reservation that extended from Quincy to Stoughton. They settled on the shore of Ponkapog Pond, "The Clear Waters." The Indians were interned on Deer Island during King Philip's War when anti-Indian sentiment peaked—only a few survived to return.

During the Revolution the patriots maintained a lookout post on the summit of Great Blue Hill. Beacons were lit to signal movements of the British troops. Great bonfires that could be seen for many miles were ignited to celebrate the repeal of the Stamp Act, the signing of the Declaration of Independence, and the British evacuation of Boston. After the war the patrons and proprietor of nearby Billings Tavern built a club on the summit.

In the early 1800s the Quincy end of the hills became the center of the nation's granite industry. Quarries proliferated, providing stone for King's Chapel, Bunker Hill Monument, Quincy City Hall, and the banks of Boston. Fallen Atlantic white cedars, preserved in the oxygen-free waters, were "mined" for their valuable timber. Iron ore was dug out of the bogs and smelted with charcoal made from the hills' remaining timber. In the east of the Reservation, along the new Quarry Footpath, are the remains of the Lyons Turning Mill, built in 1898 to supply cut and polished granite columns and slabs to builders.

In 1830 Harvard erected a twenty-foot tower on the summit of Great Blue Hill to determine a meridian line from Cambridge observatory. In 1885 Lawrence Roach, a maverick meteorologist from MIT, established one of the first weather observatories in the country on the summit, becoming Boston's first weatherman. To investigate the upper atmosphere, Roach flew weather instruments aloft on huge kites attached to the ground by piano wire. Roach died in 1912, but his work continued, with balloon replacing kite as elevator. The castlelike structure was run by Harvard until 1959 when the National Weather Service took it over. The public is not permitted into the observatory except on special occasions, but readings are still taken, providing the longest set of temperature recordings at any weather station in North America.

By 1893 nearly a million people lived within ten miles of the Blue Hills. Boston's parks had become so successful that they were already overcrowded. More and more, rich man and slum dweller alike looked to these hills for rest, exercise, and relaxation. More than a hundred individuals owned sparse woodlots in the hills; on the southern slopes piggeries abounded. Yet the Blue Hills became the centerpiece and among the first acquisitions of the Boston Metropolitan Park System.

Charles Eliot, landscape architect to the Park System, probably gave more attention to the Blue Hills Reservation than to any other metropolitan park. He would allow no construction to begin in the Reservation until he had developed a complete plan that would minimize environmental alterations while providing the public with "sublimely picturesque views of scenic natural beauty." Hundreds of men idled by the depression of the early 1890s were hired to clear brush, plant trees, and fight forest fires. Park police, predecessors of the MDC police, patrolled the trails and carriage roads. The Blue Hills Reservation was an immediate success: on one Sunday in 1895, 2,100 people climbed to the summit of Great Blue Hill.

By 1900 the Reservation included 4,857 acres, acquired at a cost of $352,897.79 from the hundred or so owners; $223,348.35 had been spent on labor and supplies in developing it. In 1905 a bridge of native granite was constructed on top of Great Blue Hill as a memorial to the late Eliot. The buildings that now house the MDC police were erected in 1904 as Reservation headquarters and stables. The refreshment pavilion beside Houghton's Pond was built in 1920. In 1929 the Great Blue Hill observation tower, designed by Arthur Shurcliff, was built; ten years later the Chickatawbut observation tower followed. One of the earliest and longest corduroy log nature trails in the country was built in 1949 out on Ponkapog bog, now a National Environmental Study Area. In the late 1950s the first and still highest downhill ski area inside Route 128 was opened on the west flank of Great Blue Hill.

Activities:

More than five hundred miles of trails and paths wind through the quiet valleys and knobby granite outcroppings of the Blue Hills Reservation. An outing to Houghton's Pond, less than a half hour from downtown Boston, can include a bit of ballplaying, an ascent of Great Blue Hill, a picnic, a cool dip, and still leave time for sitting around, exploring, and fishing. Be sure to pick up the two free brochures, with maps, at Trailside Museum or the MDC police station.

Bulletin boards: Located at Houghton's Pond, Ponkapog golf course, Chickatawbut parking lot, Wampatuck parking lot, Trailside Museum, and Paul's Bridge. Hiking and riding maps posted in summer, ski-touring maps posted in winter. Also listings of current activities are offered by Trailside Museum, MDC, and Friends of the Blue Hills.

Trailside Museum: Operated by Massachusetts Audubon Society, this is the best place for an introduction to the natural history and history of the Reservation. The excellent displays include snakes, frogs, owls, minerals, a transparent beehive, and a collection of Indian artifacts. Outside is a wildflower garden (best seen in the spring), foxes, hawks, a bobcat, and a pair of river otters that send a tingle of delight through observers.

The museum also sponsors a wide variety of day and evening programs about the outdoors for adults and children. Call (617) 333-0690 for information. Open 10:00 A.M. to 5:00 P.M. Tuesday through Sunday and Monday holidays. Admission: one dollar adults, fifty cents children. Address: 1904 Canton Avenue, Milton, MA 02186.

Friends of the Blue Hills: This nonprofit trust organization is dedicated to protecting, preserving, and investigating the Blue Hills and Neponset River Reservations. Guided hikes, ski touring, trail maintenance, flora and fauna censusing, forest-fire fighting, historical research, and environmental monitoring are some of the activities sponsored by the FBH. The public is welcome for most activities. Contact Friends of the Blue Hills, 1904 Canton Avenue, Milton, MA 02186; or call (617) 326-0079.

Hiking: The Reservation has two hundred miles of hiking footpaths. Trail maps are posted on bulletin boards, but obtain your own free at the Trailside Museum, MDC, or from the FBH—there are an awful lot of trails out there and it can be very confusing without a map in hand. You may want to bring a compass and canteen, but definitely bring your binoculars because a lot of the country is above treeline. With your map you can plan a quick dash up Great Blue Hill, a long easy lope around Ponkapog Pond, or a strenuous jaunt along the Skyline Footpath.

The Skyline Footpath, marked with blue dots, starts at the end of Burma Road in the Neponset River Reservation, circumambulates Little Blue Hill, then drops to Route 138 (where there is parking). Continuing across Route 138, the footpath makes a rapid ascent to the summit of Great Blue Hill, then sets out over the height of land for an additional eight miles. A rugged footpath, running through the heart of the reservation, the Skyline Footpath can also be reached from numerous side trails.

The fastest way to the summit of Great Blue Hill heads up from the museum parking lot, following red- and green-dot footpaths. An easier ascent follows the observatory road from the lower side of the parking lot behind the museum. The easiest walks up Great Blue Hill begin across the street from the Houghton's Pond parking lot.

From the Chickatawbut parking lot it is a twenty-minute dash to the wooden tower on the top of Chickatawbut Hill. Great Dome Footpath, in the Quincy (northeast) end of the Reservation, climbs Great Dome overlooking Quincy, then descends alongside Indian and nineteenth-century quarries. Another fine trail skirts the Great Cedar Swamp. There are an awful lot of other trails, so get your brochure and map and explore.

A very pleasant three-and-a-half-mile trail circles Ponkapog Pond, easy walking all the way. Park at the golf course, follow the road through the links, and turn either way at the pond. Don't miss the Ponkapog Log Boardwalk, which extends nearly half a mile across a floating bog (see "Nature study" below). The entrance to the bog walk is beside a small dirt parking lot (no vehicle access) across the dirt road from former Camp Dorchester.

Burma Road, the trail that runs through the Fowl Meadows, is another outstanding place for a nature walk. The trail is actually a long earthen causeway, nearly level, running through an extensive marsh and swamp of the Neponset River. Good birding, great jogging and ski touring, and extremely pleasant strolling. Parking lot on Brush Hill Road near Paul's Bridge.

Fishing: Houghton's Pond, St. Moritz Pond, Ponkapog

Outlet, and the Blue Hill River are all stocked with trout, and also have bass, catfish, and sunfish. Ponkapog Pond: stocked with northern pike; also bass, sunfish, and pickerel.

Swimming: Houghton's Pond, formerly Hoosicwhicsick Pond, is the nearest freshwater swimming-hole to the south of Boston. Lifeguards, a sandy bottom, and lack of waves make it an especially good place for children. The usual slightly murky·pond water is clean and refreshing. Crowded on weekends.

Ski touring: Three hundred miles of marked ski trails. Six sections of the Reservation have been particularly laid out for touring and marked according to degree of difficulty. Trail maps in free brochures.

Ponkapog golf course is laid out with the easiest ski-touring trails and is a good place for beginners. The season begins here when only three or four inches of snow has fallen in Boston.

Friends of the Blue Hills runs ski-touring workshops and guided trips on weekends and holidays.

Picnicking: The area around Houghton's Pond is perhaps the nicest developed picnic area inside of Route 128, with something enjoyable for everyone to do. Picnic tables and grills beneath shady pines, and three playgrounds. Use swimming-area bathrooms. Lots of hilltops for pack-it-in/pack-it-out picnics. Nearby open fields and ballfields for playing.

Boating: Launch cartop rowboats or canoes on Ponkapog Pond from Frenchman's Beach in Randolph.

Alpine (downhill) skiing: Two-hundred-and-fifty-foot vertical drop on three slopes, novice to advanced. Chairlift and two J-bars. A great place to learn to ski with ski instruction available. Ski rentals and restaurant. Open from 9:30 A.M. to 4:30 P.M. and 7:00 P.M. to 10:00 P.M. seven days a week.

Tennis: Six asphalt courts behind Houghton's Pond; four at St. Moritz Pond. First come, first served.

Bicycling: A good place for youngsters, oldsters, and families is Blue Hill River Road, a flat abandoned road that begins behind Houghton's Pond.

Horseback riding: Between two and three hundred miles of bridle trails. Among the stables are: Belliveau Riding

Academy, 1244 Randolph Avenue, Milton, (617) 698-9637; Brookedale Stables, 629 Willard Street, Quincy, 471-9547; Lazy S. Ranch, 300 Randolph Street, Canton, 828-1681; The Paddocks, 1010 Hillside Street, Milton, 698-1884; Redsam Stables, 384 High Street, Randolph, 963-9828.

Golf: At thirty-six-hole Ponkapog golf course, a beautiful championship course, with twenty-seven of its holes laid out by one of the world's most accomplished golf-course architects, Donald Ross.

Rock climbing: Lots of crags and ledges. Contact the Appalachian Mountain Club or FBH.

Birdwatching: Burma Road in Fowl Meadow, Ponkapog Outlet and bog, and throughout Reservation. Bird list and bird walks by Trailside Museum and FBH; call or write for information and list.

Nature study: The Ponkapog Log Boardwalk (see "Hiking" above for directions) leads in to the most fabulous natural environment close to Boston. The Boardwalk courses through a swamp filled with highbush blueberries, blue flag iris, Atlantic white cedar, lambkill or sheep laurel, and leatherleaf, then on to the floating mat of sphagnum moss. Out on the floating bog, cotton grass and marsh Saint-John's-wort begin to appear. Three species of insectivorous plants grow out of the sphagnum: bladderwort, sundew, and pitcher plant. And to round out the bog's delights, rose pagonia and snake's mouth orchids can be seen here as well.

Elsewhere in the Reservation a recent wildflower survey found 975 lady's slippers in one small patch, and also rare white and double-headed lady's slippers. Friends of the Blue Hills and Trailside Museum run wildflower walks and inventories, as well as walks and talks about every other aspect of the Reservation's natural environment. Please don't pick any of the flowers: collection could easily wipe them out and is also against the law in the Reservation.

Camping: Appalachian Mountain Club rents twenty cabins on Ponkapog Pond to the public. Reservations are needed five months or more in advance. Telephone: 963-9856.

Reading:
Metropolitan Park Reports of 1893 and 1895. Also free

brochures by FBH available at Trailside Museum, MDC, or from FBH.

Directions:

MBTA: Red Line to Mattapan. Canton and Stoughton Bus to Blue Hills in Milton and Canton: get out at Trailside Museum (ski slope), Hillside Street (to Houghton's Pond), or Ponkapog Pond (golf course).

From Ashmont station take Randolph Avenue bus to Chickatawbut Hill.

Train: From Boston's South Station to Route 128 station. Use abandoned I-95 bridge to cross Route 128. Burma Road and Skyline Footpath junction just ahead.

Bicycle: Arnold Arboretum to Arborway to Forest Hills, up Hyde Park Avenue to Neponset Valley Parkway, right on Route 138 to Trailside Museum (follow Claire Saltonstall Bikeway). From western suburbs take Hammond Pond Parkway to West Roxbury Parkway, to Turtle Pond Parkway, to Neponset Valley Parkway (follow Cape bike route) to Route 138.

Auto: Route 128 to Route 138 north. Or Blue Hill Avenue to Route 138.

Parking: Plenty at more than a dozen lots.

Telephone: 698-5840

17. STONY BROOK RESERVATION
Turtle Pond Parkway, West Roxbury and Hyde Park
600 plus acres   *MDC   1894

Activities: hiking, bicycling, picnicking, ice-skating, nature study, fishing, jogging, tennis, ballfields, swimming pool

Map: free MDC map including Stony Brook from MDC, 20 Somerset Street, Boston, MA 02108

Hours: sunrise to sunset

Admission: free

Allusion was made by Mr. Hills before the Park Commission yesterday afternoon to Muddy Pond Woods as a desirable locality for a park. As few people away from the immediate vicinity are acquainted with the

locality, a brief description may be desirable. The name is derived from a sheet of water of several acres, situated just south of the old Dedham Turnpike, at an elevation of some 300 feet above the Neponset river. The name is certainly a misnomer, for it is a delightful sheet of clear water capable of great improvement or enlargement. The surroundings are as wild and picturesque as anything to be found among the White or Green mountains. There are precipitous cliffs with rugged rocky faces, dense forest and undergrowth, innumerable small streams forming beautiful natural cascades. . . . The upland views from all quarters are superb. . . . For an inland park nothing could be more desirable, if cost, convenience, and beauty of scenery are to be considered.

Boston Traveller
June 19, 1874

On the second night of the 1874 Boston park hearings Thomas Hills, chairman of Boston's Board of Assessors, proposed that the Muddy Pond Woods in West Roxbury be included in any Boston park system. At the time of Mr. Hill's proposal, Muddy Pond Woods was an unoccupied tract without even a road through it; nobody could remember anyone ever having lived there, because the area was composed of jagged little rock hills and small valleys filled with glacially deposited rocks and boulders. But if the local folks found little cultivable or pastureland here, and if the terrain was too rugged for any roads, they did find plenty of trees to feed their hearths. Like the Blue Hills, Muddy Pond Woods was apparently logged and logged again, and beset by raging brush fires.

The course of Stony Brook has carved a central valley, through hills of granite and diorite. The brook appears headed for the Neponset River, less than a mile away to the south, when suddenly it veers to the north, its natural drainage blocked by a heap of glacier-dumped rubble. After running to Hyde Park, the stream has been conduited and makes its way under streets and buildings through Boston's South End before arriving by the Back Bay Fens near the Museum of Fine Arts. Unlike the rock hills in the woods, Bellevue Hill, at 338 feet the highest point in Boston, is a drumlin, formerly cleared of trees and used as pastureland.

By 1894, when the Metropolitan Park Commission was given the go-ahead to acquire lands, Muddy Pond's name had been changed to Turtle Pond and Muddy Pond Woods had become Stony Brook. Carriage roads were laid out and fire-protection measures were undertaken. Parkways were laid out to connect the Stony Brook Reservation with the Blue Hills and the Arboretum in the Boston Park System.

The Reservation is covered predominantly with red and white oaks, with pines, stands of beech, and hemlock groves on the north-facing cliffs. Blueberries and huckleberries make up the forest understory, spiked by whorled loosestrife, wood sorrel, wintercress, and yellow stargrass. Dense thickets of sweet pepper-bush surround the pond, with yellow birch trees towering above.

Activities:

The forested portion of this Reservation is quiet and underused, in part because of repeated fires, but it is nonetheless a place of real mountain beauty within the Boston city limits. The best views are had from Bald Knob, especially of Great Blue Hill across the Neponset Valley. The developed area in the south of the Reservation has complete facilities, including picnic tables, a swimming pool, ice-skating rink, and ballfields.

Hiking: Ten to twelve miles of trails. Crags and hilltops to explore. Lots of wildflowers.

Bicycling: Four miles of paved bicycle trails; some fairly steep grades, but good for families. Begin just south of Turtle Pond.

Picnicking: Shaded picnic tables with grills in south portion of Reservation. Swimming pool, ballfields, and bathrooms. Hilltops and the far side of Turtle Pond are good places for informal picnics.

Fishing: At Turtle Pond and Mother Brook Dam. Fishing piers at both sites. Catfish, perch, sunfish, and occasional bass and pickerel at both sites.

Ice-skating: Turtle Pond and flooded field on Bald Knob Road. Skating rink at developed area on Turtle Pond Road.

Jogging: Quiet woodland jogging along bike trails.

Tennis: Two asphalt courts in good condition at Connell Field.

Ballfields: Three softball fields near developed area; one ballfield at Connell Field.

Swimming pool: Open 10:00 A.M. to 8:00 P.M. all summer. Admission $1.00. In developed area.

Thompson Center for the Handicapped: This facility is specially designed for the recreational pleasure of disabled children and adults. Available by reservation only for groups. Telephone: 361-6161.

Directions:
Auto and bike: Arborway to Forest Hills station, to Washington Street. Proceed three miles to left on Turtle Pond Parkway. Parking area at Turtle Pond. Developed area two miles ahead.
Or: Hammond Pond Parkway to West Roxbury Parkway to Turtle Pond Parkway.
Public Transportation: Arborway Green Line or Orange Line to Forest Hills station. Dedham bus to Turtle Pond Parkway to developed area.
Parking: Plenty.

Telephone: 364-9683

18. GOVERNOR HUTCHINSON'S FIELD
Trustees of the Public Reservations, Next to 224 Adams Street, Milton
10 acres   *Trustees of the Public Reservations   1898

Activities: walking, scenic, historic site
Hours: dawn to dusk
Admission: Free

My House is seven or eight miles from town, a pleasant situation and many a gentleman from abroad says it has the finest prospect from it they ever saw.

Governor Thomas Hutchinson
Letter to King George III

In 1743 Thomas Hutchinson, last colonial governor of Massachusetts Bay Colony and author of the first volume of *The History of Massachusetts Bay,* purchased land at the top of Milton Hill to escape the rising anti-British sentiment beginning to find vent in Boston. More than a hundred years earlier Milton Hill had been one of Indian Sachem Chickatawbut's plantations.

Hutchinson had Sir Francis Barnard, himself a former royal governor, design a house and garden on the slope looking toward Boston and the harbor. After the Boston Tea Party, in June 1774, Hutchinson was forced into exile, his house and property confiscated. After the Revolution, his house was sold at auction and then occupied by James Warren and his wife Mercy Otis Warren, the rebel pamphleteer. The house was torn down in 1946, having passed through several families and served as a Red Cross quarters during World War II.

Hutchinson was an avid gardener of "imagination and taste" who devoted himself to ornamental plantings and grafting. One of the most interesting aspects of his garden was the construction of a "Ha-Ha." This "sunken fence" of puddingstone and granite formed an invisible barrier between formal garden and surrounding horse or cow pasture. The Ha-Ha feature of landscape gardening derived its name "from the French expression of surprise and anger, 'Ha!', as it is a feature not discovered from the garden until one is almost on to it." The last remnant of Hutchinson's Ha-Ha is next to St. Michael's Church on Randolph Street and is included in the National Register of Historic Places.

The property was donated to the Trustees in 1898 by John M. Forbes, the great industrialist and railroad magnate, and his sister, Mrs. Mary F. Cunningham.

Little remains of Hutchinson's garden except the Ha-Ha and some copper beech and Scilla believed to be descended from the governor's plantings, but the view from the grassy slopes of the meandering Neponset, the harbor islands, and the "town" of Boston remains simply spectacular.

Activities:

A small but intriguing place to walk around, take photographs, or read the Sunday paper. No facilities.

Directions:

Directly across the street from the Museum of the American China Trade.

Auto or bike: Gallivan Boulevard to Dorchester Avenue, through Dorchester Lower Mills, across the Neponset, continue on Adams Street to top of hill.

Nearby:

Museum of American China Trade—tour of ornate early nineteenth-century mansion formerly owned by John M. Forbes, filled with elegant Chinese imports of the period. Adults, three dollars, children, a dollar fifty. Worth the price.

19. NEPONSET MARSHES
Milton
Approximately 700 acres   *MDC   1899

Activities: walking, birdwatching, nature study
Hours: dawn to dusk
Admission: free

One of the constant activities of Bostonians has traditionally been the filling of marshes to create land for building. We now know that salt marshes are a critical part of our ecosystem. Each acre of salt marsh produces more organic matter than an acre of the most productive Iowa wheatfield. Food fish, including flounder and mullet, use the marsh as a breeding ground. Spawn, small fish, shellfish, and vegetable matter are flushed out of the marsh at each high tide, providing food for striped bass, tuna, swordfish, and other large sea animals. Marshes also eliminate many man-made pollutants before they reach the sea. As scientists over the last thirty years have increasingly realized the vital function of salt marshes, the state and federal governments have responded by placing stringent restrictions on the filling of marshes. It is therefore ironic that the largest surviving salt marsh immediately south of Boston was preserved not for environmental reasons, but rather, in the words of Charles Eliot, "to protect the view."

Neponset Marsh is the large grassy tract that you see on your right after passing Neponset Circle heading out of Boston on the Southeast Expressway. It was particularly the view from Milton Hill that the Metropolitan Park Commission was trying to protect. As early as 1774 Governor Hutchinson, who lived on the hill, declared that his friends thought the view of the green grasses and snaking Neponset River "the finest prospect that ever they saw" (see Section 18, Governor Hutchinson's Field).

The marsh grasses were cut as fodder for at least two hundred years, but when the railroad, steam-powered tractor, and electric trolley came, the need for hay had declined, and so apparently the marshes were lying unused by the late 1890s. When the Park Commission decided to purchase the Neponset Marsh, most of the owners were willing to either give their marshes to the Commission or sell the land at half the assessed value. The many narrow ditches through the marsh were cut during the seventeenth and eighteenth centuries to keep the marsh from ponding, which would have hampered salt-marsh hay production. They were re-cut in the 1930s by the Civilian Conservation Corps as a mosquito-control measure.

The marsh contains two relatively distinct zones: a low marsh and a high marsh. The low marsh is submerged during each daily high tide and exposed to the air at each low tide—the predominant plant is salt-marsh cordgrass. The high marsh is awash only during the highest tides ("spring" tides) of each monthly cycle, and the predominant plant is salt-meadow cordgrass. The Neponset Marsh is a large open tract and a natural nesting and feeding place for many bird species, making it a favorite spot for birdwatchers. In an hour's walk in season, one is almost sure of seeing a marsh hawk, a flock of snowy egrets, and several species of duck. Kingfishers, kestrels, great blue herons, bitterns, and a wide variety of other marsh birds may be seen here.

Activities:

To enter the marsh, cross the stream that parallels Christopher Drive, then follow a trail that snakes through a stand of cattails. The marsh itself is flat and grassy and easy walking. Wear boots or plan on wet feet. The bird calls and whispering grasses will help you forget the roar of the nearby Expressway. Bring your binoculars.

Directions:

Public transportation: Red Line (Ashmont) to Ashmont. Take Wollaston Beach-Ashmont bus to Squantum Street. Get out at Christopher Drive.

Bike: Dorchester Lower Mills to Adams Street, to Squantum Street, to third left on Christopher Drive.

Auto: From Boston take Southeast Expressway to East Milton exit, turn right on Adams Street, then right on Squantum Street, then third left on Christopher Drive.

Parking: Along Christopher Drive. Cross stream to begin walk.

20. NANTASKET BEACH
MDC Nantasket Headquarters, Nantasket Avenue, Hull 02045
2 miles long   MDC   1899

Activities: swimming, jogging, picnicking, amusement
park, birdwatching
Hours: dawn to dusk
Admission: free

*No finer stretch of beach can be found on the Atlantic Coast than at
Nantasket.*

Boston Beacon 1898

Nantasket is a long sandy barrier beach connecting several drumlins and rocky outcrops. Almost completely developed as a summer
resort, except for the beach itself, this is nevertheless one of the
loveliest and most popular beaches in the vicinity of Boston.

The first white man to settle in Nantasket was John Oldham, an
immigrant to Plymouth who was expelled by that colony for
disagreeing with the church. Oldham arrived at Nantasket in 1624
and in the following year was joined by several other Plymouth
dissidents. They were all planters and soon set out their first crops.
The beach was also the site of a Plymouth Colony storehouse, from
which the Pilgrims traded with the Indians in the Boston region.
Before the 1630 arrival of the Boston Puritans, small fishing boats
were plying the offshore waters here in search of cod. But apparently the sandy soil was infertile and the life hard at Nantasket, for
in 1629 one settler was in such poor condition that he petitioned a
cruising Plymouth boat to remove him from the long peninsula. In
1830 the total population of Nantasket and the islands off its
shores was 193. The beach was already becoming a popular resort,
aided by weekend ferry service from Boston. The first hotel on the
beach, The Sportsman, was doing a thriving business, counting
Daniel Webster among its customers. Farming, though, was the
principal occupation of the inhabitants, supplemented by shipping
and fishing.

The first of the Grand Hotels in Nantasket, the Rockland
House, was built in 1854. Over the next half century Nantasket
Beach became one of the most famous resorts in the Northeast,
second only to Newport in the wealth of its clientele and a favored
rest spot of presidents. As the resort grew, a clique of local citizens
took over the town government and for the next fifty years their
organization, known as the Old Ring, controlled the town in a
most corrupt manner, an era documented in Dr. William M.
Gergen's delightful book, *Old Nantasket.* Nantasket was the only
"wet" town between Boston and Provincetown. Not only were

there legal barrooms but innumerable illegal ones as well, with the proprietors paying off town officials for "protection." Prostitution, gambling, and pickpocketing were also among the town's biggest businesses. To ensure their continued control, the Old Ring fixed many town elections.

By the 1890s the beach was disappearing beneath a profusion of casinos and honkytonks. In an attempt to ensure public access to the beach and a modicum of safety from pickpockets, the Metropolitan Park Commission purchased a mile of beach. The public beach could be patrolled by men not beholding to the Old Ring. Building setbacks kept prostitutes, gamblers, and bars away from playing families. Sunshelters, bathhouses, and a police station were constructed. But the fear of crime—wallets and pocketbooks often didn't make it from the ferry dock to the beach—began to cause the crowds to dwindle.

Paragon Park was built in 1905 to attract new visitors. The amusement park was equipped with a huge mural of the Jamestown Flood, a tall lighted tower, oriental dancing girls, a wild-west show complete with more than a hundred cowboys and Indians, and a resident circus. Paragon Park suffered from severe fires in 1916 and 1923, so that little remains of the ornate park as it was originally built.

Activities:

Today Nantasket is a popular and crowded developed beach two miles in extent. The soft white sand is as fine to play in today as it was in 1900, and if the crime is long gone, a bit of the honky-tonk atmosphere remains across the beach road. Families still find much pleasure in going to the beach, the old folks sitting in the shade 'neath pavilions built by the Metropolitan Park Commission nearly eighty years ago, and then going on the rides, pitching skee ball, or playing Pac Man.

Swimming: Clean white sand and clear, relatively warm water. Lots of space for long walks, games, or running around. Bathhouse, toilets, and first aid station. Gentle dropoff and lifeguards make this a fine safe beach for children. Lots of snack bars across the street. Good wet sand for castles.

Picnicking: On the beach or under pavilion.

Jogging: Along the beach or on promenade.

Birdwatching: Good sea and bay ducks in the winter as well as cormorants, sandpipers, and plovers.

Paragon Park: Giant rollercoaster is one of the biggest in the world. Twenty-five or so other rides both for kiddies and those with stronger stomachs. High double waterslide. Penny arcades, "games of skill," ice-cream stands, and bars.

Reading:

Old Nantasket by Dr. William M. Bergen is one of the funniest town histories you will ever read. A member of the Old Ring, the author tells the story of Nantasket's heyday with charming outrageousness.

Directions:

MBTA: Red Line to Quincy. Summer Nantasket bus runs all the way to the beach.

Boat: Ferryboats make a delightful excursion to and from Nantasket several times each summer day. Massachusetts Bay Line boats leave from Rowes Wharf, near Aquarium station on the MBTA Blue Line; call 542-8000 for information. Bay State, Spray, and Provincetown line boats leave from Long Wharf, also near Aquarium station; call 723-7800 for more information. Round trips: adults, six dollars, children, three dollars.

Auto or bike: Route 3A from Neponset Circle, continue to Hingham Harbor, then follow signs to beach.
Auto: Route 128 to Route 3 to Route 228 to Nantasket.
Or: Route 3A south from Neponset Circle, left on Washington Street in Hingham; follow signs to the beach.
Parking: Plenty except on the hottest Sundays and holidays, when you should try to be there by 11:00 A.M.

Telephone: 925-9898

21. WORLD'S END RESERVATION
Martin's Lane, Hingham
249 acres   *Trustees of Reservations   1967

Activities: strolling, scenic viewing, nature study, ski touring, fishing, jogging, birdwatching
Map: available from the warden at the entrance
Hours: 10:00 A.M. to sunset
Admission: small fee charged

. . . an island of beauty where we can still enjoy the satisfaction of lying in a field of warm grass and looking at the sky; where we can still watch wildlife undisturbed by the noise and confusion of the city; where we can still walk on beaches washed by the sea without seawalls and hotdog concessions; and where we can turn momentarily to simple pleasures such as seeing a child explore the mystery of the coming spring.
Samuel Wakeman
Chairman of the Committee to Preserve World's End

If there is a natural heaven on earth in Greater Boston, a place that eighteenth-century romantic theorists could have used to define one of their favorite words, "picturesque," it is World's End. At the top of Martin's Lane, where you turn off Rockland Street, a gate once defined the bounds of the great estate owned by the Brewer family, known as World's End Farm. The estate included Cushing Neck, the peninsula between the Weir River and Hingham Harbor, and World's End, the two "islands," each composed of two smoothly rounded drumlins, connected to each other and the shore by sandbars.

The first settler of the area was Abraham Martin, who arrived in

Hingham in 1635. Martin dug a well almost directly across the road from the present attendant's cottage and gave the little lane, which he may have laid out, his name. At first World's End was separated from Cushing Neck by a sandbar that was flooded during high tides, but by the end of the 1600s stone dams had been constructed along the harbor and river, providing a permanent crossing and transforming the salt marsh into a freshwater marsh, known henceforth as "Dammed Meadows."

For the next 230 years the territory served as pasture, woodlot, and hayfield for nearby farmers who erected only two small buildings on World's End in all that time. Hingham became an important seaport and shipbuilding center, and even the shallow Weir

River bustled with shipping. A huge ringbolt, fastened to a rock where the river narrows before entering the bay, was used by ships winching themselves into and out of the river against the tide or wind.

John Brewer, a wealthy Bostonian, and his wife Caroline began

their estate in 1855 with the purchase of twenty-four acres on Cushing's Neck, building a house on the west side of Martin's Lane in the same year. Only one structure was standing in the entire World's End–Cushing's Neck area, an old barn. By 1882 the Brewers owned the Neck and World's End in their entirety, as well as two neighboring islands in Hingham Harbor.

In the late 1880s the Brewers hired Frederick Law Olmsted to plan roads, landscape, and subdivide World's End into houselots. Olmsted, most famous for his park-making, was also among the first to lay out subdivisions taking advantage of topography and scenery to enhance the sought-for rural values of a development— the two most notable examples of his work of this sort being Chicago's Riverside district and Sudbrook outside Philadelphia. Because only three trees were growing on World's End at the time, Olmsted designed gently curving roads with rows of tree plantings. The property was subdivided into 163 building lots. By 1900 the roads had been built and lined with double rows of trees on each side. English oaks were the most widely planted trees, and walnuts, chestnuts, Norway maples, basswoods, and larches, among other species, were also established. Fortunately, for some now-obscure reason, the lots were never sold; now many of those ninety-year-old trees have grown with room to spread their limbs.

The farm, which had expanded to include sixteen buildings and employ more than a dozen workers, continued as a great estate through the mid-1930s.

In 1944 the estate was purchased by Helen Brewer Walker, John's granddaughter who had married the estate's manager in 1920. The estate had become too unwieldy to be run as a farm and so the Walkers felt constrained to sell a portion of the tract as house lots. Fortunately again, the subdivision and those which followed were on Cushing's Neck and not World's End. Slowly the old estate was demolished, there now being only traces left.

In 1945 World's End was considered briefly as a site for the United Nations. In the early 1960s it was proposed as a site for a nuclear power plant. The Trustees of Reservations had tried to acquire the property in 1940 and so when the Metropolitan Area Planning Council gave World's End its highest acquisition priority as an open space in the mid-1960s, the Trustees were ready to move. In an extraordinary fund-raising effort $450,000 was raised from 1,800 individual donors, most of whom lived in the South Shore community. The property was purchased and turned over to the Trustees.

Walk out to the granite shores of Rocky Neck by bearing right past the entrance on old roads that have rarely felt a tire, past the overgrown thickets of buckthorne, chokecherry, cranberry viburnum, and old orchard trees. A boardwalk extends across the "Dammed Meadows," a favorite haunt of ducks, snowy egrets, and redwing blackbirds. Keep your eyes open for the ruffed grouse, warblers, and sparrows that nest in this quiet area.

Out at the end of World's End, jonquils bloom in the overgrown fields each spring as they have for a hundred or more years. The fields are mown only often enough to keep woody species from developing, but not often enough to keep masses of pasture roses from tinting the summer fields pink. An interesting assortment of trees will be found in the narrow valley between the two hills, site of the sheepfold, one of only three structures ever built on World's End. Nothing but islands lie between the height of the last drumlin and Boston; below are the cottages of Sunset Point.

Activities:

To maintain the wonderful feeling at World's End, picnicking and "conduct which disturbs the tranquility of the Reservation" are prohibited. To further protect the environment of World's End and ensure that it does not suffer from overuse, the parking lot is intentionally kept small. All this protection has kept World's End a most romantic place to saunter or loll around on the grassy slopes.

Walking: Six miles of pasture roads and woodland trails. Mostly easy walking. Don't forget to see Rocky Neck.

Jogging: Along the Olmsted-designed roads. Not for groups.

Fishing: Five miles of shoreline, with bass, flounder, mackerel.

Reading:

The Trustees have published *History of World's End,* complete with maps and photographs. It is presently out of print but soon to be reissued.

Directions:

Route 3A south through Hingham Harbor; at rotary take Rockland Street toward Nantasket; Martin's Lane just ahead at the lights, turn left. Entrance and parking at end of lane.

Parking: Small lot but worth the wait if it is full.

22. GREAT ESKER PARK
Elva Road, North Weymouth   02191
238 acres   Weymouth Park Department   1965

Activities: walking, nature study, picnicking, birdwatching
Map: free by sending SASE or at Park Department Head-
quarters on Elva Road
Hours: dawn to dusk
Admission: no charge

The Great Esker along the Back River is one of the most unusual
natural features in the region. A long high ridge like the Great
Wall of China, it forms a towering rampart between suburban
Weymouth and the marshes of the river. There are other eskers in
the region, but this is by far the most spectacular, and the park
between the esker and the Back River is beautiful.

Eskers were formed about twelve thousand years ago near the
end of the last Ice Age. As the mile-thick glacier melted, retreating
to the north, streams and rivers fed by meltwater coursed through
and beneath the ice. The glacier had picked up huge amounts of
dirt, rock, sand, and clay, and as it melted, it released this burden
into its streams. The debris settled to the bottom of the streams,
forming stratified deposits of sand and gravel. When the glacier
disappeared, these internal deposits remained as long sinuous
ridges. The park also contains several kettlehole ponds.

At least seven thousand years ago Indians began to inhabit the
base of the esker, along the Back River. Shell middens tell us that
clams and other shellfish were abundant, and wildfowl must have
filled the marshes. At the outlet of the tidal kettlehole pond, now
known as The Bathtub, the natives erected fish weirs. When the
shopping mall along Route 3A was constructed, an Indian burial
ground was discovered. If you keep your eye to the ground, this is
a good place to discover arrowheads and spear points.

Like the Indians, the English settlers of Weymouth hunted
along the marshes. At the outlet of The Bathtub, where the Indian
fish weir had probably been, the settlers built a tidal-powered grist
mill. The settlers harvested salt hay along the river using horses
with oversized shoes.

In 1909 when the United States Naval Ammunition Dump was
built across the river, the Great Esker was taken as a security
buffer. A road was laid along the crest of the long ridge for
military patrols. The Navy excavated part of the esker for the
gravel used in building the runways of Weymouth Naval Air

Station. In 1965 the Town of Weymouth purchased the Great Esker for use as a park.

The steep-sided esker is mantled with a woodland of hickory, red oak, black cherry, black locust, and sassafras. The wildflowers of the forest floor include whorled loosestrife, pipissewa, sarsaparilla, Canada mayflower, blueberries, and a rich tangle of raspberries. The marshes below the esker are a likely place to sight a great blue heron, snowy egret, or marsh hawk, in addition to flocks of ducks and numerous shorebirds.

Activities:

No facilities.

Walking: The crest of the ridge and the fingers of land around The Bathtub are beautiful quiet places to walk. The view from the crest takes in the river on one side and Weymouth on the other.

Picnicking: The fingers of land that encircle The Bathtub are especially delightful places for pack-it-in/pack-it-out picnics.

Directions:

Route 3A south from Boston; cross Fore River Bridge, then proceed one mile to right on Green Street; then left on Elva Road to the end.

Or: Route 3A south from Boston; cross Fore River Bridge. Continue one and a half miles to shopping center on right before Back River Bridge. Turn in to the shopping center and park behind it along the far fence.

Telephone: 337-4742

22A. STODDER'S NECK

This short neck of land protruding into the mouth of the Back River is a twenty-acre MDC park. Gravel companies mined the hill here for years, but the MDC has planted grass and trees and laid out trails to make a pretty little area suitable for jogging, picnicking, or strolling. Picnic tables and a boat landing, but no other facilities. Nice views.

Directions:

Coming from Boston on Route 3A, cross the Back River Bridge and take an immediate left into the small parking lot.

22B. BARE COVE PARK

This area of 468 acres, across the river from Great Esker Park, was acquired by the Town of Hingham in 1971. It includes the naturalizing remains of the former Naval Ammunition Dump. The marshes along the river are an important wildlife sanctuary, holding one of the largest nesting colonies of great blue herons in the region. Very pleasant picnic sites have been laid out throughout the park. Other facilities include a three-mile bicycle trail, fishing dock, observation tower, and extensive trail system.

Directions:

Turn right into park after crossing Back River Bridge.

The Hingham Land Conservation Trust, P.O. Box 10, Hingham, MA 02043, publishes an excellent and informative map of more than sixty park and conservation areas in Hingham.

23. WEBB STATE PARK
River Street, Weymouth
30 acres   *State Park   1970s

Activities: picnicking, walking, nature study, fishing, bird-watching
Hours: 9:00 A.M. to dusk
Admission: free

Out on the tip of Weymouth Lower Neck, at the mouth of the Back River, a finger of low glacial deposits occupied by Webb State Park stretches into Hingham Bay. During the 1950s and 1960s this was the site of a Nike missile base, but now all that remains of the defense installation are a few blocked-off ventilator shafts, square metal mushrooms growing in a landscape of open fields.

During the early days of the Revolution, the "Alarm of Grape Island" was carried out here. The British, cut off from potential supplies by the Colonists' landward embargo, needed hay to feed their horses. One morning in 1775, three British ships set out to gather hay on Grape Island, owned by Tory Elisha Leavitt, across the channel from the Neck. Thinking the British were invading, Minutemen from surrounding towns gathered on the tip of the peninsula. After assessing the situation, they drove the British away, though not before the Redcoats had stowed three tons of hay. To prevent a repeat of the British foray, the Patriots burned the rest of Leavitt's hay and torched his barn.

The meadows where the missiles were once planted now are overflowing with wildflowers: purple clover, vetch, and alfalfa; yellow wintercress, wild indigo, clover, and field hawkweed; blue toadflax and chicory; Deptford pinks; and white hoary alyssum, clover, and daisies. The meadows also harbor nesting birds and the plaintive call of the killdeer is common all summer. Shorebirds nest and feed along the rocky shingle beach; cormorants and bay ducks cruise offshore.

Activities:

This open park surrounded by the sea is peaceful, under-used, and very easy on the eye.

Picnicking: Fine place for picnics. Only a few tables and benches, and so consider bringing a blanket or chairs. Bathrooms. Unsupervised swimming on a small sandy beach.

Walking: Beautiful gravel roads skirt the shore before ending at the point looking out to Grape Island and Boston Harbor. Good beachcombing.

Fishing: Shore casting for flounder, bass, and occasional bluefish.

Directions:

Route 3A south through Weymouth, left on Neck Road several hundred yards before the Back River Bridge rotary, continue to end.

Parking: Plenty.

24. WOLLASTON BEACH
Quincy Shore Drive, Quincy
2 miles of beachfront   *MDC   Circa 1900

Activities: swimming, fishing, picnicking, birdwatching
Hours: 8:00 A.M. to dusk
Admission: no charge

In 1625 Captain Wollaston, an English adventurer, established a settlement on Passonagisset, the hill at the south end of Wollaston Beach. Wollaston's little colony traded for furs with the Massachuset Indians and made a halfhearted attempt at agriculture. At the time, Chickatawbut, sachem of the Massachuset, had his main camp at the north end of the beach on Moswetusset Hummock, Moswetusset being another spelling of Massachuset.

Two years later, after Wollaston had returned to England, leaving his name with the beach, an ambitious lawyer named Thomas Morton took over the colony. Morton pursued the Indian trade aggressively, giving the Indians guns and rum for furs. Not being a Puritan, Morton apparently enjoyed consorting with the Indians. After renaming Passonagisset Merry Mount, he gathered the friendly Indians of the neighborhood for a celebration of dancing around a maypole. Already upset with Morton's incursions into their fur-trading monopoly and his gun swapping, Myles Standish and the Plymouth militia put a stop to the dancing, arresting Morton and sending him back to England for execution. But the king, not a Puritan, dismissed the charges against Morton. Morton returned to Merry Mount, only to be arrested again, but the site of his colony remained known as Merry Mount.

By 1900 Wollaston Beach was undergoing the sort of unplanned development that had previously blocked public access to other beaches. A few years later the beach was acquired by the Metropolitan Park Commission. The MPC laid out a carriage drive along the crest of the beach and built a bathhouse.

Activities:

Swimming: Wollaston Beach is surprisingly clean, considering its proximity to Boston. The beach is sandy and gravelly and nearly disappears during high tide, but it is nonetheless pleasant and convenient. Lifeguards, bathhouse, and bathrooms. Snack bars with excellent clams across the street. Gentle dropoff and surf.

Fishing: Surf fishing at the end of the beach near the outlet of Black's Creek.

Picnicking: In addition to picnicking on the beach, Caddy Memorial Park, across from the beach by Black's Creek, is a very pleasant little picnic area. The facilities at Caddy Park include picnic tables (bring your own charcoal grill), a wooden tower overlooking the marshes behind the beach, jungle gyms, and slides.

Birdwatching: Wollaston Beach is a fine spot during fall, winter, and spring for seeing rafts of bay ducks, plovers, sandpipers, grebes, loons, and sanderlings.

Directions:
MBTA: Red Line (Braintree car) to Wollaston station. Fifteen-minute walk down Beach Street to beach or take bus marked Wollaston Beach.
Bike or auto: Route 3A south from Neponset Circle. Left on Quincy Shore Drive to beach.
Parking: Plenty, though very crowded on hot summer weekends.

25. BOSTON HARBOR ISLANDS
Wompatuck State Park	***MDC***
Union Street, Hingham,	***20 Somerset Street,***
MA 02043	***Boston, MA 02108***
State Park	MDC Reservation

Activities: walking and exploring, picnicking, boating, camping, swimming, fishing, nature study, birdwatching, historic sites
Hours: dawn to dusk
Admission: no charge

The Boston Harbor islands are a treasure such as few cities anywhere can boast. If the Park System is Boston's "Emerald Necklace," then the harbor islands are its "Emerald Tiara," green isles set in the deep waters of the harbor that was once among the busiest in the world. Each of the islands has its own story and recreational possibilities—the emphasis here will be on those islands accessible by public transportation.

Indians arrived in the region behind the retreating glaciers and canoed out to the islands some six thousand years ago. When Captain John Smith explored the harbor in 1614, he found "many isles all planted with corn, groves, mulberries, savage gardens, and good harbors. . . . The seacoast shows all along large cornfields, and great troops of well-proportioned people." He also remarked that several of the islands were wooded.

Within a year of their 1630 arrival, the Puritan settlers of

Boston were turning to the islands for pastureland and fuelwood. Soon each island was privately owned and going its own way.

The first comprehensive analysis of the islands and their scenic and recreational potential was Frederick Law Olmsted's 1887 report to the Boston Park Commission. Olmsted assessed the acreage, ownership, and municipal jurisdiction of seventy-five islands in the harbor (he included almost every rock that poked above the surface). He found that the islands' chief drawback, from his perspective as a landscape architect, was that all had been denuded of trees. He recommended that city-funded tree plantings be commenced on all the islands, private as well as public. But little attention was paid to the report and no action was taken until nearly our own day.

Although many sticky issues remain, such as what to do about Peddock's Island and how to put all the publicly owned islands under one management, each year has seen the public's access to the islands grow. Hazards have been removed and interpretive programs have been developed, making the islands a rare urban delight.

Activities:

Freshwater is either not available or in short supply; bring a canteen or jug of water with you.

Swimming: The only developed swimming area is the sandy beach on Lovell's Island. It is the only lifeguard-patrolled beach and the only safe place for children to swim. Picnicking is permitted. At-your-own-risk swimming is allowed, but not encouraged, on the other islands. Use caution. The water is clear and cold around the islands.

Picnicking: Permitted on all the islands except Peddock's. Tables and grills provided, as are toilets. Take a blanket or chairs on weekends, because all the tables may be taken after the first boat arrives.

Boating: All the islands but Peddock's have public boat docks for landing, but boats must be moored offshore. There is room for a limited number of boats to tie up at George's Island. With a private boat you can explore the entire archipelago, certainly one of the most pleasurable outdoor activities in all New England. Public launching areas providing access to the harbor include state ramps on Shirley Street in Winthrop, Terminal Street in Charlestown, Nonantum Road in Newton on the Charles River, and River Street in Weymouth.

Fishing: Public piers on all the islands except Peddock's. Dozens of good places to cast a line from the rocky shores of each island. Innumerable flounder, cod, haddock, pollock, and hefty striped bass have been caught off these shores. Check with your local bait shop about bait and tackle (check Yellow Pages).

Interpretive programs: Staff and volunteer rangers are stationed on each island during the summer to guide walks, recall the history and legends, and point out the natural features and wildlife. Although they help enforce the regulations, most are friendly gold mines of interesting information.

Nature study: The geology of the harbor islands is described in Father Skehan's *Puddingstone, Drumlins, and Ancient Volcanoes. An Illustrated Flora of the Boston Harbor Islands* by Levering and Pastuchiv combines a complete island-by-island list of the islands' plants with descriptions and excellent illustrations of many of the more common wildflowers. Self-guiding nature trail on Lovell's Island.

Birdwatching: More than a hundred species of birds have been sighted on the islands. The gulls, blackbirds, and cormorants seem to rule the roost, but the islands are famous for their heron colonies and terns. Ducks and shorebirds flock here in the spring with a fair number remaining to nest. A fine warbler station as well. The best birding is along the less-frequented shores and in the scrubby island interiors.

Walking: All the islands have pleasant, if short, trail systems. Great for exploring, but be careful of the profuse poison ivy.

Camping: This is the finest place to camp in the region, providing a unique experience of wilderness sea-island camping. Small campsites have been developed on Lovell's, Peddock's, Bumpkin, and Grape islands. Primitive toilets. Bring your own water.

A special permit is required for all camping on the harbor islands: apply well in advance of the date you plan to camp. Free permit for state-owned Grape and Bumpkin islands by writing or calling Boston Harbor Islands State Park Headquarters at Wompatuck State Park at address and telephone above. Camping on MDC-owned Peddock's and Lovell's islands from MDC at address and telephone above; permit costs three dollars weekdays and five dollars on weekends.

Free water taxi: From Memorial Day to Labor Day a free taxi provides regular, scheduled transportation from George's Island to Gallop's and Lovell's islands. Less-frequent daily service from George's to Peddock's, Grape, Bumpkin, and Great Brewster islands.

Reading:

The Islands of Boston Harbor by Edward Rowe Snow and *Boston Harbor Islands* by Kales and Kales. The 1972 *Boston Harbor Islands Comprehensive Plan* by the Metropolitan Area Planning Council is loaded with information and a series of detailed maps for each island.

Directions:

Ferryboats depart from T and Rowe's wharves on the waterfront near Faneuil Hall and the Aquarium, throughout the summer. For round trip, adults, three dollars; children under twelve, two dollars. Call or write State Park for current schedule.

Telephone:

State Park: 749-7160
MDC: 727-5250

25A. GEORGE'S ISLAND   *MDC

Dominated by the massive star-shaped earthen and concrete embankments of Fort Warren, this twenty-eight-acre island spent two hundred years standing sentry before the gates of Boston. Beginning in 1628 with James Pemberton of Hull, the island served a succession of owners as farm and pastureland. During the Revolution some of the fields were dug up for fortifications by French sailors seeking to protect their Boston-based fleet from British attack. Around this time the island was named George's after Captain John George, a civic-minded Boston merchant.

After the many sea battles of the War of 1812, Boston purchased the island and turned it over to the federal government as a site for a fort. Construction began on the fort in 1834 under the direction of military architect Sylvanus Thayer, "Father of West Point" and designer of Fort Independence on Castle Island. Using the French five-pointed-star fort as a model, Thayer had earth moved and thousands of hand-hewn blocks of Quincy and Cape Ann granite molded into ten-foot-thick walls, gun emplacements, dry moat, bunkers, and barracks. The fort was named after General Joseph Warren, a leading patriot killed at the Battle of Bunker Hill. In 1958 the fort was designated a National Historic Site.

During the Civil War 300 guns on movable carriages and 1,500 men were stationed at the fort. The fort was also used as a military prison: Mason and Sidell, Confederate commissioners to England captured in the early days of the war, were imprisoned here, as was the Confederate vice-president, who was captured near the war's end. The ditty "John Brown's Body," which served as the basis for Julia Ward Howe's "Battle Hymn of the Republic," was composed by soldiers stationed at Fort Warren during the war. In 1946 the island was purchased by the MDC as a park.

Activities:

George's Island is the most developed of the harbor islands. Picnic area, bathrooms, snack bar, first aid station, and tot-lot. Ranger-conducted tours and tape-recorded guided tour of fort. This is the main terminal point for the water taxi to the other islands and the ferryboats from the waterfront.

25B. LOVELL'S ISLAND *MDC

This long, sixty-two-acre island, with drumlins in the middle and at the north end, was one of the wooded islands that greeted John Winthrop and the Boston settlers of 1630. Named after Captain John Lovell, it was logged bare to supply fuelwood to Castle Island's fort and the growing town of Boston, and then became a farm.

The city acquired the island after the War of 1812 and gave it to the federal government for use as a fort. Seawalls were constructed at both ends of the island in 1844. During the Civil War a company of New Hampshire infantrymen was stationed on the windswept island. After the war, a tunnel was built under the channel, connecting the island to George's Island. The tunnel was not used for communication or as an escape passage, but rather as a marine defense. Explosive charges were set in the tunnel that could be blown up by remote control, destroying any enemy armada trying to steam into the harbor. But like the rest of the harbor's fortifications the tunnel never saw action.

Activities:

The best beach on the islands is found here. Fine picnic area, bathroom, boating and fishing pier, and primitive camping. Free water taxi from George's Island.

25C. GALLOP'S ISLAND   *State Park

Until recently, this was one of the most intensively used islands in the harbor. Its first owner was Captain John Gallop, a harbor pilot. Later, vegetables and milk from the island were sold to ships anchored in the harbor. Gravel was removed from the round drumlin that dominates the island to fill in mainland marshes, perhaps in South Boston. Another portion of the drumlin was cut away when Fort Warren was built to clear a firing and lookout line. In 1819 the island was purchased by Peter Newcomb, whose wife operated a restaurant and inn on the island until his death in 1833.

During the Civil War 3,000 Union soldiers were barracked on the small island. In 1866 the island was returned to the city, which then built a quarantine hospital on it. In 1916 a new quarantine hospital was built by the U.S. Immigration Service to quarantine suspected disease carriers. During World War II the U.S. Maritime Service operated a radio school on the island. After the war several of the buildings were sold, jacked up, and floated off the island on barges—one served as a gym for Boston University. The island itself was sold as well and was used for a few years as a dump.

Activities:

The remnants of the dump have been trucked away and the hospital foundations and asphalt roads are slowly being reclaimed by beach grass, sumac, and wild roses. The view from the top of the drumlin, one of the highest points in the harbor, is outstanding. Many lovely picnic spots along the beach and on the west slope of the drumlin. Fishing and boating at pier. Bathroom. Free water taxi from George's Island.

25D. PEDDOCK'S ISLAND   *MDC

At 113 acres, Peddock's Island is the largest of the harbor islands not connected to the mainland. It is comprised of four drumlins connected by low sandy beaches and is covered by lush vegetation. Acquired by the MDC in 1968, the island is now managed by a coalition of nonprofit organizations called the Peddock's Island Trust.

In 1971 a local resident uncovered an Indian skeleton on the island. Carbon dated as at least 4,000 years old, it confirms the long history of Indian occupation of the islands. Leonard Peddock, a refugee from the failed colony at Wessagusset (Weymouth), settled on the island in 1622. Before the British were driven from Boston at the start of the Revolution, they "harvested" thirty cows and five hundred sheep from the island to supply their embargoed dinner tables.

The federal government purchased eighty-eight acres of the island in 1900 for use as a naval defense. Twelve-inch mortar batteries were installed to lob shells at invading navies. The base was named Fort Andrew after a professor of languages at West Point. During World War II antiaircraft guns were emplaced and a thousand Italian prisoners of war were held here.

The natural history of Peddock's Island is among the harbor islands' most varied. One of the most prolific black-crowned night heron rookeries in the state is in an old apple orchard here. Quail, woodcock, egret, and an occasional great blue heron also thrive here in the dense brush and marshes. The area around old Fort Andrew has some of the biggest trees on the islands: cottonwood, birch, maple, and pine. Clumps of salt-spray rose garland the shores.

Activities:

The Peddock's Island Trust offers a wide variety of history and natural-history tours of the island; unsupervised activities are not permitted. Tours leave several times a day from George's Island on a free water taxi. Camping is allowed with a special permit from the MDC (see Camping above). No private boats are allowed to land at this island.

25E. GRAPE ISLAND   *State Park

This fifty-acre island, near the mouth of the Back River, was a favorite clamming spot of the Indians, as evidenced by scattered shell heaps and other artifacts found here. The island, named for the tangle of grapevines that grew here, was cleared by early Puritan settlers and turned into pastureland. During the Revolution, the British attempted to harvest hay here, causing the Minutemen to call "The Alarm at Grape Island" (see Section 23, Webb State Park).

The island is composed of two drumlins with a low saddle between them. Though much of the island is covered by a dense brush of sumac, poison ivy, raspberries, and wild roses, the southern drumlin is covered by old grassy fields filled with wildflowers. The view from the seventy-foot hilltop is excellent.

Activities:

This is a particularly peaceful island, great for strolling or picnicking. Picnic tables, primitive toilets, and boating and fishing dock. Free camping with state permit (see Camping above). Free water taxi from George's Island.

25F. BUMPKIN ISLAND   *State Park

From the 1630s to nearly 1900, this thirty-five acre drumlin was under almost continuous cultivation. At first privately owned, in 1682 it was donated to little Harvard College by Samuel Ward. The college leased it in turn to farmers for the next 218 years. In 1900 it was sold to philanthropist Clarence Burrage, who built on the island a hospital for paraplegic children. During World War II, the island was sold to the Navy, which stationed 1,300 sailors on the small acreage. After the war most of the buildings were dismantled and those which remained burned to the ground.

Activities:

Although much of the island is covered with thickets, several old roads lead into the interior. Picnic tables and grills, fishing and boating pier, primitive toilets, and walking paths. Camping with state permit (see Camping above). Free water taxi from George's Island.

25G. GREAT BREWSTER ISLAND   *State Park

Largest of the Brewsters and the only drumlin (the other Brewsters are all rocky outcrops), Great Brewster sits just outside the entrance to Boston Harbor. The sparsely vegetated island rises a hundred feet above the waves, providing a spectacular view of the inner islands and both the North and South shores.

Windiness and high ocean waves seem to have slowed the occupation of this island: the first record of its use was when

Boston purchased it in 1848. Boston turned it over to the federal government, which built a seawall on three sides of the island to halt erosion. In 1856 Bug Light, a manned lighthouse built on stilts so that it looked like a giant insect, was erected on a sandspit off the island. In 1930 Bug Light was replaced by an automatic light.

The military occupied the island during both world wars. During World War II an elaborate bunker was built as a control station for the harbor's extensive minefields. Ninety-millimeter rapid-fire guns were emplaced on the height of land to defend against high-speed torpedo boats. After the war the island was largely abandoned.

Activities:

Great Brewster is the wildest and perhaps the most beautiful of the islands. Walking trails, boating and fishing dock, interpretive programs, picnic tables, primitive toilets. Free water taxi from George's Island.

26. WINTHROP BEACH
Winthrop Shore Drive, Winthrop
1.5 miles long   *MDC   1898

Activities: swimming, jogging, fishing, birdwatching

Soon after the settlement of Boston, most of the land around Pullen Point was granted to John Winthrop, first resident governor of Massachusetts Bay Colony. During the summer the area had been frequented by Indians who harvested clams, fish, and lobsters. Early English visitors, to what was essentially an island, found game in abundance: seafood, deer, and even turkeys. They also hunted duck, plover, and sanderling to stuff their bird pies.

In 1711 there were a mere four houses in Winthrop but all the land had been logged and much of it was under cultivation. No bridge connected the island to neighboring Revere or Chelsea until 1839. When the town of Winthrop was incorporated in 1744, there were only forty-five dwellings in the entire area and not one of them was along the beach. The farmers grew corn and potatoes, raking up kelp from the shore for fertilizer.

A real estate development in 1875 brought the first cottages to the beach. The summer colony grew rapidly, with public band concerts and clambakes as an attraction—10,000 people showed up for the 1878 clambake. Ford's Hotel, a famous resort, was built on the beach at about this time. After the Boston, Winthrop, and Point Shirley Railroad reached the beach community, known as Ocean Spray, in 1880, real estate development accelerated. Visitors took a steamship to Point of Pines in Revere and then the railroad to Winthrop.

After a storm destroyed the seawall and many of the cottages in 1898, the beachfront land was turned over to the Metropolitan Park Commission. The town agreed to pay two thirds of the cost of building a new seawall and a beach road. To forestall another disaster, the town enacted strict setbacks from the road and restrictive residential zoning for the new wave of building that followed the construction of Shore Drive. Breakwaters were built in the 1930s of granite rubble with the hope of curtailing erosion and to provide employment.

Geologically Winthrop has a granite spine covered by glacial till and drumlins. Sand pounded by wave action off three of the drumlins—Beachmont Hill, the Highlands, and Point Shirley—collected in the space between, creating the beach.

"Upon ye beach they spied great multitudes of birdes of manie kindes, they being there to pick up ye wormes and little fishes." So wrote Obadiah Turner of Winthrop in his journal for 1638. Winthrop still attracts a great many bird species, particularly in the off-season. Among those sighted by the Bird Observer were mergansers, eiders, plovers, dunlins, red knots, goldeneyes, and sanderlings. In the summer the black cormorants sitting on the breakwater are hard to miss.

Activities:

This one-and-a-half-mile beach runs between Fort Heath and Point Shirley. The beach ends at the rotary, but the rocky shore and seawall beyond are quiet places to walk and explore tidepools.

Swimming: In its center the beach is wide and sandy with lifeguards on patrol. Much of the beach is lost at high tide, but the seawall is wide enough for beach blankets and chairs. Pondlike tidepools along the beach are swimmable and extremely popular with children. No facilities.

Fishing: Off jetties at either end of the beach during high tide. Off breakwater during low tide. (Be sure to walk back before the incoming water becomes too deep.)

Jogging: On beach or along two-mile-long sidewalk along Shore Drive.

Directions:

Bike: Revere Beach Parkway to Revere, right on Winthrop Parkway, follow signs to beach.

Auto: Second right after Sumner Tunnel, Bennington Street to Saratoga Street, follow signs to beach.

Parking: Along Shore Drive. Limited on weekends.

27. REVERE BEACH
Revere Beach Boulevard, Revere
2 miles of shorefront   *MDC   1896

Activities: swimming, picnicking, birdwatching, fishing, jogging

Hours: 8:00 A.M. to dusk

Admission: no charge

"The First Public Beach in the United States"

In its heyday, from the 1880s through the 1940s, Revere Beach was one of the most famous and popular beaches in America. By the millions, people moved from the water of the beach to the promenade, and across the street to the giant amusement park. According to Revere historian Peter McCauley, "Revere Beach has always been a 'people's beach,' a playground for the masses."

In 1846, when Revere, formerly known as Rumney Marsh and North Chelsea, was separated from Chelsea and incorporated as a town, there were only two buildings on the entire four-and-a-half-mile beach. For more than two hundred years the local inhabitants had visited the beach to take clams, mine sand and gravel, and crop marsh hay. Both buildings on the beach were taverns, the Robinson Crusoe House at Point of Pines, built in 1834, and the Neptune House, built in 1845. By 1875 another half-dozen private houses and inns had been added to the windy beach. Then things began to change rapidly.

In 1875 the Narrow Gauge Railroad opened, running from

Boston directly over the crest of the beach to Lynn. Hundreds of hotels, cottages, and taverns immediately followed the railroad's completion. In 1881 the 1,700-foot-long Great Ocean Pier was built with a vast dancehall, rollerskating rink, cafe on the end, and

a landing on the side for excursion steamers from Boston. By 1885 the beach had become such a popular resort that the town installed gaslights along the length of the beach in a celebration with eleven bands playing. But because development was allowed to occur helter-skelter, by 1895 the beach itself was completely obscured under the railroad tracks and a profusion of cottages, bathhouses, and other businesses. On the water side of the tracks, the tightly packed buildings were built on pilings so that there was no beach except at low tide. People had to cross the busy railroad tracks and squeeze between buildings just to reach the low-tide beach.

In 1896 the Metropolitan Park Commission decided that the people of Greater Boston needed a public beach and that Revere Beach could be improved to meet that need. At the time there were no public beaches in Massachusetts, or for that matter, in the entire country. Under the direction of Charles Eliot at the Olmsted firm, the beach was acquired, all the buildings along the shore were removed, and the Narrow Gauge tracks were moved three hundred yards to the west. All buildings were banned from the shore side of the boulevard, which ran along the line of the former tracks, except for the Park Commission's own shade pavilions and bandstand. A police station and bathhouse were constructed, the latter charging "25¢ for a suit, towel, and locker; locker has Yale Lock, a mirror, brush, and comb. 10¢ for children's trunks. 5¢ to check a bicycle." And Revere Beach became not only the first, but also the most popular beach in the region.

Across the boulevard from the beach, amusements and restaurants began to expand. There were dozens of fine seafood restaurants, hot saltwater baths, ballrooms, and beer gardens. Giant merry-go-rounds, funhouses, and lindy loops, bicycle races, fireworks, and circus acts encouraged crowds to stay for the evening. Over the years at least eight roller coasters operated along the amusement strip.

The amusement park and beach began slowly to decline after World War II, until finally in 1978 the MDC returned its attention to its first beach. The amusement park and the old bathhouse were demolished, and the beach itself was cleaned up. The old MDC Police Station was completely restored.

Activities:

Revere Beach is a long barrier beach, of which two miles is owned by the MDC. The beach is lined by a seawall and sidewalk suitable for jogging or people watching. The old Victorian shade pavilions and bandstand have recently been rehabilitated, and the green benches beneath, overlooking the beach, are very popular with the older set. Plenty of snack bars are open across the street.

Swimming: Fine gray sand, good for castles on the lower beach; portions of the upper beach are rocky. Beach is MDC-monitored, and has fairly clean water. Lifeguards, bathrooms, and bathhouse.

Fishing: Surfcasting along the beach in the early evening.

Birdwatching: According to the Eastern Massachusetts Bird Observer, Revere Beach is a very good place for winter birding. Loons, grebes, and eiders may be seen along the breakwater; plovers, sandpipers, and dunlins along the rocks; and buffleheads, goldeneyes, and other sea ducks offshore.

Reading:

Peter McCauley's *Revere Beach: A Pictorial History* has numerous pictures of the old amusement park.

Directions:

MBTA: Blue Line to Revere Beach station. Beach directly across the street.

Bike: Boston's North End to Rutherford Avenue in Charlestown, to Broadway in Everett, to Revere Beach Parkway all the way.

Auto: Route 1A north through Callahan Tunnel. Take Revere Beach Parkway exit and follow signs to beach.

Parking: Plenty, but very crowded on hot summer weekends.

28. NAHANT BEACH
Nahant Beach Parkway, Nahant
1.5 miles   *MDC

Activities: swimming, fishing, picnicking, jogging, tennis, ballfields, bicycling

When the Trustees of Reservations surveyed the Massachusetts coast in 1892, it was discovered that Lynn Beach, today known as Nahant Beach, was the only beach open to the public in the entire Boston region, and only because the beach was a public highway.

The earliest settlers of Nahant in 1629 found that the beach was the summer residence of Poquanum, known as "Black William," a lesser sachem of the Massachuset Indians. Apparently not understanding the English property system, Poquanum sold the entire peninsula to at least two individuals; once for a "suit of clothes," the second time for "two pestle stones."

As the Nahant "islands" became settled, the beach was used as a causeway. Except during the highest spring tides and during storms, the hard-packed fine-grained sand of the beach was suitable for horsedrawn carriages. In 1824 the town and the state both granted funds for the erection of a sand fence the length of the beach in an attempt to control erosion and storm overwash. In 1848 a carriage road was built along the back of the beach on the line of the current roadway. Three years later much of the new road was washed out by a storm. After it was rebuilt a great quantity of rocks, pebbles, and sand was dumped along the causeway and planted with cedars in a further attempt to stop the action of wind, waves, and tides.

Nahant Beach is a typical barrier beach composed of sand worn off nearby headlands and transported by longshore currents. The low dune between the parking lot and the beach is covered with beach grass and banks of salt-spray rose. At the toe of the low dune grow beach pea, seaside goldenrod, and gray-green dusty miller. Across the road a salt marsh lies between the mudflats of Lynn Harbor and the beach.

Activities:

Walking: Walk the beach in the winter and watch the birds.

Swimming: Clean white sand and a beautiful wide beach make this one of the most attractive beaches near Boston. A gentle dropoff and long sandflats when the tide is out make it a particular favorite of children as well as adults. Bathrooms, bathhouse, bubblers, snack bar. Lifeguards on duty until dusk.

Picnicking: Bring your own blanket and chairs.

Jogging: Two-mile paved trail behind beach. Also along the packed sandflats during low tide.

Bicycling: Along paved trail behind beach.

Fishing: Surf fishing in the early evening for flounder, cod, and striped bass.

Tennis: Three courts in excellent condition. Play a set, then go for a swim.

Ballfields: Two ballfields for softball.

Directions:

Auto: Route 1A from Sumner Tunnel, right in Lynn to beach.

Bike: Broadway in Everett to Revere Beach Parkway to Route 1A.

Parking: Large lot behind dune. Two dollars per car. Arrive by 10:30 A.M. on weekends.

Offshore:

Egg Rock is that two-acre oval feldspar rock out in Nahant Bay. It is officially known as Henry Cabot Lodge Wildlife Sanctuary, named for Senator Lodge, whose summer home on Nahant's Eastern Point overlooked the rock— Lodge donated it to the state in 1925. It was always a favorite place of nesting birds; the early settlers of Lynn and Nahant mined the long accumulated bird droppings as fertilizer for their farms. Pine trees that grew on the crest of the rock were cut and used for chair caning. In 1856 a lighthouse and test site for submarine bells were built, the lighthouse remaining in use until 1923. Gulls and double-breasted cormorants nest here in the summer and purple sandpipers and great cormorants flock here in the winter.

29. CUTLER PARK
Needham and Dedham banks of Charles River
80 acres   *MDC   1962

Activities: nature study, birdwatching, walking, picnicking, jogging, fishing

Cutler Park comprises the largest remaining freshwater marsh on the middle Charles, a broad green carpet of sedges, grasses, and rushes, punctuated by an occasional blue flag iris. Sandwiched between Route 128 and the river, the area was once a water reserve for the towns of Newton and Brookline. The tumbledown building at the end of the Kendrick Street trail supplied water to Newton around the turn of the century and the marsh was maintained as an emergency supply until the early 1950s. The glacial

ridges along Route 128 were mined for sand and gravel to fill Boston's Back Bay and the marsh was mined for muck to fertilize farmers' fields. The farmers also cropped the marsh hay each year, calling the area Great Plains.

Birders have identified at least 137 species here, particularly along the shores of Cutler Lake and in the boggy swamp between the lake and the river. This is as good a place as any near Boston for hawk watching: red-tailed hawks nest nearby; brightly colored kestrels and ring-tailed marsh hawks are sighted regularly. Among the birds around the lake are ducks and geese, common snipe, Virginia rail, herons, and plenty of catbirds, mockingbirds, and blackbirds. Species found between the river and the lake include northern orioles, eastern kingbirds, scarlet tanagers, and the long-billed marsh wren.

Trails at either end of the park lead into red pine plantations, probably a reclamation effort of the Civil Conservation Corps (CCC) forty-five years ago. The trail from Riverdale is a gravel causeway across the marsh leading out to a quiet, deeply shaded hummock along the Charles. When the marsh is tinted purple by late summer's loosestrife, the vines along this trail are lush with juicy grapes.

When the park was acquired by the state in 1962, it was named for Leslie B. Cutler, a state senator from Needham who fought long and hard in the Legislature for the protection of wetlands and the preservation of the Charles River marshes as a flood-prevention measure.

Activities:

Walking and jogging: Kendrick Street trail forms a one-and-a-half-mile circle around Cutler Lake. The pine needle cushioned trail is excellent for jogging. Riverdale trail is less than a mile of easy walking.

Picnicking: Pleasant place, particularly Riverdale hummock; no facilities.

Fishing: Cutoffs from both trails lead to the Charles; also from Kendrick Street Bridge and Cutler Lake.

Birding: Very good.

Directions:

Bike or auto: To Kendrick Street trailhead—Route 9 to Hammond Pond Parkway, right at rotary to Newton Street, which becomes Brookline Street, right on Dedham Street then first left down Nahanton Street, which becomes Kendrick Street after crossing the Charles, left between Red Cross building and Polaroid building to trailhead.

Parking: Limited.

Bike or auto: To Riverdale trail—VFW Parkway in West Roxbury, right on Route 109, one mile to right on Pine Street, one mile to trailhead, just beyond last street on right.

Parking: Very limited.

30. BROOK FARM AND SAWMILL MARSH
Baker Street, West Roxbury, MA 02132
180 acres   Lutheran Church and MDC   1871

Activities: walking, picnicking, historic site, birdwatching, nature study
Hours: 8:00 A.M. to dusk
Admission: no charge

In the summer of 1841, a group of idealistic Unitarian ministers, disgruntled over the "bloodlessness" of their faith, formed themselves into the Brook Farm Institute of Agriculture and Education. Many members of the group had met at the Hedge (or Transcendentalist) Club. Organized by Reverend George Ripley, they purchased the two-hundred-acre Brook Farm in outer Roxbury. According to historian Lindsey Smith, "Ripley proposed to eliminate the competitive fervor and the class conflict which marred American life and to combine intellectual, manual, and managerial labor in a harmonious social system." The basis of the system was to be Christian love and hard work.

Soon an increasing diversity of people joined the Utopian farming experiment and a school was established for paying and scholarship students, based on the most progressive theories of the day. After long days in the fields, classrooms, and communal kitchens, the Farmers entertained themselves by acting out plays, discussing serious issues, or having a dance. Other evenings, the young people strolled down to Cow Island on the Charles or in to Boston for music or a lecture. Among the more famous residents of Brook Farm were Nathaniel Hawthorne, John Sullivan Dwight, and Elizabeth Peabody. Regular visitors included Ralph Waldo Emerson, Theodore Parker, William Ellery Channing, the young Robert Gould Shaw, and Margaret Fuller, feminist and editor of the Transcendentalist magazine, *The Dial.* Emerson often lectured to the Farmers from Pulpit Rock, the puddingstone outcropping from which Reverend John Eliot had preached to the Indians two hundred years earlier.

In 1843, the idyllic complexion of the community began to change as the mathematical socialism of Fourier gained credence among the Farmers. Soon the name of the farm was changed to Brook Farm Phalanx and the farm became a center of Fourierism. Skilled craftsmen and laborers joined in the Farm's attempts at communal industry. Residences and workshops were constructed and a new magazine, *The Harbinger,* was published. But the Farmers' road was becoming rocky: students began to leave the school as their parents became frightened by Fourier's ideas and an outbreak of smallpox. Also, the collective business sense of the community was unwieldy and ineffectual.

After a long period of fundraising and three trying years of construction, a huge new central building, called a "phalansery," was erected. But by a stroke of terrible luck, on the day of the building's dedication in 1846, it accidentally caught fire and burned to the ground. Soon a discouraged exodus began and a year later the six-and-a-half-year experiment ended. In 1849 the land was sold at public auction.

Brook Farm had provided pastureland to dairy cows since the 1600s. Sand and gravel had been excavated from an esker and a kame terrace on the back of the property. Muck from the marshes was dug as "poor man's manure." In 1865 the Union Army turned the farm into a military camp, Fort Andrew.

In 1871 the land was purchased by G. P. Burkhardt and donated to the Lutheran Church. In the same year the church founded Gethsemane Cemetery and the Lutheran Orphanage here. The tallest obelisk in the cemetery is a monument to Burkhardt. The orphanage operated until 1974.

Sawmill Brook runs all the way from Hammond Pond before it enters the Charles at the foot of the property. Oaks, elms, hickories, and ashes rise above the glacial rubble and rocky ledges of the property's uplands, providing habitat for migrating songbirds. Maples, willows, blueberries, and hornbeams, sedges, and grasses in the MDC-owned swamps and marshlands below shelter herons, hawks, nesting ducks, muskrats, foxes, and sunbathing turtles. During the summer, the fields and orchards are full of blossoming flowers and shrubs.

Activities:

Although Brook Farm ended 135 years ago, it lives on in the minds of idealists and lovers of literature. Cow Island has been buried since the 1950s by a dump, but many reminders of Brook Farm may still be found. Sawmill Marsh is also worth visiting for its natural and scenic values—the view of the Blue Hills and Prudential Tower from the highest hill in the cemetery is quite good. Remember that this is privately owned church land that must be given due respect.

Map key:

1. Orphanage built on site of original Brook Farm house in 1871.
2. Repair shop, probably a workshop built by the Brook Farmers.
3. Cemetery office.
4. Granite gateposts, originally on Baker Street.
5. Margaret Fuller Cottage, actually the guesthouse built by the Brook Farmers.

6. Munitions storage vault of Fort Andrews.
7. Cannon from the U.S.S. *Constitution.*
8. Foundation of the Brook Farm barn, burned 1920s.
9. Gethsemane Cemetery.
10. Pulpit Rock.
11. Esker pocked with gravel pits.
12. The Dell, favorite gathering place of Brook Farmers.

Reading:
Lindsey Smith's *Brook Farm* is an excellent and readable account of events at Brook Farm. The Metropolitan Area Planning Council has done an extensive inventory of the property.

Directions:
From Arnold Arboretum take VFW Parkway, continue past Westbrook Village, right at Baker Street lights, Gethsemane Cemetery entrance just ahead on left. Park car by empty orphanage and walk.
Parking: Limited.

31. HEMLOCK GORGE
Newton Upper Falls, Wellesley, and Needham
23 acres   *MDC   1895

Activities: walking, nature study, fishing, picnicking, scenic and historic site
Hours: dawn to dusk
Admission: free

This scene of extraordinary picturesque and romantic charm is formed by the swift passage of the river, in the falls and rapids, through a wild, rocky gorge, with precipitous banks clothed with a splendid growth of hemlocks, and spanned by the grand arch of Echo Bridge. . . .
Sylvester Baxter
Boston Parks Guide 1895

The Metropolitan Park Commission in 1893 considered Hemlock Gorge and Beaver Brook the most beautiful small natural areas in the Greater Boston region. Fed by the melting glacier, a more powerful Charles cut its way through layers of Roxbury pudding-

121

stone in a geologically short 10,000 to 12,000 years, leaving this steep-walled gorge with falls at either end. The mature hemlocks and white pines that have taken hold on the river's west bank may well be the biggest trees along the entire length of the river.

The upper falls of the Upper Falls, now the Silk Mill dam, was first dammed in 1688 by John Clark, who ran a sawmill there. By 1782 the mills around the falls were grinding snuff, turning machine screws, drawing wire, and driving a blacksmith's bellows and hammers. In 1821 Thomas Handasyd Perkins, the great merchant and manufacturer, built cotton and silk mills on an enlarged dam here. In 1964 the remaining silk-mill buildings were converted into office, industrial, and restaurant space.

The lower falls of the Upper Falls, alongside Boylston Street, at the 1906 MDC Circular Dam, became the site of a sawmill and iron foundry in the 1780s. Later a nail factory and cotton mill operated along the millrace. In 1907 most of the buildings around the dam were destroyed by fire and the rest were torn down for the widening of Boylston Street. The brick and stone building beside the dam is a barn built in 1750, part of the Ellis Farm that stretched in the direction of Wellesley.

Built of enormous blocks of granite in 1878 by the Boston Water Works, Echo Bridge carries the Sudbury Aqueduct across the Charles River Valley. Part of Boston's second waterworks, the aqueduct carried water from Farm Pond in Framingham seventeen miles to the Chestnut Hill Reservoir, dropping only a foot per mile. Soaring seventy-nine feet above the river, the central span is the second largest masonry arch in America. With seven spans in all, the bridge is an outstanding example of the monumental civil architecture of the nineteenth century. In 1982 the bridge was officially designated a National Historic Landmark. Steps leading down the east shore of the river end at a platform beneath the bridge; you will find the best echo you've ever heard here.

Activities:

Echo Bridge is worthy of an excursion itself. Take a close look at the massive granite blocks of which it is constructed. The reservation is a small, beautiful natural area consisting of the shores of the Charles and the gorge. No facilities.

Walking: An easy half-mile trail leads around the reservation and over the aqueduct, a pleasant walk with excellent views. Steps lead to the top of the aqueduct on the Newton side. You may not be able to cross a little inlet on the west shore, but the area is small enough to double back.

Picnicking: Many moss-covered knolls and nooks to toss down a blanket in. Very pleasant place to picnic. No facilities.

Fishing: Sunfish, catfish, and enormous carp.

Reading:

Charles River Dams, available from the Charles River Watershed Association (see Section 33, Norumbega), gives complete histories of the dams.

32. CHARLES RIVER PATHWAY
The banks of the Charles in Newton, Weston, Wellesley, and Needham
MDC and Newton Conservation Commission

Activities: walking, birdwatching, nature study, picnicking, fishing
Map: see below

In 1969 the Newton Planning Department recommended that the City of Newton develop a continuous walkway along the Charles River in Newton. Their idea was to actualize Charles Eliot's earlier proposal to preserve the banks of the Charles River in their natural state as a recreational and educational resource for the population of Greater Boston. Included in this walk are a number of sites taken before 1900 by the Metropolitan Park Commission, including Norumbega (Section 33), Riverside, Quinobequin Road, and Hemlock Gorge (Section 31); another site, Cutler Park (Section 29), was added in 1962. The hoped-for connecting of these sites had been almost forgotten after Eliot's death in 1897.

In response to the Planning Department recommendation, in the mid-1970s the Newton Conservation Commission applied for and received a matching grant from the Ford Foundation to develop a Charles River Pathway. Landscape architect William D. Giezentanner was hired to plan the pathway. Although the pathway is not yet complete, and though sections run near the noise of Route 128, the portion that follows is the longest extended river walk in the region and captures much of the natural beauty of the Charles.

Map:

A necessity for this trip is a map. The simplest and easiest to follow is the Arrow "Map of Newton" available at most area bookshops and newsstands.

Path Directions:

Start your walk at Riverside Park (see directions below). Riverside was a popular place for outings after the Civil War. As outdoor recreation continued to grow, the Boston Canoe Club and the Newton Boat Club built large boathouses here, each equipped with hundreds of canoes for its members. By 1898, with special excursion trains stopping regularly at Riverside train station, the facilities had grown to include a swimming pool, dormitories, a restaurant, tennis courts, ballfields, picnic areas, and a running track. In 1920 the forty-acre site was taken over by the MDC, which over the years allowed portions of the area to be used for Route 128 and the Massachusetts Turnpike. In 1959 the semi-abandoned wooden boathouses and pavilions were consumed by a fire. Now the site is slowly becoming a natural area again. This is a fine place for a picnic.

Cross the footbridge and turn right, walking along the river until you come to the abandoned railroad bridge (near Riverside MBTA station). Turn right and use the bridge to cross Route 128. On the far side bear right to the river and follow its shoreline through the Martin golf course for nearly one and a half miles, crossing Concord Avenue. Continue until you come to a railroad right-of-way where you turn left. Walk up the right-of-way, then take a right on Concord Avenue, cross Washington Street (Route 16). Turn left on Washington Street and proceed to the driveway between 2776 and 2774 Washington Street, where you'll turn right and take a short walk down to Cordingly Dam.

Cordingly Dam is built on the Lower Falls, the most spectacular cascade on the Charles. First dammed in 1703 or earlier, the Lower Falls powered an ironworks' forge and trip-hammer and a grist mill. By 1800 fulling, saw, snuff, paper, and leather mills all operated on the banks around the dam. Paper manufacturing was the main work for the next century in the little industrial town that had grown up around the Lower Falls mills. The last of the paper mills closed its doors in the 1920s.

Continue on Washington Street and at the lights take a right on Quinobequin Road. This road was a Metropolitan Park Commission carriage drive laid out as part of the Charles River Reservation by Charles Eliot in the 1890s. About a quarter of a mile after you pass under Route 128, if you are walking along the grass, you will notice a small hump. This is part of the 1848 siphon that carried the Cochituate Aqueduct across the river. To your right is the siphon bridge. To your left, the buried aqueduct ascends a steep hill to a siphon chamber where it returns to the hydraulic grade.

Continue on Quinobequin Road, noticing the diversity of trees and flowers along the way. Pass under Route 9 to Hemlock Gorge (Section 31). Walk through the Gorge on the left side, stopping to explore or picnic, then climb the steps and cross the Sudbury Aqueduct Bridge to the Needham side of the river. Turn left just beyond the end of the bridge and walk down to Eliot Street. Turn left on Eliot Street, then right on Chestnut Street to the old Upper Falls railroad station, now a museum with exhibits about this historic mill town along the Charles.

Turn right at the station on Oak Street. Continue up Oak Street to Needham Street, where you turn right and cross the river. After crossing the river, immediately cross the street, and follow a path along the right side of the river to Kendrick Street. Here you have two options: turn left and cross the bridge and turn left again in to Newton's Novitiate Park and Winchester Street Recreation Area; or turn right, walk a few hundred yards down the road, then turn left between the Red Cross and Polaroid buildings in to Cutler Park (Section 29).

Novitiate Park and Winchester Street Recreation Area comprise a fifty-seven-acre natural area on the Newton side of the river. The tract was part of the Kendrick Farm, owned by the Kendrick family from 1658 to the 1850s. It is a fine place to walk around, picnic, fly a kite, watch birds, or launch a canoe.

Activities:

This pathway provides an excellent opportunity to study the flora and fauna of the Charles River and its history, or merely to stroll along enjoying the natural beauty. Walk a portion of the pathway if you haven't the time or energy for the full distance. This portion is approximately eight miles long: do it with two cars, one parked at Novitiate Park on Kendrick Street and the other at Riverside station.

For public transportation, begin the walk at Riverside MBTA station by walking behind the car barns to the abandoned RR bridge and the river. You may cut off the pathway by turning left on Route 9 and walking ten minutes to Eliot MBTA station. Or continue to Kendrick Street, where you can pick up a bus to Newton Highlands MBTA station (call Hub Bus Lines for weekend schedule: 661-0202).

Reading:

Charles River Dams, available for a dollar fifty from the Charles River Watershed Association, is filled with the history of the dams you will see. You might try writing to the Newton Conservation Commission (1000 Commonwealth Avenue, Newton, MA 02159) for a copy of the *Charles River Pathway Plan* by William D. Giezentanner, which is filled with maps and information. The Newton Conservators publish a free map of Newton's parks, including several on this walk; write Newton Conservators, Box 11, Newton Center, MA 02159.

Directions:

MBTA: Riverside D Green Line to Riverside station.
Auto: To Riverside—heading north on Route 128, bear right in to Massachusetts Turnpike exit, then turn right on Recreation Road to end.
Or: Take Commonwealth Avenue west, cross Route 128, then in a half mile turn left on Park Road. Cross over the Mass. Pike, then take third left on to Recreation Road to the end.

33. NORUMBEGA

33A. NORUMBEGA PARK CONSERVATION AREA
*Newton Conservation Commission

Activities: historic site, nature study, walking, picnicking

After crossing the Back Bay, Commonwealth Avenue was extended in 1897 to the Charles River. The Commonwealth Avenue Street Railway soon began service the length of the landscaped road, from Chestnut Hill to the Charles River, serving commuters primarily. To promote weekend and summer riding, the trolley line built Norumbega Park across the street from its car barn and turnaround. Picnic grounds were laid out, ornamental trees were planted, and a zoo, merry-go-round, elk park, and swings were built. In 1904 the Totem Pole Ballroom with a capacity of 3,000 was opened to attract trolley riders for evening dancing.

The round-trip trolley ride from the Chestnut Hill terminal cost ten cents and included admission to the park. Thousands came for outings. Hundreds of canoes and paddleboats drifted on the river. Electric launches, charged by the railway power plants, also plied the calm waters of the area that came to be called the Lake District. During the thirties and forties the facilities expanded to include numerous rides, an arcade, and game rooms. Tommy Dorsey, Glenn Miller, and Benny Goodman regaled crowds at the Totem Pole. In the late forties the park began to decline and it finally closed in 1959. In the sixties it was torn down; one portion became the Marriott Hotel, another section survives as a Newton conservation area.

The Norumbega Park Conservation Area includes thirteen acres of riverbank, woods, fields, and remnants of the old amusement park. The park is now quiet and shady, a peaceful natural area overlooking the Charles River where you may fish or have a pack-it-in/pack-it-out picnic—or stroll around remembering "the good old days." No facilities.

Directions:
Heading west on Commonwealth Avenue, turn right on Woodbine Street just before the hotel. Limited parking at end.

33B. CHARLES RIVER WATERSHED ASSOCIATION
This organization, founded in 1965, is dedicated "to protect,

improve, and expand the natural resources and recreational opportunities of the Charles River watershed, and to enhance their enjoyment by the inhabitants." The CRWA runs public educational programs about the river and activities that use and clean up the river. One of the most interesting current programs is Adopt-a-Brook, which focuses on local involvement in the river's tributaries.

If you drop in, you can pick up the *Charles River Profile,* an introduction to the river. You can also purchase CRWA's two fine booklets: *Charles River Canoe Guide,* a complete guide to canoeing the Charles and its tributaries; and *Charles River Dams,* a detailed look at the river's history, with special attention to its many dams.

Address: Charles River Watershed Association, 2391 Commonwealth Avenue, Auburndale, MA 02166. Telephone: 527-2799.

33C. CHARLES RIVER CANOE SERVICE

Activities: canoeing

Located in the basement of the MDC engineer's building, this is the most complete recreational canoe service in the region, offering instruction, hourly rentals for the Lake District or daily rentals to take away, sales, and guided tours of the Charles and other rivers of the region. Open April 1 to October 31. Weekend hourly rate: $4.50 an hour, $3.50 each additional hour; $16.00 daily maximum. For rentals, park at Duck Feeding Station and walk over.

Address:
Charles River Canoe Service, 2401 Commonwealth Avenue, Auburndale, MA 02166.

Telephone: 527-9885

33D. DUCK FEEDING STATION   *MDC
The duckiest place in the region for much of the year. A fine place to dispose of last week's Wonder Bread or stale bagels. Bring the kids.

Directions:
Commonwealth Avenue west to entrance to Route 128

north; bear right and keep on bearing right.

33E. NORUMBEGA TOWER AND PARK *MDC

Activities: walking, birdwatching, picnicking, historic site

Professor Eben Horsford, a somewhat eccentric Harvard historian, believed that Norseman Leif Ericksson had a settlement along the Charles River. Citing evidence that was never accepted by other historians, Horsford proved to his·own satisfaction that Ericksson and his band occupied a site on a bluff overlooking the river. To honor these supposed first explorers, Horsford had Norumbega Tower erected on that site.

This area includes not only the tower, which you should surely climb, but also about a mile of riverbank overlooking the Flowed Meadow, a vast area also known as the Lakes District. The Flowed Meadow was created when the Moody Street Dam in Waltham backed the river up, flooding formerly cultivated fields, creating a conflict between mill owners at the dam and the farmers upstream.

Activities:
A beautiful trail winds along the shoreline beneath many big trees, providing a long excursion around the Flowed Meadows. The marshes and woodlands here are excellent for birdwatching. Picnic near the base of the tower or overlooking the river.

Directions:
Follow Norumbega Road from the Duck Feeding Station.

33F. COMMONWEALTH AVENUE IN NEWTON

Activities: jogging and bicycling

This is probably the most beautiful electric car ride in the world.
Country Rides by Trolley
Circa 1910

In the world of the long-distance runner no name is more likely to cause a cold sweat than "Heartbreak Hill." Actually four hills,

129

rising from 80 to 230 feet, Heartbreak Hill is the four-mile stretch of Commonwealth Avenue in Newton from the intersection of Route 16 (Washington Street) to the Boston line near the Chestnut Hill Reservoir. It is the most difficult hurdle runners face on the long haul from Hopkinton to Boston during the annual Boston Marathon, and its accomplishment is a true feat of heroism. It is a favored place for spectators who watch the struggling but noble racers.

From Norumbega to Chestnut Hill, Commonwealth Avenue covers a distance of 5.7 miles, meandering (just look at Commonwealth Avenue on a map) beneath mature shade trees, past many fine homes. Commonwealth Avenue was first proposed in the 1880s by the owners of several large farm estates in the rural districts of Newton. They hoped that a transportation link to Boston would open the area to residential development, allowing them to sell or develop their properties at a large profit. The city was enthusiastic about the idea of the road, knowing that it would increase tax revenues, but it balked at undertaking the cost of construction.

In 1893 it was agreed that the private property owners would build the road under the direction of Newton's city engineer, and that the city would pay for such improvements as sewers and waterlines. To attract "a desirable class of wealthy persons" to Commonwealth Avenue and its attendant side streets, the road was laid out as a stately boulevard. Shade trees were planted on both sides of the road and along a median strip that was to contain a trolley line and separate local from through traffic. As fast as the road could be built, house lots and homes along the way were sold.

As road construction and the housing boom progressed, starting at Chestnut Hill and proceeding toward Norumbega, the trolley line followed, providing another amenity for new residents. The road was completed in 1896; the trolley line was completed in the following year. And immediately construction began on Norumbega Park.

Activities:

The north lane of Commonwealth Avenue and the median strip provide a terrific course for joggers. The north lane has numerous barriers to block through traffic, increasing its value not only to joggers but to bicyclists. Auburndale Playground is a good place to limber up at the beginning of your workout or to relax when it's over.

Directions:
Commonwealth Avenue in Newton, from Chestnut Hill to Route 128. Park along the north side of the street.

34. HAMMOND POND WOODS
Between Beacon Street and Route 9 on the Newton-Brookline boundary
64 acres   *MDC   Circa 1908
110 acres   *Newton Conservation Commission   1963–1974

Activities: walking and hiking, picnicking, fishing, nature study, ski touring, rock climbing, birdwatching
Map: for the free map that includes Hammond Woods, send SASE to Newton Conservators, Box 11, Newton, MA 02159
Hours: dawn to dusk
Admission: no charge

The Hammond Woods are one of the most interesting and beautiful forests in New England, rich in every variety of ferns and lichen, and abounding in rare plants and brilliant flowers.

> King's Handbook of Newton
> 1889

Hammond Pond Woods, the most pristine and least known of large open lands in the Boston region, is a forest-covered "wilderness" set among puddingstone hills, ledges, and outcrops. Puddingstone, so named because it resembles lumpy tapioca pudding, is the hallmark of these woods. Hundreds of millions of years ago mountains to the west of here pushed up as high as or higher than today's Rockies. Movements of the earth and the ceaseless erosion of wind, water, and ice slowly tore the mountains apart, tumbling them down creeks and rivers to the sea in the form of rocks with their edges taken off, sand, and mud. Over millions of years water-rounded stones and silt accumulated to a depth of thousands of feet and metamorphosed into puddingstone.

When Thomas Hammond settled in New Cambridge (Newton) in 1650, he must have laid out his fields and pastures on the

Chestnut Hill side of his property, for his lands on the west side of Hammond Pond were too rocky for agriculture or even grazing. At some time a swamp north of the pond was cleared in an attempt to raise cranberries.

As Newton grew, surrounding farms logged the area for fuelwood, but it appears not to have been settled or cultivated. In 1835 the Worcester Turnpike (Route 9) was built along the south edge of the woods as the direct route between Boston and Worcester. Fifteen years later Beacon Street was constructed along the north edge of the woods. In 1852 the New York and New England Railroad extended its tracks through the woods and on to Needham, providing Newton Center and other villages along the line with rapid commuter service to and from Boston, and also a route for soil going from Needham to fill the Back Bay.

Residential development followed the railway lines. Wealthy Boston Brahmin families built estates on the Chestnut Hill side of Hammond Pond, making this one of the most prestigious neighborhoods in Boston. Commuters began moving in large numbers to Newton Center. Ice was cut on Hammond Pond and shipped via the Worcester Turnpike to the iceboxes of Boston. Only the ruggedness of the woods allowed them to remain undeveloped, itinerant gypsy caravans being the only occasional residents.

On the eve of the twentieth century when there was a proposal to subdivide the woods into house lots, a wealthy Newtonite named Edwin Webster purchased the entire area. Webster immediately sold half the land to the Metropolitan Park Commission. On the rest of the land, Webster and his heirs erected an estate and laid out a deer park, but otherwise the woods were allowed to remain wild.

The Metropolitan Park Commission's successor, the MDC, built Hammond Pond Parkway through the middle of the tract and then in the 1950s permitted Chestnut Hill Shopping Center, the first shopping center in the country, to be built on the shore of the pond. In 1968, after the demise of Webster's last direct heirs, the city of Newton purchased 103 acres of the woods as conservation land with the aid of state and federal money. Unfortunately, the MDC allowed a new shopping mall, a temple, and an apartment building to be built on or adjacent to its "parklands." This questionable sale of public parklands by a government conservation agency acting against the public interest illustrates the need for private citizens to monitor the activities of government agencies and to get involved in the political process to prevent similar incidents. In 1973 and 1979, after considerable lobbying by local residents, the city added two especially lovely parcels to its holdings, the Vale and the Houghton Gardens, consolidating Hammond Pond Woods as one of the finest public open spaces in the region.

Activities:

Hammond Pond Woods would be a most pleasant woodland anywhere; that it is so close to Boston is our good fortune. Although trails cross Hammond Pond Parkway and MBTA tracks at fence openings, this area is best enjoyed by keeping all four of its sections in mind. Each

133

portion of the park has its own special delights. Be sure to send for the Newton Conservators' map.

Houghton Garden: One of the estates that abutted the woods was owned by Mr. and Mrs. Clement Houghton. In 1906 they dammed a little stream running from the pond and began laying out a forest garden. Sowing seeds and planting sprouts, clearing little groves, and cutting paths in the little glen around their pond, the Houghtons transformed their bit of woods. Numerous varieties of phlox, azalea, and rhododendron, and hundreds of other flowers and shrubs were planted, as well as such exotic trees as a dawn redwood and a Douglas fir. After the land was purchased by Newton in the late 1970s, the garden was restored by the city and the Chestnut Hill Garden Club. Only a brief walk from the Chestnut Hill MBTA station or a few steps from parking along Suffolk Road, Houghton Garden is an exquisite place for a stroll, particularly during the spring and summer.

Hemlock Grove: Above the pond, through a little notch in the hills near the Chestnut Hill shopping-center parking lot, the well-rooted trunks of these old-growth hemlocks create a feeling of timelessness like the columns of a Greek temple. (You have to ignore the traffic on the "parkway" for this one.)

Gooch's Caves: This area of moss-crowned puddingstone ledges is pockmarked with shallow caves and overhangs, making it a really neat place to explore or to have a pack-it-in/pack-it-out picnic.

The Vale: A narrow little valley, carved by water flowing from the springs at its head, provides a wet habitat for marsh marigold, skunk cabbage, violets, false hellebore, beeches, willows, and a large assortment of ferns. Along the base of the Vale a pathway leads by a swampy temperate jungle: a walker's or naturalist's sanctuary.

Deer Park: A dozen or so deer can be watched, as they watch back, through the fenced enclosure along Hammond Pond Parkway or from Suffolk Road.

The Ledges: These vertical puddingstone and sandstone ledges have a trail at their base and along their crest. From the crest we look directly into the tops of the hickories, ashes, and oaks growing below.

Walking and hiking: Ten or so miles of very lovely trails.

Easy and interesting walking.

Jogging: Along woods roads; several possible circuits.

Nature study: At least 375 species of plants have been identified in the woods. The Newton Conservators (see address under Map above) publish a booklet, *Geology of Newton,* which describes several sites in the woods.

Fishing: Hammond Pond, reclaimed in the 1970s. Bass, pickerel, catfish, and sunfish. Popular ice-fishing spot.

Picnicking: Many places for informal picnics among the ledges or along the western shore of the pond. No facilities.

Ski touring: All woods roads and trails used by local skiers during the winter. Casually maintained. Novice to intermediate. Easy access from MBTA.

Birdwatching: The northwest corner of the pond is a favorite stopping place for migrating birds. Feedable mallard ducks nest around the pond. Red-tailed hawks nest in the woods.

Rock climbing: Crags on the west shore of the pond are a very popular practice area. Also try the ledges.

Directions:

MBTA: Green Line Riverside to Chestnut Hill station. Left on Hammond Street, then walk behind shopping center, bearing right to park entrance.

Bike: Beacon Street through Cleveland Circle, past Boston College to right on Hammond Pond Parkway. The park is on both sides of the Parkway.

Auto: Beacon Street or Route 9 to Hammond Pond Parkway.

Parking: Parking lot on Hammond Pond Parkway next to end of shopping center. Plenty of room.

35. CHESTNUT HILL RESERVOIR
Chestnut Hill Driveway and Beacon Street, Brighton
*MDC   1867

Activities: jogging, picnicking, historic site
Hours: dawn to dusk

If you've ever jogged or driven around Chestnut Hill Reservoir you may have noticed the assemblage of ornate buildings around the reservoir and across the street. Not only are these buildings in fact part of our water supply, but, with the reservoir itself, they comprise one of the most significant sites in the history of America's public waterworks. The reservoir was constructed by the City of Boston between 1866 and 1870 as a receiving reservoir for the Cochituate Aqueduct; it had become apparent that the earlier Brookline Reservoir (see Section 37) could not satisfy Boston's peak water demands. Two basins were excavated and embanked at the base of the fields sloping from the Lawrence Farm, now Boston College.

An influent gatehouse, since demolished, was constructed at the end of the aqueduct; an intermediate gatehouse was placed between the reservoirs; and an effluent gatehouse led into the city's water mains. A carriage drive, with an ornate arch at its entrance, was laid out around the reservoir so that the populace could enjoy pleasure drives around the basins.

In 1879 a terminal chamber, designed by City Architect G. A. Clough, was constructed across Beacon Street from the reservoir, bringing the new Sudbury Aqueduct's waters to the reservoir and the city. A small high-service pumping station had been built in Roxbury to supply water to the higher districts of Boston that could not be served by gravity, but by the 1880s that too had proved inadequate to the city's growing population. And so a new high-service pumping station was built across the street from the reservoir on the designs of then City Architect Arthur Vinal. To house the pumping engines, Vinal designed a "Richardson Romanesque" building, using the same Longmeadow fieldstone and Milford granite that Richardson used on Trinity Church. Water was pumped to a distribution reservoir on the top of nearby Fisher Hill, whence it flowed to Boston's hills by gravity.

One of the engines installed in Chestnut Hill High Service Pumping Station was a huge triple-expansion steam engine designed by Erasmus Leavitt. This was the first engine of its type in America and its frame was so large it had to be cast at Germany's Krupp Ironworks. In 1973 the Leavitt engine was designated as the nation's second National Historic Mechanical Engineering Landmark.

In 1895, when the Boston water system was included in the newly constituted Metropolitan Water System, Edmund Wheelwright, architect of Horticultural Hall and the concession stand

and gazebo at Jamaica Pond (Section 7), designed an addition to the High Service works to accommodate a yet larger pumping engine. Wheelwright also designed a new gatehouse with a bronze cheneau or crested roof across the street from the High Service building. In 1897 the Metropolitan Water Commission determined that the water pressure was too low even in the lower sections of Greater Boston, therefore the commission ordered the construction of a low-service pumping station. The massive gray building that enclosed the low-service pumps was designed by Shepley, Rutan and Coolidge, successor firm to H. H. Richardson, and constructed of Indiana limestone in the beaux arts style. The grounds of the reservoir were landscaped at the time by the Olmsted firm.

Although both pumping stations have been replaced by more modern facilities and the upper basin of the reservoir is filled in for Boston College's football field, the lower basin is still in use. It is the second largest reservoir in the Metropolitan District, with a capacity of 523 million gallons and a depth of 32 feet. The old waterworks buildings, so substantially constructed, remain; perhaps they should be reused as a Museum of American Waterworks.

Activities:

In addition to serving the region as a water supply, Chestnut Hill Reservoir has become one of the most popular jogging circuits in Greater Boston.

Jogging: Excellent 1.7-mile course around the reservoir.

Picnicking: Under the big old oaks planted by the Olmsted firm more than eighty years ago. Small tot-lot and a few picnic tables. Nearby swimming pool. Ballfields across the street.

To visit the High Service Pumping Station call the Superintendent.

Directions:

MBTA: Cleveland Circle station on the Riverside Green Line or Beacon Street Green Line. Reservoir a short distance up Beacon Street.

Auto or bike: Beacon Street in Boston to Cleveland Circle; reservoir just beyond lights.

Telephone: 734-9194

36. LARZ ANDERSON PARK
Newton Street, Brookline
66 acres   *Brookline Park Department   1948

Activities: picnicking, nature study, walking, birdwatching, historic sites, ski touring, sledding
Hours: 8:00 A.M. to dusk
Admission: no charge

Weld, as the estate of Larz and Isabel Anderson was known, was always on the itinerary of princes and kings when they visited Boston. The estate was put together between 1848 and 1891 by William Fletcher Weld, scion of the owners of the Black Horse Line, one of America's greatest clipper-ship fleets. Purchasing several old farms on the slopes of Goddard Hill, crossed by tree-lined roads, Weld's property amounted to eighty-three acres. On the summit of the hill he erected a mansion house.

In 1897 Isabel Weld Perkins married Larz Anderson, a Kentuckian who had graduated from Harvard. His personal fortune was estimated at eight million dollars, hers at sixteen million dollars. In 1899 Mrs. Anderson purchased the Weld estate in Brookline. Larz Anderson served as a diplomat in England, Belgium, and Japan. Though the Andersons loved to travel and owned homes in Washington, D.C., Boston, and Maine, Weld was their home base. They had former Boston City Architect Edmund Wheelwright design a palatial addition to the mansion and a carriage house. The carriage house, designed to resemble a castle in Chamonix, France, held the Andersons' prize-winning horses and collection of carriages. Later, when they began to collect expensive automobiles—an adjunct of their love for traveling—these too found a home in the carriage house.

The Andersons also had vast gardens laid out on the estate in the English, Italian, and Japanese styles. Classical statues and trees molded by the art of topiary bordered the terraced gardens. On the flat section of the property at the western base of the hill, the first private polo and golf grounds in America were laid out. Larz died in 1937 and was buried in the National Cathedral. When Isabel died in 1948 she left the estate to the Town of Brookline.

The town loaned the carriage house and collection of carriages and cars to the Veteran Motor Club of America, which opened the Antique Auto Museum of Massachusetts here, later the Museum of Transportation in Boston.

Because the town was unable to afford the expense of maintenance, the gardens were allowed to decline, the site of the main garden eventually being converted into a skating rink. The mansion house, after repeated assaults of vandalism, was torn down in 1954, its fixtures sold at a public auction. The polo field was converted into ballfields. But, all in all, the beauty and dignity of the former estate remain, making this a most picturesque town park.

Activities:

Larz Anderson Park is a high, rounded drumlin with great old beech, linden, and evergreen trees and open sloping fields overlooking Boston and the western suburbs.

Walking: Explore the romantic remains of the gardens and mansion at the top of the hill. Take in the fine view of Boston. Relax around the classic duck pond. Look at the fine detail of the carriage house.

Picnicking: Very nice picnic area around the pond. Tables, grills, sun and rain pavilion, bathrooms, and kids' play area. Ducks to feed and paths to wander. Two ballfields. Great place to fly a kite. Please help keep it clean.

Ice-skating: Excellent rink on hilltop surrounded by remnants of the old gardens, including statuary, site of an old well, and balustrades. Fee charged.

Sledding: The slopes of the hill provide some of the best sledding in the region.

Ski touring: Good place to ski; steep slopes on the hill and easy grades at the base. Track laid down by locals. Novice to intermediate.

Directions:

Public Transportation: Arborway bus from Cleveland Circle goes by Goddard Avenue. Entrance is a five-minute walk up Goddard Avenue.

Auto: Jamaicaway to Arborway. Right on Pond Street after passing Jamaica Pond. Continue up hill to park entrance on right.

Parking: Plenty.

Telephone: 232-9000

37. BROOKLINE RESERVOIR
Boylston Street and Warren Avenue, Brookline
*Brookline Park Department

Activities: jogging, strolling, sitting, historic site
Hours: dawn to dusk
Admission: free

Brookline Reservoir was created in 1848 as the receiving reservoir for Boston's first waterworks, the Cochituate Aqueduct system (see Section 97, Lake Cochituate). Between Lake Cochituate and here, the aqueduct ran 14.3 miles, dropping only 3.81 feet before spilling its water out through the small granite effluent chamber at the western end of the reservoir. The reservoir was constructed from a small pond surrounded by country estates by excavating and raising an embankment along Boylston Street. A large conduit buried in the embankment allowed water to proceed directly from the effluent chamber to the intake gatehouse at the other end of the reservoir.

The intake chamber, now used as a sportsmen's club, is an outstanding example of Greek Revival architecture. Designed by waterworks engineers John B. Jervis and Ellis Chesbrough, the fine stonework, the layered columns of the entrance, and the architrave window casements make it one of the most interesting and earliest waterworks structures surviving from pre-Civil War America.

Because the Olmsteds, Charles Sprague Sargent, H. H. Richardson, and Charles Eliot all lived around the corner, the grounds of the reservoir were laid out near the end of the nineteenth century by the Olmsted firm with particular grace.

Activities:
No facilities.
Jogging: Paved circuit of 0.7 mile. Level and very popular with local runners.
Strolling: A pleasant place to walk around. Plenty of shady benches.

Directions:
MBTA: A ten-minute walk west on Boylston Street from Brookline Hills Station on the Riverside Green Line.
Bike: Chestnut Hill Avenue from Cleveland Circle. Reser-

voir just over Route 9.
Auto: Boylston Street (Route 9) to Warren Street or Chestnut Hill Avenue.

38. PROSPECT HILL PARK
*Totten Pond Road, Waltham, MA 02154
254 acres   Waltham Park Department   1895

Activities: picnicking, walking, viewpoint, nature study, alpine skiing, children's animal farm
Hours: 9:00 A.M. to 6:00 P.M.
Admission: no charge

Prospect Hill is the steeply rising western rampart of the Boston Basin; the view of the region from the 478-foot summit is the finest to the west of Boston. Like the Blue Hills, Prospect Hill is a batholith, a huge mass of molten rock that pushed upward but cooled before reaching the surface. Tilted up at a sharp angle over the declining Boston Basin by geomorphic forces, the softer stone above the batholith has been worn away by eons of wind, water, and glacial erosion, leaving this jagged diorite mount. The large boulder near the summit is a glacial erratic.

Climbing these heights, the earliest settlers of Waltham (at first a territory of Watertown) could see the waves of new colonists arriving in Boston under full sail. In 1632, merely a year after the first colonists settled the reaches of the Charles beyond the second falls, a young farm servant named Thomas Hawkins secretly met local Indian Sachem Cutstomach on Prospect Hill. In exchange for three beaver pelts, Hawkins gave Cutstomach "an old flintlock, a horn of powder, and some bullets." Within a week the other colonists knew of Hawkins's dealing and proceeded to reprimand and whip him for selling a gun to an Indian.

In the 1700s Daniel Harrington built a tavern on Prospect Hill from which his customers could enjoy a view over the agricultural town. The tavern was on an old road that ran over the hill, connecting the farms at either end. In the nineteenth century a recluse with a taste for the long view built himself a home, known locally as the Hermitage, on the precipitous east slope of the hill. In 1895 Prospect Hill became one of the first large town-owned parks in the region.

Hickory, ash, oak, and black birch grow amid the glacial rubble and rocky outcroppings here. The forest floor is covered with Canada mayflower, Solomon's seal, wild oats, hay-scented fern, wild raisin, and huckleberries. Chipmunks and red squirrels are everywhere scurrying over the leaves.

Activities:

A paved "mountain road" leads to both summits of the hill and cars are permitted. Though there is some litter near the summits, most of the park is clean and quiet, considering its proximity to Waltham's center and Route 128. The best view is had from the lower southern summit, the higher summit being a radar station.

Picnicking: Lots of picnic sites, all with tables and fireplaces (bring your own wood or charcoal grill), most set in the shade of tall pines. Some sites have great views, particularly those near the summits; other sites have swings or rain shelters. Your choice of isolated sites or group areas. Small fee for large groups. Bathrooms near park entrance. Small children's zoo behind office.

Walking: Along road, interesting but rugged trails on the steep east slope.

Bicycling: Good place to practice hill climbs.

Alpine skiing: 250-foot vertical drop. Two T-bars. Night skiing. Lift ticket $2.00 to $8.50 depending on time and age.

Directions:

Bicycle: Route 20 to Lexington Street in Waltham, to Totten Pond Road.

Auto: Route 128 to Totten Pond Road exit in Waltham, or Route 20 to Waltham, right on Lexington Street, one mile to left on Totten Pond Road.

Parking: Plenty.

Telephone: 893-4837

39. BEAVER BROOK AND WAVERLY OAKS
Trapelo Road, Belmont and Waltham
59 acres *MDC 1893

Activities: walking, picnicking, play area, wading pool, duck feeding, open-field sports, ballfields, tennis, nature study, ice-skating, fishing, sledding
Hours: dawn to dusk
Admission: free

In the early 1890s, along with Hemlock Gorge, Beaver Brook was considered one of the most beautiful scenic natural areas in the Greater Boston region. The area's impending development in 1891 inspired landscape architect Charles Eliot to organize the Trustees of Reservations, and later the Metropolitan Park System, in his effort to save this "charming scene of sylvan beauty." The mighty oaks, little ponds, and twisting ridges had already been immortalized in James Russell Lowell's poem, "Beaver Brook." With the creation of the Metropolitan Park System, Beaver Brook—also known as Waverly Oaks after the great white oaks that grew there—was the first site acquired.

The area had been explored early in 1631 by John Winthrop, first governor of Massachusetts Bay Colony. Winthrop named the area Beaver Brook because "the beaver had shorn down divers great trees there, and made divers dams across the brook." Watertown was soon settled by Puritan colonists and it appears that the Beaver Brook area came under cultivation; the rich bottomlands of the little valley were particularly attractive to farmers.

In 1819, a ruined old mill on the upper dam was replaced by a new grist mill. The outlet stream of the lower dam powered a sawmill and a satinet mill, which wove cloth (with a wrap of cotton and filling of wool) used for trousers. Once there were many more great old white oaks in the neighborhood, but most were cut down to supply the shipyards of Medford, then their stumps were removed for use as ship's keels. Next the hickories succumbed to the logger's ax, providing wood to smoke bacon, and, because it was the best fuelwood, Beacon Hill residents sought it.

When the area became a reservation in 1893, just twenty-eight mature white oaks were left. Lowell had counted 750 yearly growth rings in a tree blown down by a storm. Louis Agassiz, the country's most prominent natural scientist, estimated the biggest tree as a thousand years old. The park commissioners had the deadwood of the trees pruned—the greatest oak required an amazing 2,800 individual cuts. Every cut was tarred and cavities were filled with cement. Four or five of these great trees remain, their boughs casting a wide circle of shade over the grass.

Most of the oaks grow along several ridges that are, in fact, glacial eskers, long piles of sand and gravel deposited on the bed of rivers running through or beneath the melting glacier that had covered New England. The valley of the brook forms a notch through the surrounding uplands, though the picturesque glen was probably cut when the stream was more potent. From the bottom of the reservation, the stream winds its way through marshes to the Charles.

Activities:

Though small in area, Beaver Brook is a pleasant place to wander and explore, to picnic or feed the ducks.

Picnicking: Tables are scattered around beneath the trees; get there early for the best sites; charcoal grills allowed. Lots of places to throw down a blanket.

Play area: One of the most popular around; kids love it. Wading pool.

Nature study: Privet, barberry, buckthorn, and English hawthorne are remnants of the area's domestic past, as are household herbs that may be found scattered around the reservation. Wildflowers abound along the brook between Trapelo Road and the lower pond and in the "Bowl." Good birding along the lower streamcourse.

Sports: Two rough ballfields, good for softball. Open field for Frisbeeing or putting practice.

Tennis: Four new asphalt courts, busy on weekends and warm evenings.

Ice-skating: Upper pond.

Sledding: Steep hill above lower pond. Many gentle slopes as well.

Directions:

Public transportation: Waverly bus from Harvard Square, Red Line station. Get off at end of line in Waverly Square, then walk for two minutes up Trapelo Road.

Bike or auto: From Harvard Square, out Mount Auburn Street, bear right on Belmont Street beyond Mount Auburn Cemetery, go 1.5 miles, bear right on Trapelo Road, go through Waverly Square, park ahead.

Parking: Scattered parking lots all around reservation.

40. ROCK MEADOW
Mill Street, Belmont
70 acres   *Belmont Conservation Commission   1968

Activities: walking, nature study, birdwatching, ski touring
Hours: dawn to dusk
Admission: no charge

In the nineteenth century mental health reformers believed that tranquil country scenery could ease the anguish of the insane. Toward that end Harvard University's McLean Asylum moved its residential treatment facility from the Massachusetts General Hospital to rural Belmont. During the years from 1875 to 1886 Frederick Law Olmsted was hired to landscape the new hospital's grounds. Ironically, after Olmsted's mental health failed in 1895, he was sent to McLean, where he lived until his death in 1903.

As an adjunct of the asylum, McLean purchased the Rock Meadow Farm, just up Mill Street, to raise food for the asylum's patients. In 1968 the farm was purchased as a conservation area by the town of Belmont with assistance from state and federal conservation programs.

Just above Waverly Oaks on Beaver Brook, the grassy fields of Rock Meadow's glacial hills overlook the marshes of the brook. Around the turn of the century the farm was a favorite stamping ground of ornithologist and first president of the Massachusetts Audubon Society William Brewster, and the marshes and thickets of the area still attract birds in profusion. Orioles, meadowlarks, bobolinks, and an occasional bluebird may be sighted in the upland portions of the property. Bitterns, herons, and marsh hawks may be seen in the marsh.

The open fields of the area provide habitat for an abundance of wildflowers: dogbane, honeysuckle, rough-fruited cinquefoil, vetch, milkweed, burdock, and mustard. Buckthorns, which have invaded the fields, are themselves being invaded and shrouded by bittersweet vines. In the wetlands along Beaver Brook purple loosestrife, swamp candles, tall meadowrue, and five or six fern species may be found, as well as the spectacular yellow Canada lily.

Activities:

Rock Meadow is a beautiful natural area of fields, great old trees, and wetlands only fifteen minutes from Harvard Square. If you're studying nature or walking around at Beaver Brook, Rock Meadow is just a short distance up Mill Street and provides another view of the brook and a diversity of wildlife. No facilities.

Walking: Pleasant walking along old farm roads that wind through the fields, over the low hills, and along the wetlands. If your visit includes walking or nature study, look for a small trail through the brush that crosses the brook. The far side of the brook is quiet and wild.

Ski touring: Good ski touring on the old farm roads. Easy grades. Track laid down by local skiers. Novice to intermediate.

Directions:

Public Transportation: Bus from Harvard Square to Waverly. Walk five minutes up Trapelo Road, then turn right on Mill Street. Continue up Mill Street for ten minutes to entrance on left.

Bike: Follow Concord Avenue from Harvard Square, through Belmont center, then up the hill to left on Mill Street. Entrance on right.

Auto: From Fresh Pond rotary in Cambridge take Concord Avenue through Belmont center, up the hill, then left on Mill Street. Entrance on right.

41. MOUNT AUBURN CEMETERY
580 Mount Auburn Street, Cambridge, MA 02138
170 acres   Proprietors of the Cemetery of Mount Auburn   1831

Activities: strolling, historic site, nature study, birdwatching

Map: free maps of cemetery, its notable graves and trees, at entrance office or send SASE

Hours: May 1 to October 1, 8:00 A.M. to 7:00 P.M.; rest of year until 5:00 P.M.

This is a cemetery; please respect its sanctity.

America's first garden cemetery

If it is possible by natural means to lose the dreadful associations of dissolution in the grave, a burial in some one of the lovely places of Mt. Auburn seems sure to assist it. All that meets the eye there above and around the grave is pure and beautiful.

Reverend Nehemiah Adams
1834

In 1825 a young doctor from Harvard Medical School, Jacob Bigelow, called together a small group of his friends to consider the idea of a country cemetery. Boston's graveyards were filled to overflowing, there was fear that water was leaching through grave-sites and into the city's wells, and the area needed outdoor recreation space, for the Common was the only park in nearly the entire region. Bigelow's idea seemed to address all three problems. A committee was formed to approach landowners about acquiring a parcel for such a rural graveyard, but it was several years before any action was taken.

Around 1830 George Brimmer bought the former Stone farm, overlooking the Charles, known to generations of Harvard students as "Sweet Auburn," to prevent it from being developed. When approached by the site committee, he agreed to sell them the land at his cost, $6,000. Unable to either pay for the land or generate the public support their project required, Bigelow's committee sought and received the assistance of the recently formed Massachusetts Horticultural Society, an organization composed primarily of wealthy individuals interested in ornamental gardening. Backed by the Society, legislation was put through on Beacon Hill, lots were sold for sixty dollars each, and experimental gardens were planned. General Henry Dearborn, president of the Horticultural Society, laid out the grounds for tree, shrub, and flower plantings, as well as for pathways and carriage roads. In 1831 the cemetery was opened by its first president, U.S. Supreme Court Justice Joseph Story.

The cemetery had immediate success in selling graves, but was also perhaps a bit too successful in attracting outings: less than a year after opening there were numerous complaints about the dust raised by the many carriages and horseback riders using the roads and paths. Until the 1880s, when Boston and Cambridge began to develop parks, Mount Auburn remained one of the most popular destinations for excursions in the region, in particular following late-afternoon dinner parties.

After Story died the cemetery and the Horticultural Society

parted company. Bigelow was elected president of the cemetery. Bigelow, also a student of architecture and sculpture, designed the Egyptian Revival entrance gates (recent excavations in Egypt had made that country's burial practices well known), the gothic chapel just beyond, and Washington Tower on the height of land at the center of the grounds. He commissioned R. S. Greenough to sculpt Governor Winthrop, Thomas Crawford to do James Otis, and Randolph Rogers to carve John Adams's image. The stonemasons of the region honed their craft on the gravestones and monuments sought by tasteful citizens. Among the most notable monuments are the Asa Gray Garden, Mary Baker Eddy's tomb, a sphinx by Martin Milmore, and the Chickering Monument by Thomas Ball.

Among the famous citizens of Massachusetts buried here are scientists Louis Agassiz and Asa Gray; actor Edwin Booth; social worker Dorothea Dix; preachers William Ellery Channing and Edward Everett; architect Charles Bulfinch; poets Amy Lowell, Oliver Wendell Holmes, and Longfellow; Harvard Presidents Lowell and Eliot; Boston Mayor Josiah Quincy; historian Francis Parkman; Senator Henry Cabot Lodge; and industrialist Abbot Lawrence. In all, more than 77,500 individuals have been interred here, many of them just ordinary people. An average of about 700 people a year still find their final resting places here amid the great citizens of the past.

Thousands of trees have been planted on the grounds over the last hundred and fifty years, many now grown to substantial size. Approximately two thousand trees of three hundred and more species have labels with their common and scientific names and places of origin. The cemetery publishes a free guide map to 150 of the most notable trees, Niko fir to weeping flowering cherries. Many budding botanists from Harvard have come here to sort out their dogwoods and viburnums.

Activities:

Ten miles of paved carriage roads are open to cars but are best enjoyed on foot, as are the many grassy footpaths. The roads and trails wind over small hills, into quiet little glens, and around the banks of half a dozen noble ponds. Be sure to pick up a free map of the paths and roads and notable graves and memorials at the entrance office. The view from Washington Tower is one of the best in the Boston Basin. Remember, this is a cemetery and loud or active sports are inappropriate.

Birdwatching: Mount Auburn has some of the best birding in the vicinity of Boston. At least 213 species have been sighted here. The abundance of trees and shrubs seems particularly attractive to spring and fall warbler migrations—some thirty-five species have been seen here in recent years.

Reading:

Mt. Auburn Cemetery: A Proper Boston Institution by Barbara Rotundo is a fine account of the history of Mount Auburn. Available at office.

Directions:

MBTA: Red Line to Harvard Square; Watertown or Waverly bus to Mount Auburn Street one mile from Harvard Square.

Bike: Mount Auburn Street in Harvard Square one mile toward Watertown.

Auto: Mount Auburn Street out of Harvard Square for one mile.

Parking: Plenty of scattered sites around the cemetery.

Telephone: 547-7105

42. CHARLES RIVER BASIN

The waters and shores of the Charles River from Watertown Square to the Charles River Dam
18.5 miles of riverbanks   *MDC   1883 to 1982

Activities: walking, jogging, bicycling, sailing, picnicking, boating, tot-lots

Map: good map in MDC regional map; free for SASE from MDC, 20 Somerset Street, Boston, MA 02108; or call 727-5215

Hours: dawn to dusk

To the River Charles
River! that in silence windest
Through the meadows, bright and free,
Till at length thy rest thou findest
In the bosom of the sea!

. . . .

Thou hast taught me, Silent River,
Many a lesson, deep and long;
Thou hast been a generous giver;
I can give thee but a song.

Henry Wadsworth Longfellow

In 1843 an eccentric but visionary Scotsman named Robert Gourlay proposed that the Charles River be lined with parks and pleasure drives. It is only in our own time, in 1982 to be exact, that Gourlay's dream has reached completion. With the construction of a bicycle trail on the site of the old abattoir (slaughterhouse) in Brighton, the continuous circuit of parks, jogging and bicycle trails, boathouses and landings, picnic areas and recreational facilities along the banks of the Charles River Basin reached fruition. From the last falls on the river, just beyond Watertown Square, to the new dam that extends from the North End to Charlestown, the river's banks have been turned into one of the world's outstanding urban water parks: eighteen miles of metropolitan shoreline in Boston, Newton, Watertown, and Cambridge devoted to public recreation.

For thousands of years the lower Charles River was an estuary, flooded up to the first falls in Watertown twice a day by the incoming tide. When the tide went out, the river became a thin ribbon of water flowing between broad mudflats and salt marshes. The Indian inhabitants of the region walked out on the flats to hunt, dig clams, and gather oysters, and lived in villages along the shore beyond the reach of the tide. At the Watertown falls they built a fish weir to trap the seasonally migrating alewives, shad, and salmon that entered the river each spring to spawn.

At its widest point the river was perhaps twice as broad as it is today. The south bank was not the present Esplanade but rather Boston Neck, the site of our present Washington Street in the South End. The Cambridge side of the river reached almost into the modern Central Square. From east to west the waters of the river extended from the foot of our Boston Common to our Kenmore Square. It was so wide in its lower reaches that when Captain John Smith explored it in 1614, he was sure it was a great river continuing into the interior. Therefore, he named it after his patron, Prince Charles of England.

The Puritan settlers of Boston and the surrounding towns used and altered the river almost from the time of their arrival in 1630. They initially established Newtowne (Cambridge) as their capital with the thought that the river and marshes would shield them from any attack of the French Navy. In 1632 they built a fish weir at the last falls in Watertown and two years later a dam, a grist mill, and a footbridge were constructed at the site.

In 1631 a ferry began service between Boston's Copps Hill and Charlestown at the mouth of the river. Two years later a second ferry began operating between "Sweet Auburn" (in Watertown) and Brighton. In 1648 the first horsebridge in America was built at the Watertown falls to replace the earlier footbridge. But because of intervening marshes the route from Watertown or Cambridge to Boston was a long one, better than ten miles. The distance was shortened to eight miles in 1662 when the Great Bridge was built along the line of the present Anderson Bridge in Cambridge. The next bridge over the Charles, and the first to link Boston directly with the towns across the river, was the Charles River Bridge, a 1,503-foot structure built in 1786 along the line of the Copps Hill–Charlestown ferry. The first direct bridge between Boston and Cambridge was the West Boston Bridge, built in 1793 and running 3,483 feet from West Boston (near the present Charles Circle) to Pelham's Island (Kendall Square).

Although the river itself was not dammed in its lower reaches, its coves and bays were. North Cove was dammed to power a grist mill in 1643 and then filled beginning in 1807 to create a commercial and residential district between today's Haymarket Square and North Station. Between 1814 and 1821 the Back Bay was dammed along the line of present Beacon Street by the Boston and Roxbury Mill Corporation. Between 1859 and the 1870s the dam's receiving basin was filled to create the exclusive Back Bay district (see Section 3, Commonwealth Avenue Mall). In the 1880s the full basin was filled to create the Back Bay Fens (see Section 4, Back Bay).

After the Back Bay was filled, expensive residences lined the Boston side of the river along Beacon Street and Bay State Road. Unfortunately the expanded population of the towns around Boston was pouring its raw sewage into the Charles, and the flats, exposed at each low tide, were laden with a six-inch coating of wastes. Each summer, when the stench of the flats became intolerable, the wealthier citizens of the area would flee to the country or seaside; those left behind demanded that the city or state do something about the Charles.

The "Boston Park Report" of 1876 had recommended taking a two-hundred-yard-wide strip of land along the river for use as a park "laid out with walks, drives, saddle-paths, and boat landings, and ornamented with shrubbery and turf." Charlesbank (see Section 5, Charlesbank) was the first attempt to use the riverbank as parkland, and it dealt with only a few hundred yards out of nearly eighteen miles of riverbanks. Several problems combined to prevent even thinking about parkland along the rest of the river: a waterside park would only be beside the river at high tide—during low tide it would face the stinking flats; sewage was still flowing into the river from communities and industries; and the expense of remaking the Charles would be great.

Nevertheless by 1890 two ideas had become inextricably linked: damming the river at its mouth and lining its banks with parkland. Because the issue of the Charles crossed town lines and involved both parks and sanitary improvement, in 1893 a joint board consisting of the new Metropolitan Park Commission and the state Board of Health was constituted. Charles Eliot was appointed secretary to the joint board, serving also as the primary advocate for creating a beautiful river park. On his European travels in 1884 Eliot had been particularly impressed with the Alster Basin in Hamburg, Germany. The Alster Basin, a dammed tributary of the Elbe, was lined with boat landings and linear parkland—it was the model Eliot chose for the Charles.

In 1894 the joint board issued the most comprehensive plan for the Charles ever undertaken. But though the board recommended damming the river, thus creating a freshwater basin, and lining it with parks, it acknowledged some major obstacles in achieving those goals. There was a fear that if the river were dammed, the demise of its currents would allow Boston Harbor to silt up. Another issue was the industries still using the river for transportation. The final problem was the great expense of an undertaking that had never been attempted in America: damming a river where it entered the sea. For the next ten years the proposal of the joint board was debated.

During those years an outstanding civil engineer, John Freeman, was hired to study the river's problems. After addressing all the potential problems, Freeman concluded that the river could be successfully dammed. In 1903 construction of a dam across the mouth of the Charles to keep out the tides and maintain the basin at a constant, full level was authorized. By 1910 the dam was completed according to Freeman's designs, with a lockhouse designed by Guy Lowell, architect of the Museum of Fine Arts. The Boston side of the river was lined with a seawall along the top of which was a long promenade for strollers.

Meanwhile work had begun on the Cambridge side of the river in 1881. In that year the Charles River Embankment Company was incorporated "to construct a seawall, fill the lands behind it, and develop them for residential purposes, and to lay an esplanade 200 feet wide along the river." Now the site of MIT, at the time the area was a sewage-coated mudflat and marsh known as Oyster Banks. In 1870 Charles Davenport, owner of the Davenport Car Manufacturers, builder of carriages and railroad cars, began to acquire the flats and marshes down to the low-water mark. In exchange for permission to fill along the river and a low tax rate, Davenport and his partners in the Embankment Company agreed to construct a public esplanade along the river. The seawall was erected and filling began, but the company failed during the depression of 1893. The area was taken over by the city, but completion of filling awaited the damming of the river.

About this time, the new Cambridge Park Commission began to consider the recreational potential of their side of the river. Charles Eliot was hired by the Commission in 1891. Eliot developed a plan for a pleasure drive along the Cambridge side of the Charles, now Memorial Drive. The first site selected for an actual river park in Cambridge was Captain's Island, a low hummock below Cambridgeport surrounded by marshes. The island was part of a grant to Captain Daniel Patrick, "trainer and driller of the colony's militia from 1632–1637." A powder magazine was erected on the island at that time to store the colony's ordnance. After passing into private ownership, the island was repurchased by Massachusetts in 1817 and a new powder magazine was built on it in the following year. With construction of a new West Boston Bridge in 1893, Cambridgeport was soon crowded with new homes and industries. In 1899 the Olmsted firm was hired by the Park Department to lay out a park on the site. The city filled the marshes and the landscape architects laid out a beach and playing fields along the river, converting the old powder magazine into a bathhouse complete with lockers and matrons. From the turn of the century until the 1930s, when river pollution caused its abandonment, Magazine Beach was a popular, if the only, public beach in Cambridge.

In 1910, after the river was dammed, Cambridge completed the filling of the Davenport embankment. Two years later MIT decid-

ed to relocate on the filled lands from its crowded quarters on Boylston Street in Boston. Over the next twenty years Welles Bosworth, architect of the new MIT, worked out the design for a public esplanade, providing strollers with a series of shaded benches, lights for the evening, and more than a mile of walkway along the river.

By the late 1920s it had become apparent that the Charles was not being used much for recreation. The dream of Charles Eliot and others of a basin filled with sailboats and surrounded by playing and exercising families was nowhere to be found. In 1928 a committee was formed by industrialist J. J. Storrow to study potential improvements for the river. Storrow, a leading backer of the original dam and Boston-side embankment, had become interested in the river during his undergraduate days at Harvard when he was captain of the rowing crew. His committee found that the embankments on both sides of the river were little more than concrete walkways, with few trees and no lawns for playing or picnicking. There were no public boat rental facilities or boat landings and the crews who did use the river found that the steep seawalls on both sides of the basin created a severe chop that made sailing and boating unpleasant if not downright dangerous. But no action was taken on the committee's report.

A few years later Storrow died. He had become a millionaire managing the huge investment banking firm of Lee, Higginson and Company. To honor his memory and his love of the Charles, Storrow's wife donated a million dollars to the MDC, hoping to remedy the Charles River Basin's problems. Using these funds, a system of lagoons and islands planted with trees and lined with benches and walkways was created using the designs of landscape architect Arthur Shurcliff, giving us the Charles River Esplanade that we know and love today. In addition, the shores of the Esplanade were sloped to eliminate the chop in the basin and several boat landings were constructed along the river.

Even while the Esplanade was under construction it drew crowds back to the river. In 1929 a wooden bandstand was erected on the Esplanade and Arthur Fiedler and the Boston Pops began to hold concerts there. In 1939 two sisters of Edward A. Hatch, a prominent realtor and auctioneer, donated $240,000 for the construction of a band shell to memorialize their late brother. Specifying that the shell not be used for "sectarian, political, or controversial purposes," the sisters had architect Richard A. Shaw design a bandstand with polished granite surfaces. In 1940 Boston area musicians were polled for the names of the world's greatest musicians and those names were carved into the shell. Fiedler conducted concerts in the Hatch Shell for forty years, with 400,000 people showing up for his last July Fourth concert in 1979.

In the 1950s and 1960s a new series of problems appeared on the river. Saltwater seeping in through the dam's locks was collecting and stagnating in low spots on the basin bottom, saltwater being heavier than freshwater. The stagnant saltwater caused noxious fumes to rise to the surface of the river, releasing a rotten-egg odor into the air. The dam itself was becoming inadequate to the task of releasing stormwater. It had been designed to keep out the storm tides and collect the stormwaters coming down the river, releasing them at low tide. As development of new roads and parking lots decreased the land's ability to absorb rain runoff, stormwater flowed immediately into the river. This trend reached a climax in 1968 when Hurricane Diane caused the river to overflow the basin, resulting in millions of dollars worth of damage—the storm tide on the ocean side of the dam was too high to release the river's flow. Another issue that rose to public attention was the problem spawning fish returning from the sea, such as herring and shad, had getting through the dam. And finally, so many pleasure boats were using the one narrow lock on the dam that there was often a long wait for passage.

In 1974 the U.S. Army Corps of Engineers began construction of a new Charles River Dam. The new dam includes fish ladders, three locks, and six 3,000 horsepower diesel engines capable of pumping 630,000 gallons per minute each. These powerful engines maintain the basin at a constant level even in the most severe storm.

Activities:

Strolling: The Esplanade is surely one of the grandest urban walking spaces in the world. Cross the little footbridge over the Lagoon. Watch the sailboats on the river. Sit on the grass and let the cooling breezes waft the city's traffic out of your mind.

Other pleasant places to stroll include the Embankment in front of MIT, the north shore of the river from Watertown Square to Arsenal Street Bridge, and the parkland along Soldier's Field Road.

Jogging and bicycling: A bicycle and jogging trail circles the entire Charles River Basin. The complete circuit is 18.5 miles long, but any number of shorter circuits can be used. One popular circuit of 2.4 miles runs along the inside and the outside of the Esplanade. Another circuit begins at the Esplanade (or any other point), crosses the Harvard Bridge (Massachusetts Avenue), heads up the Cambridge Embankment to Longfellow Bridge, which it crosses to return to the Esplanade. The entire 18.5-mile circuit takes about three leisurely hours on a bicycle. Caution should be used when crossing roads.

Picnicking: Artesani Playground on Soldier's Field Road in Brighton is the most popular tot-lot and picnic area around Boston, with a wading pool, complete play area, picnic tables, and fireplaces (bring your own grill). Plenty of parking, but rather crowded on hot weekends.

Magazine Beach on Memorial Drive in Cambridge has a wading pool, nearby swimming pool, cartop boat-launching ramp, picnic tables under great shade trees, ballfields, and tot-lot.

The Esplanade and the length of Charles River Road in Watertown are fine places for informal picnics. Many other quiet stretches of the river are suitable for picnics.

Other tot-lots are scattered around the Esplanade and all along the river.

Sailing: Community Boating is the Charles River sailing center. Public sailing began here in 1936 and the boat-house was built in 1940 with funds from Mrs. J. J. Stor-row. Community Boating has run the boating program since 1950. The present fleet includes more than a hundred boats, from thirteen-footers to a twenty-four-footer.

Members may take out boats as often as they like during the season, from April 1 to November 1. Hours run from 1:00 P.M. to dusk on weekdays and 9:00 A.M. to dusk on weekends and holidays. Membership rates for the full season are from twenty dollars for senior citizens and forty-five dollars for youths (16–17) to eighty-five dollars for adults.

Community Boating provides free lessons to members. Those folks who already know how to sail may go right out after a test.

The Junior Program, which costs only one dollar a season for children 11–17, is a great way for children to learn sailing.

Community Boating is between the Hatch Shell and Longfellow Bridge. Address: 21 Embankment Road, Boston, MA 02114. Telephone: 523-1038.

Boat launching: Good boat-launching ramp for all types of boats at Daly Recreation Area on Nonantum Road in Brighton. Plenty of parking. An outstanding motorboat trip begins here, cruises up the river, through the locks, and out to the harbor islands. Cartop boats may be launched at Magazine Beach.

Boat excursions: Fifty-minute trips on the river begin at the Hatch Shell landing and Science Museum; three dollars for each adult, one dollar per child. Contact MDC Public Information for time and schedule. Telephone: 727-5215.

Charles River Dam: The new dam includes an excellent multimedia show describing the river and its dams. Also a chance to look at the huge flood-control pumps and the locks. Telephone: 727-0488.

Reading:

The Charles by Arthur B. Tourtellot. *Boston: A Topographical History* by Walter Muir Whitehill has a good description, complete with maps, of the construction and filling of the Back Bay basins. A good history of the Basin is contained in "The Charles River Basin" by Charles Eliot II, published by the Cambridge Historical Society. Be sure to send for the *Charles River Profile* from the Charles River Watershed Association (see Section 33, Norumbega).

Directions: (to Esplanade)

MBTA: Arlington Street station then walk up Arlington Street, cross Beacon Street, then take the Fiedler footbridge over Storrow Drive to the Esplanade.

43. FRESH POND PARK
Fresh Pond Parkway, Cambridge
*Cambridge Park   1892

Activities: jogging, picnicking, walking, ski touring
Hours: dawn to dusk
Admission: free

Fresh Pond was the name that early settlers of Newtowne, as Cambridge was once known, gave to the large, spring-fed, glacier-created kettlehole pond in the western part of the town. Once visited by Indians and a site of their clambakes, the pond was separated from the main body of the town by a long low ridge, a moraine set down ten or twelve thousand years ago as the retreating glacier briefly paused. In 1634 the west shore of the pond was divided into farmlots and in the following year the swamps and marshes to the north were also divided. Many of the smaller farms around the east shore of the pond were consolidated into one large farm by Justin Holden in 1691, though the west shore remained dominated by the Coolidge farm.

In 1796 Fresh Pond Hotel was built on the hill overlooking the pond, thus beginning Fresh Pond's recreational history. Other farms were becoming the estates of wealthy Bostonians. But the desire of these people for peacefulness was soon thwarted.

In the 1830s Frederick Tudor, soon to become Boston's greatest ice merchant, began cutting ice on the pond and shipping it to Southern plantations, Caribbean hotels, and the gin mills of India. In rapid order the ice surface was divided among competing merchants, double-walled icehouses sprang up on the shore, and a railroad spur, the "Ice Railroad," was constructed, connecting the icehouses directly with Charlestown's wharves. As many as eight hundred workmen and several hundred horses worked on the ice each winter. In the peak years of the industry, around 1845, 95,000 tons of ice were shipped out.

The Cambridge Water Works, a private company, in 1856 built a steam engine on the pond's shores, to pump water to a reservoir on the Fayerweather estate off Brattle Street, from which it flowed to customers by gravity. In 1865 this waterworks was bought out by the City of Cambridge, though many feared pollution from the ice businesses and farms along the shore. To control the pond's commercial and agricultural use, Cambridge annexed the west shore from Belmont in 1880, but the problems remained. Finally, in 1892 the city took control of and removed all the farms and icehouses around the pond to ensure the quality of the water. The landscape architecture firm of Olmsted, Olmsted, and Eliot was hired to lay out the territory around the pond as a park.

Since the 1870s the pond had attracted increasing numbers of boaters and picnickers. Several companies rented boats and some of the larger picnics drew as many as eight thousand revelers from Cambridge and Boston. Because the water commissioners felt the need to curtail boating on the pond, they had their landscape architects design carriage drives and bridle paths around the pond as a consolation measure. The hill overlooking the pond was christened Kingsley Park and laid out as a small "country park," with a picnic area, tree plantings, benches, and a pavilion. Within twenty years, though, the rural park was formed into the present golf course, much as had happened at Boston's Franklin Park.

The path around the pond, now paved, is one of the most popular jogging spots in the Boston area. In the clumps of vegetation between path and golf course, tufted timothy, a remnant of the old farms grows amid pasture rose, dogwood, milkweed, and Queen Anne's lace. Grapevines use the fence as an arbor. Meadowsweet, thistle, elms, black cherries, and buckthorns grow behind the fence, and at the very edge of the pond silver maple, hop hornbeam, weeping willow, and old crabapples proliferate. The high path from Kingsley Park to the clubhouse leads through the nearest thing to an old-growth forest in Cambridge.

Kingsley Park, behind the pumping station, has an expanse of grassy slopes. From a lookout on a bluff over the pond the hills of Waltham and Arlington loom in the distance, a view created by the landscape architects on the site of the old Fresh Pond Hotel.

Activities:

Tennis courts limited to Cambridge residents. Fine golf course.

Jogging: Two-and-a-half-mile loop, mostly level, makes this one of the best and most popular jogging circuits in the region.

Picnicking: Blanket picnics, sunbathing, or tossing a ball around at Kingsley Park. Swings and jungle gyms for kids. Plenty of benches. Bubblers and toilets. Trails through woods overlooking pond.

Ski touring: On the golf course and around the pond. Winter joggers tend to pit the circuit path.

Directions:

MBTA: Red Line to Harvard Square. Then take Belmont bus to Fresh Pond Parkway. Or walk a mile and a half up Concord Avenue, which begins by forking left at Cambridge Common.

Auto or bike: Concord Avenue from Harvard Square or Fresh Pond Parkway from Memorial Drive.

Parking: Either side of water pumping station on Fresh Pond Parkway or at golf-course clubhouse on Huron Avenue.

44. MYSTIC RIVER RESERVATION
Mystic Valley Parkway, Medford, Arlington, Malden, and Somerville
*MDC   1899

Activities: walking, jogging, bicycling, birdwatching, sailing, picnicking, ballfields, tennis
Map: free in MDC regional map and in MDC biketrails map (see "Maps" in Introduction)
Hours: dawn to dusk
Admission: no charge

Medford, unlike the other towns of colonial Massachusetts, was the private reserve of a wealthy Puritan, Matthew Craddock. Craddock sent several hundred of his employees to settle his lands between 1630 and 1641. The first arrivals found a healthy tribe of Indians living along the river, the Pawtuckets, led by Sagamore John, but by 1633 most of the natives had died during a smallpox epidemic. Craddock's men farmed and fished, and on the Mystic River's banks they built a thirty-five-ton bark, *The Blessing of the Bay,* the first boat launched in the English colonies. In 1637 they erected the first bridge across the Mystic River, Craddock Bridge. In 1641 Craddock died and the land was divided into a regular town.

For the next two hundred years Medford and the other towns along the Mystic River were primarily devoted to agriculture, using the river's marsh hay for feed and catching the river's fish.

In the nineteenth century Medford became a major industrial city, and the river was lined with shipyards, mills, and brickworks. Toward the end of the century, the area along the Mystic was reached by the trolleys of the West End Street Railway, and with the trolley came the real estate speculators and residential development. Somerville was already on its way to becoming one of America's most densely populated cities. And all these new settlers, many of whom worked in the factories and mills along the river, needed outdoor recreation.

In 1900 the Metropolitan Park Commission took 270 acres of land along both sides of the river for parkland. A parkway was laid out to connect the Mystic River Reservation with crowded Everett and Revere Beach on one side, and the Middlesex Fells Reservation on the other. Between 1906 and 1908 a dam was built, changing the river from a tidal estuary to a freshwater basin. It was hoped that this dam, by keeping the river full of water, would increase its recreational attraction. But too many industrial wastes were spilling into the river and it could not attract the crowds, and so its development was not completed until our own day.

Activities:

The Mystic River Reservation is generally a narrow strip of greensward bounded by the river and the road; several areas have developed facilities.

McDonald Park: Completed in 1981, this pleasant park near Wellington Circle has been laid out for bicycling and picnicking. Approximately one mile of bike trails wind along the river and over newly planted little hillocks. Plenty of benches have been placed for leisure-time walkers. This is also a nice place for a blanket picnic. An observation tower provides a fine view of the marshes and the river. Toilets at MDC Police Station.

Hormel Stadium: Fields for football, rugby, baseball, and running. Reservations required for ballfields: call 438-5690. Also six tennis courts, first come-first serve, and skating rink.

Blessing of the Bay Sailing: This MDC sailing facility rents boats and provides lessons. Open Memorial Day to Columbus Day. Address: Shore Drive, Somerville, MA 02143. Telephone: 628-9610.

Jogging: Jogging path through the mowed grass along much of the river between Wellington and Mystic Lakes, a distance of four miles. Use caution when crossing roads.

Picnicking: Many shady lawns where you may toss down a blanket along the river. Several tot-lots. No facilities. Developed picnic area at Sandy Pond Beach on Upper Mystic Lake with tables, grills, and nearby bathrooms and swimming.

Swimming: Small, pleasant freshwater beach on Upper Mystic Lake. Picnic area. Bathhouse, bathrooms, and lifeguards.

Fishing: Bass, pickerel, sunfish, and catfish from Mystic Lake.

Directions:
Mystic Valley Parkway in Medford, Arlington, Somerville, and Winchester.
Parking: Plenty, though Sandy Pond Beach is crowded on hot summer weekends.

45. MIDDLESEX FELLS RESERVATION
Headquarters, Pond Street, Stoneham, MA 02180
2,060 acres   MDC   1894

Activities: hiking, ski touring, picnicking, nature study, jogging, horseback riding, swimming pool, tot-lots, ballfield, zoo
Map: free at headquarters weekdays during business hours or send SASE
Hours: dawn to dusk
Admission: free

The Fells forms a region of great natural beauty, which has long served as a recreation ground for the large population in its immediate vicinity . . . while it is a favorite resort of excursionists from Boston, Cambridge, and other localities.

Sylvester Baxter
Metropolitan Park Report of 1893

One of the speakers at the Boston park hearing of 1869 was an elderly journalist and reformer from Medford named Elizur Wright. Wright began his statement by declaring: "What is wanted is not a local breathing hole. . . . Of such we have some, and should have more,—oases in the great desert of brick and mortar." Wright hoped the City Council would think big: "If Boston makes a park only for the present municipality, a larger Boston will soon have to make another."

Wright had developed five criteria for what he thought was wanted in a park that would serve not only Boston but the communities north of the city as well, where as yet there was no public open space. First, it should be of at least two thousand acres.

Second, it should be surrounded by enough land to screen out "nuisances." Third, it should include "a great variety of scenery and eminences overlooking the whole city, the sea, and the interior of the country." Fourth, it should be well wooded and have lakes. And, fifth, it should be a "museum for the study of every branch of natural history, as well as an attractive retreat in the domain of wild nature herself." Wright knew of a place that met all these conditions: Five Mile Woods, known since 1879 as Middlesex Fells.

First explored by Governor Winthrop in 1632, in 1634 a portion of the tract was granted to Governor Craddock, "where he has impaled a park where he keeps his cattle, till he can store it with deer." Much of the rest of the land was used as common land by the people of Charlestown. "It was common practice to allow cattle and swine to roam in the woods until deep snow came." Sawmills were established along several of the brooks that tumbled out of the hills: lumbering began early here.

In an effort to control cutting in the woods, the selectmen of Charlestown passed a resolution in 1653 "that no inhabitant of the town or any other town shall under any pretense whatever cut down any tree upon the Common, . . . without first acquainting the selectmen therewith. . . ." In 1689 it was Malden that was worried about overuse of Five Mile Woods, for they warned their Charlestown neighbors "against cutting off wood and timber from the common lands." Meanwhile, Stoneham residents were logging the Cedar Swamp to make posts, shingles, and clapboards. Malden forbade the cutting of saplings "under penalty of paying five shillings per tree." Finally in 1694 the common land was divided and turned over to private ownership. Over the next two hundred years the area was repeatedly logged and swept by fires.

The ponds in the woods had been turned into reservoirs to supply drinking water to the surrounding towns. Melrose, Medford, and Malden each had a pumping station or gatehouse on Spot Pond by 1890. In the western section of the woods the town of Winchester had dug out Turkey Swamp and enlarged several ponds to make itself three reservoirs. In 1886 the Appalachian Mountain Club published a map and description of the Fells, it already having become a popular excursion destination for Club members, as well as other folks. In 1879 Sylvester Baxter, later secretary to the Metropolitan Park Commission, coined a catchy name for the tract, "Middlesex Fells," after the old English name for rocky windblown hills.

By 1893 nearly 1,600 acres of land in the Fells were in the

public's hands, but because much of this was water supply and so not suitable for recreation, the Metropolitan Park Report of that year recommended acquisition of an additional 1,500 acres for parkland. With the approval of funds to purchase the land by the Legislature, in the following year acquisition began and 1,583 acres were designated as the Middlesex Fells Reservation. Several parcels were donated to the Reservation, including the Trustees' Virginia Wood and two hills donated by Wright's children.

A plan for the Reservation was drawn up by Charles Eliot, who had roamed here during his youth. Hundreds of unemployed workers were hired—a depression was on at the time—to clear fire roads and remove brush. Contractors were hired to build carriage roads, bridle paths, and facilities. Names were assigned to hilltops and glens after Indian legends and the adventures of the Puritan explorers. As work progressed, parkways were laid out connecting the Fells to other parks in the region. Soon a trolley line penetrated the Reservation and the crowds began to flock to the woods of the Fells for picnics, horseback rides, and hikes.

In 1897 the Metropolitan Water Commission acquired Spot Pond as a receiving reservoir for the new Wachusett aqueduct system. The water level was raised five feet, covering the rocks that had given the pond its name. A massive brick and limestone pumping station, designed by Shepley, Rutan, and Coolidge and powered by Leavitt and Holly engines, was erected on the east bank of the pond. The station pumped water to a distributing reservoir on Cairn Hill, from which the water flowed by gravity to the higher elevations of the northern water district.

Oaks and white pines predominate in the forest that now covers the Fells. Cool dark hemlock groves, stands of beech, and a scattering of hickory and ash fill out the woods. Red maple, yellow birch, and hop hornbeam are found along streamcourses and near wetlands. The upland forest floor is carpeted with huckleberries, wild oats, yellow stargrass, sweet fern, Canada mayflower, pipsissewa, blueberries, mapleleaf viburnum, and spring violets. Less common wildflowers of the woods include shinleaf, false foxglove, wood anemone, ragged fringed orchis, and Indian pipe.

With the growth of automobile use, carriage drives became highways, urban mountaineers discovered that they could journey to the White Mountains in the time it had taken their parents to reach the Fells, and the Fells was slowly forgotten as a major recreation area. It was neglected and allowed to slowly decline after the Metropolitan Park Commission was merged into the

MDC. The ultimate injury, however, awaited our own day: the permanent division of the Reservation by the multilaned Route I-93, exactly the sort of "nuisance" that Elizur Wright was fearful of. Yet in the woods and vales the trees have been growing taller, the flowers wilder, and the sheltering quiet more valuable with each passing year.

Activities:
Though the crowds flock to the Zoo and swimming pool, or storm the summits of Bear Hill and Pine Hill (too often leaving their litter behind), Middlesex Fells has hundreds of acres of woodlands awaiting the modern re-explorer.

Hiking: At least fifty miles of hiking trails and old woods roads run through the Fells. Start at the Bear or Pine hill towers to get your bearings, then head out around the quiet reservoirs or hike the long Skyline Trail that runs between the two towers. In the eastern section of the Reservation, clamber over the open ledges around Cairn Hill or consider the towering trees of the Virginia Wood. There are many more good trails and areas worth poking around—free maps are available at Park Headquarters, just north of the entrance to the Zoo.

Picnicking: Developed picnic areas with tables, grills, and bathrooms can be found at the swimming pool near the north entrance to the park and at the Zoo. The Sheepfold, pastureland for hundreds of years, has shade trees, picnic tables, open fields, a softball diamond, and many places to wander. Many of the hilltops are fine places for a picnic.

Ski touring: The old carriage roads and fire roads provide very good wilderness skiing, the circuit trail around the Winchester reservoirs being particularly lovely. Good trails are found elsewhere in the park; well maintained but not prepared. Novice to intermediate. Be sure to obtain a map.

Jogging: Many of the woods roads are well graded and suitable for jogging. Winchester Reservoir circuit is popular as is the east side of Spot Pond along the sidewalk.

Ice-skating: Natural ice-skating on Doleful, Dark Hollow, and Fellsmere ponds. Artificial skating rink at Wright's Pond.

Fishing: At Fellsmere, Doleful, and Quarter Mile ponds

for sunfish, perch, catfish, pickerel, and bass. No fishing in reservoirs.

Swimming: At pool near north entrance to park.

Horseback riding: Stoneham Ranch, 106 Pond Street (a quarter mile north of Zoo) Stoneham (telephone 438-9837) conducts guided horseback riding through the Fells.

Zoo: The Walter D. Stone Zoo at 149 Pond Street, Stoneham (telephone 438-3662) is the busiest section of the Fells and the most popular with kids. A four-story enclosed aviary is delightful, with more than a hundred species of exotic birds. The main zoo has pairs of gorillas and orangutans, pigmy hippos, lions, tigers, giraffes, and more. Picnic area.

Directions:

Public transportation: Stoneham bus departs from Government Center in Boston every half hour. Goes through eastern section of Fells and by the Zoo. Call Hudson Bus Lines for information, 395-8080.

Bike: McGrath Highway in Somerville to Fellsway.

Auto: Route 93 north to exits 7, 8, and 9.

Parking: Room for half a dozen cars at trailheads. Large formal parking areas at Bellevue Pond (at the base of Pine Hill), Zoo, and Sheepfold.

Telephone: 438-5690

46. PINE BANKS PARK
***1087 Main Street, Melrose, MA 02176**
150 acres   Trustees of Pine Banks Park   1905

Activities: picnicking, walking, jogging, ballfields, ski touring, children's zoo

Hours: 8:00 A.M. to dusk

Admission: no charge

This large old park on the Melrose-Malden line was one of the first large parks in the region donated to the citizenry by an individual. Elisha Converse owned the Boston Rubber Shoe Company, largest manufacturer of galoshes in America and largest factory in Melrose. Converse was active in the parks movement and one of the earliest members of the Trustees of Reservations. To show his appreciation to his workers and the two towns that most of them lived in, he purchased a large tract of land across the way from his factory and began to lay it out as a park.

The area he purchased had been part of Thomas Lynde's farm in the early 1600s, and in 1653 a road was laid out through the area between Winnesimett (Chelsea) and Reading. Converse oversaw the construction of parkways, picnic areas, and playing fields, and the planting of ornamental trees and shrubs. Almost immediately Pine Banks became a "famed resort for outing parties" and favored site for Christian revival meetings. When the park was completed to Converse's satisfaction, he donated it to Melrose and Malden, specifying that it be administered by representatives from each town.

During World War I the local people had Victory Gardens here. During World War II the top of one of the park's hills was blasted out and an antiaircraft gun was installed.

The two wooded hills in the park have very different origins: the hard-rock hill behind the picnic area is believed to be a solidified volcanic vent; the higher hill, named Mount Ephrim after Converse's brother, is a glacial drumlin. In addition to putting out a healthy crop of huckleberries and wildflowers, and serving as a nesting site for red-tailed hawks, Mount Ephrim is one of the most popular sites in the region for fossil hunters.

Activities:

Picnicking: Very pleasant picnic area with tables, grills, swings and slides, toilets, and a little pond for duck feeding and fishing. Children's zoo next to area. Reservations needed on weekends for a developed picnic site (table and fireplace).

Walking and hiking: Four miles of trails wind through woods and over hilltops. Nice walk up Mount Ephrim.

Ballfields: Six fields; reservations needed for evenings.

Ski touring: Several miles of trails laid out for skiing. Novice to intermediate.

Directions:

Main Street in Melrose and Malden. Pine Banks is on the border between the two towns.

Parking: Plenty.

Telephone: 324-0822

47. BREAKHEART RESERVATION
Lynn Fells Parkway, Saugus
600 acres   *MDC   1934

Activities: swimming, hiking, picnicking, jogging, bicy-cling, fishing, ski touring
Map: free at office (near entrance)
Hours: 10:00 A.M. to 8:00 P.M.
Admission: free

The area now within Breakheart Reservation was once a common shared by Wakefield and Saugus and known as the "600 Acres." The area was divided before 1750 by the residents of those two towns and turned over to private ownership, but it was still considered public enough to be used as a muster and training ground during the Civil War. Around the turn of this century the entire tract was purchased by Benjamin Johnson and a Mr. Clough for use as a private hunting reserve, called "Wakesau," after Wakefield and Saugus. They dammed the spring-fed brook in the reserve to increase waterfowl habitat. Later the two men sold their property to the Breakheart Hill Forestry Company, which logged the area.

In 1934 the MDC acquired this area for use as a reservation, but it was not developed until 1960, when the ponds were cleaned up and new dams were built to increase the water depth. During the Depression the MDC had leased the tract to the CCC, which built fire roads and conducted forestry work. During World War II, Breakheart served as a base for Military Police and the Quartermaster Corps.

Activities:

Though most visitors to Breakheart congregate around the clear waters of artificial Pearce and Silver lakes, there is much more to explore here. Trails lead through a mixed forest of hemlock, white pine, and oak to the tops of rocky hills. Eagle Rock, a bare knoll across from the swimming area, looks almost straight down on the lake and south to Boston. Castle Hill, with a few trees on its summit to provide some shade, is the highest eminence within thirty miles north of Boston.

Swimming: Two sandy beaches on the north end of Pearce Lake. Lifeguards, bathrooms, shallow area for kids. Excellent, clear, cool water.

Picnicking: Near bathing beach; tables and grills. Also tables at Pine Top area. Many other places on the rocky summits and around the lakes suitable for blanket picnics. Bathrooms and water at swimming area. Bring your own grill.

Hiking: Many miles of trails, most of which do not appear on the map. Pick a summit and head for it.

Jogging: Several miles of paved park roads closed to cars make a terrific jogging course.

Bicycling: On closed roads. Good for beginners, children, and families. Wide and little trafficked; you can go all out here.

Ski touring: Along six miles of park roads plus several miles of additional tracks laid out along a sewer line. According to locals, this is an excellent place for ski touring, never too crowded.

Fishing: Both lakes occasionally stocked with trout. Also the usual perch, sunfish, and catfish.

Directions:

Bike: Charlestown to Broadway in Everett north to Main Street through Malden and Melrose to right on Lynn Fells Parkway. Park entrance two miles on left.

Auto: Route 1 north to Saugus, Lynn Fells exit, entrance a quarter mile on the right.

Parking: Plenty, though crowded on weekends; arrive early if you want to go swimming.

48. LYNN WOODS
Pennybrook Road, Lynn
2,200 acres   *Lynn Park Department   1882–1889

Activities: hiking, nature study, picnicking, jogging, ski touring, historic sites, birdwatching

Map: for fifty cents from Park Department at Pennybrook Road entrance or send SASE

Hours: 8:00 A.M. to dusk

Admission: no charge

*Such is the gift which the good God, working through social history and
natural history, and statute laws, and the hearts of men, has given to
the present and future people of Lynn.*

Edward Everett Hale
Circa 1890

Lynn Woods, one of the largest municipal parks in America and by
far the largest in the region, has the clear potential to be one of the
most beautiful as well. Tree-covered hills, open summits, and
reservoir banks create many a pleasing prospect from the trails and
woods roads that form a network through this forested reservation.
Unfortunately this park is the site of more litter, broken glass,
dump remains, and vandalism than any other park in the region.
Nonetheless, the great beauty and long history of this park make it
definitely worth visiting.

The area was first explored by William Wood in 1629. A Mr.
Tomlin, builder of a grist mill along Strawberry Brook in 1633,
appears to have been the first settler. During the 1650s the hills
became a retreat for pirates who anchored along the Saugus River.
They built a hut and dug a garden near a tall crag that served as
their rendezvous for several years. Their rowdy life came to an end
when all the pirates but one were captured by the authorities and
sent back to England for execution. Tom Veal, the escapee, set up
his abode in a nearby cave. According to legend, during the
earthquake of 1658 a boulder fell in front of Veal's cave, sealing
him in to his death. Since then the cave has been known as Pirate's
Dungeon.

Because the region was too rugged for cultivation, in 1706 the
town decided not to lay out roads in or subdivide the Woods.
Walls were built, but unlike those in other towns, these did not
indicate individual property bounds, but rather common pastures
separated by animal species. That is, although animals were individually owned, oxen, sheep, horses, and pigs grazed in their own
common pastures.

In 1750 John Adam Dagyr, a Welsh shoemaker, arrived in Lynn
and began the industry that would make Lynn the largest shoemaking city in America. After the Woods' white birches were harvested for shoepegs to attach soles, Lynn Woods was all but forgotten
except as a source of fuelwood. Landings, as in Blood's Swamp
Landing and Dungeon Landing, were clearings to which Lynnmen
dragged their winter-cut logs for six or seven months of seasoning.

In 1843 a dam was built across a stream, creating Breed's Pond as a water supply to drive shoemaking machinery.

In 1852 a "confirmed spiritualist" named Marble purchased Dungeon Rock and its surroundings after a pirate treasure there was revealed to him in a dream. For the next twelve years, using automatic writing as his guide, Marble blasted and dug into the hard rock of his claim, but not one piece of eight ever turned up.

In 1870 Breed's Pond was purchased by the town as a reservoir. Twelve years later, when the state Legislature passed the Park Act of 1882 allowing towns and organizations to purchase parkland, Lynn was among the first to respond. A private citizens' group, Lynn Trustees of the Public Forest, raised $20,000 and purchased 160 acres of the Woods for the public's pleasure. In 1889 the town purchased 996 additional acres and received the Trustees' 160 acres as a donation, making of Lynn Woods the first large forest park in the region. When Walden Pond (named after Lynn Mayor Edwin Walden) and Glen Lewis Pond were built as reservoirs in that same year, the town's total holdings in the area increased to 1,600 acres.

The picturesque rocky hills of Lynn Woods are covered with red and white oaks, tall white pines, shagbark hickories, and many acres of huckleberries and lowbush blueberries. Some of the steeper slopes are mantled by exquisite hemlock groves. Solomon's seal, sarsaparilla, raspberry vines, sweet fern, and yellow-flowered rockrose enliven the forest floor. Around the streams and swamps, where tremendous jack-in-the-pulpits sprout, gray birch, red maple, hop hornbeam, and spruce grow.

The Woods is divided in two by the long arm of Walden Pond. The summits of Burrill Hill and Mount Gilead, in the southern section, are among the North Shore's finest viewpoints, overlooking Boston Harbor, Boston, the Blue Hills, and a sea of green leading the eye to the distant horizonal humps of Mounts Monadnock and Wachusetts. Both hilltops attract migrating and nesting songbirds, and the bright orange flash of a towhee or oriole may distract your distant gaze. You are also likely to spy a red-tailed hawk soaring over the lower hilltops.

The northern section of the Woods, lying between Walden Pond and the long, steeply rising Bow Ridge, is bisected by Ox Pasture Road. Giant boulders have been glacially plucked off the top of the ridge and cascaded down the slope, making a pleasantly grotesque rock garden. Hay-scented fern, Indian cucumber root, and starflower are among the predominant wildflowers sprouting around the tumbled rocks.

Activities:

The northern section of Lynn Woods is the cleaner of the two sections, but even in the southern section many fine places may be discovered. When the winter's snow hides the litter and debris, this park is a real wonderland. Bring a flashlight to explore Pirate's Dungeon.

Walking and hiking: Nearly thirty miles of woods roads and trails. The trails around Birch and Walden ponds, along Hemlock Ridge, over Burrill Hill and Mount Gilead, and out the Ox Pasture are particularly enjoyable. A little bushwhacking is in order here to find the more pristine spots: try exploring the slope and ledges of Bow Ridge or the relatively untrammeled banks along the west end of Walden Pond. Be sure to pick up or send for a map.

Jogging: Fifteen or twenty miles of woods roads have good gravel or pine-needle running surface. Many possible circuits, choosing fairly level or hilly routes.

Picnicking: Though there are no tables or facilities, there are many pretty places to picnic: the shores of the ponds, Mount Gilead, and the ledges above Ox Pasture Road being among the best.

Ski touring: Excellent ski touring on the many woods roads and wide trails. Beautiful in the winter, with many miles of easy grades. Lynn Woods Ski Touring Center (598-4212) prepares trails and offers rentals, instruction, and refreshments.

Directions:

Public transportation: Train from North Station to Lynn. Take Central Square, Lynn—Pine Hill bus to Thistle Street, where several trails enter the Woods.

Bike: North on Route 107 through Lynn Center. Left on Chestnut Street to Broadway, to Lynnfield Street. Continue straight on Great Woods Road, where Lynnfield Street jogs right.

Auto: To northern entrance (Ski Touring Center and north section of Woods) same as "Bike" above. To southern entrance (Park Department Headquarters), follow Route 1 north from Boston. Walnut Street exit east to Lynn. Continue one and a half miles to left on Pennybrook Road. Continue to end.

Parking: Plenty at both entrances.

49. RED ROCK PARK AND KING'S BEACH

49A. RED ROCK PARK
Lynn Shore Drive, Lynn
*MDC

Activities: picnicking, strolling, birdwatching, scenic area, bicycling

Red Rock Park is a high landscaped bluff along the Lynn shore overlooking the Atlantic Ocean. The wide walkway along the escarpment is not only a breezy place for a spring or fall stroll with a spectacular view of the ocean, it is also an excellent place for jogging or bicycling. The walkway connects to Nahant Beach walkway, making nearly a four-mile route along the seashore uninterrupted by street crossings. Open grassy areas on the bluff are suitable for picnics. The boulder-strewn beach below the bluff is a fine place for wandering or birdwatching when the tide is out. Use the Nahant facilities.

Directions:
Lynn Shore Drive north of Nahant Beach.
Parking: Along road.

49B. KING'S BEACH
Lynn Shore Drive, Lynn
*MDC

Activities: swimming, fishing, picnicking

The King family was one of the first families to settle the colonial town of Lynn, being signatories to the original deed of purchase for that town from the Indians. The Kings settled in the Swampscott section of Lynn, where they owned a large tract of land that included inland farms and much of the shoreline. By 1653 the family was actively engaged in farming, fishing, and shipping. This beach has been known as King's Beach since that time.

Although the area around the beach has been almost completely developed, the beach itself is a half-mile crescent of clean gray sand. The beach becomes very narrow when the tide is in, but when the tide is out you can walk for two miles below the Lynn bluffs to Nahant. Lifeguards, bathhouse, and bathrooms. Picnic with a blanket or chairs on the beach. Surf fishing in the evening.

Directions:
Just beyond Red Rock Park on Lynn Shore Drive.
Parking: Limited parking.

SOUTH PARKS

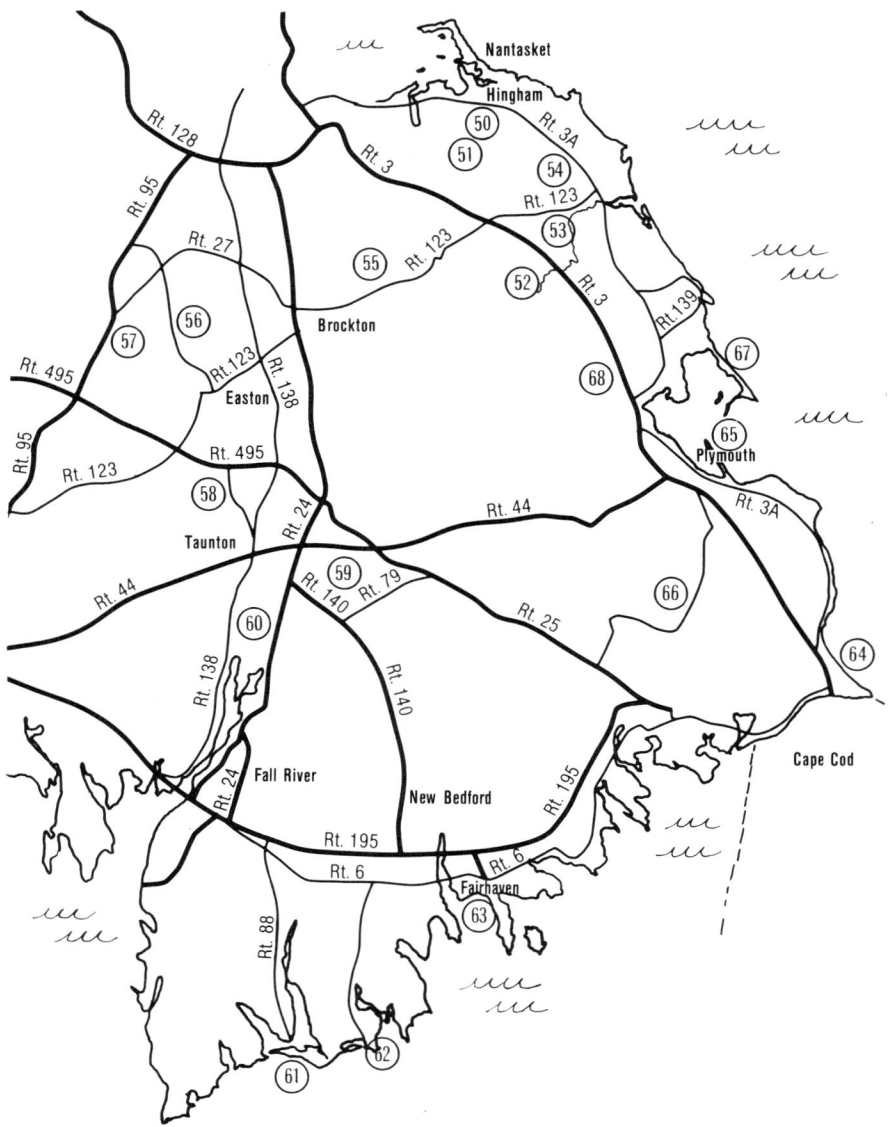

South Parks
Quick Guide to Outdoor Activities

	WALKING	PICNICKING	SWIMMING	JOGGING	NATURE STUDY	SKI TOURING	FISHING	BIRDWATCHING	HIKING	CANOEING & BOATING	ICE-SKATING	PROGRAMS	CAMPING	HORSEBACK RIDING	TOWERS, ZOOS, ETC.	HISTORIC SITES	BALLFIELDS	TOT-LOTS	BIKE TRAILS	TENNIS
50. Whitney and Thayer Woods	•	•		•	•	•		•	•					•						
51. Wompatuck State Park	•	•		•	•	•	•	•	•			•	•	•					•	
52. North River					•		•	•		•						•				
53. Norris Reservation	•	•		•	•	•		•	•											
54. Black Pond Reserve	•				•			•												
55. Ames Nowell State Park	•	•			•		•	•	•	•										
56. Borderland State Park	•	•		•	•	•	•	•	•			•				•				
57. Moose Hill Sanctuary	•				•			•	•			•								
58. Watson Pond State Park		•	•				•			•								•		
59. Massasoit State Park	•	•	•	•	•	•	•	•	•	•		•	•	•						
60. Dighton Rock State Park		•											•			•				
61. Horseneck Beach Reservation	•	•	•	•	•		•	•		•			•						•	
62. Demarest Lloyd State Park	•	•	•		•		•	•		•										
63. Fort Phoenix Street Reservation		•	•				•									•				
64. Scusset Beach State Reservation	•	•	•	•	•		•					•	•					•	•	
65. Plymouth Beach	•	•	•	•	•		•	•												
66. Myles Standish State Forest	•	•	•	•	•	•	•	•	•	•			•						•	
67. Duxbury Beach	•	•	•	•	•		•	•												
68. Malachi Brook Wildlife Sanctuary	•	•		•	•			•	•											

50. WHITNEY AND THAYER WOODS
Cohasset and Hingham
799 acres   *Trustees of Reservations   1933

Activities: hiking, nature study, picnicking, horseback riding, ski touring
Hours: sunrise to sunset year-round
Admission: no charge

Like much of the rest of New England, this large tract of undeveloped forest land was occupied by farms for one hundred and fifty or more years. Abandoned in the 1870s, the only evidence of the former inhabitants are a few old overgrown cellar holes, lichen-covered stone walls that separated sheep and cow pastures, old roads, and periwinkle, a persistent garden groundcover. After the turn of the century, the land was purchased by the Whitney Woods Association and used for horseback riding. The Association gave 640 acres to the Trustees of Reservations in 1933, and over the years since then other parcels have been added to the property by purchase and donation.

The forest floor here is covered with club mosses, partridgeberry, sarsaparilla, pipsissewa, whorled loosestrife, and tall Indian pipe. During the spring, colorful bunches of violets and marsh marigold grace the streamcourses, where seven or eight varieties of fern, including the rock-loving polypody, can also be found. Shagbark and pignut hickory, white ash, red and white oak, red maple, and sweet birch make up the forest, with an occasional holly as a treat. From Turkey Hill there is a view of Boston and Cohasset Harbor.

Activities:

Situated on Route 3A, this woodland is a good place to wander after a hard week in the city or a hot day at the beach. It is always clean, peaceful, and quiet.

Hiking: Twelve miles of old woods roads wind over the tract. Mostly easy walking. Trail connects to Wompatuck State Park nature trail.

Picnicking: Several picnic tables in a lovely pine grove just beyond Sohier Street entrance and parking lot. Pack-it-in/pack-it-out picnics in the woods. No fires or grills. No facilities.

Ski touring: Along twelve miles of woods roads. Wide and

well maintained, though no preparation. Connection to Wompatuck makes this part of a vast skiing area.

Horseback riding: Along the twelve miles of woods roads. Hingham Riding Stables, Turkey Hill Lane, Hingham (telephone 749-9734) rents horses for riding in the woods.

Directions:

Route 3A to Cohasset; parking lot on right where Sohier Street goes left to South Shore Music Circus.

Parking: Plenty, but limited in the winter months.

51. WOMPATUCK STATE PARK
Headquarters, Union Street, Hingham, MA 02043
2,877 acres   Massachusetts State Park   1967

Activities: hiking, picnicking, bicycling, nature study, bird-watching, camping, cross-country skiing, fishing, horse-back riding
Map: free from Visitor Center or send SASE
Hours: 8:00 A.M. to dusk
Admission: three dollars a car or a state season pass

Only twenty miles from downtown Boston, Wompatuck contains some of the oldest forest groves in eastern New England. Situated in the towns of Hingham, Cohasset, Norwell, and Scituate, the park's woodlands, wetlands, fields, and granite outcroppings shelter many types of flora and fauna—and the bicycling is among the best in the region.

On July 4, 1665, the area now in the park was included in the lands deeded to Massachusetts Bay colonists by Indian Sachem Josiah Wompatuck of the Massachuset tribe. The deeded area, soon settled by small farmers, included all the land now in Hingham and Cohasset. Shipowners also held title to much of the land, using the largest native trees to build ships along the Fore and Back rivers.

During the 1700s, the Stockbridge Mill used the power of one of the brooks to manufacture shingles. Farmers let their horses, cows, and oxen graze the fields. The woodlands were valued as a source of fuelwood. But as in so much of New England, the soil was thin and farms were abandoned for the opportunities of the frontier. From the middle of the nineteenth century until the 1920s, the pink granite of the area was quarried. Tiffany's of New York owned one of the quarries, which they mined for expensive residential interior slabs and mantlepieces.

By the middle of our own century, few residents or industries remained. In 1941, the U.S. Navy purchased the area and turned it into a huge ammunition dump. Ordnance was stored in massive concrete bunkers scattered around the reservation. Rumors used to be heard that parts of the nation's first atomic bomb were stored here in special bunkers during World War II. When the federal government conveyed the area to Massachusetts in 1967, all the bunkers were filled and sealed, though the land to the north of the park was retained as a military reservation.

The park is covered by a second-growth oak and hickory forest that filled in the fields and woodlots of the former settlers. As an indication of how long ago the area was abandoned, the Forest Sanctuary Climax Grove, composed of large old white oak, hemlock, and beech trees, has been dated back 175 years. This grove and two others in the park are the nearest things to virgin forest in the entire region. Other common trees of the park include oak, red maple, ash, birch, and occasionally a native holly. Among the common shrubs are swamp azalea, witch hazel, sheep laurel, and bayberry. Wildflowers include lady's slipper, partridgeberry, meadowsweet, dwarf cinquefoil, starflower, spring violet, and the crimson cardinal flower.

The area is also a natural sanctuary for deer, rabbits, racoons, skunks, turtles, and frogs. Among the birds regularly sighted are marsh hawks, green herons, goshawks, owls, grouse, quail, and warblers.

Prospect Hill, a pine-covered knoll in the south end of the park, at 247 feet is the highest point in Hingham. Nearby is famous Mount Blue Spring, source of some of the purest water in the state. Once the spring water was commercially bottled, but today it's free for the taking—bring some jugs. The native holly can be seen across from the Mount Blue parking lot, but please don't pick any foliage. A feature of the Climax Grove Nature Study area is Burbank Boulder, a balancing glacial erratic dragged here during the last ice age.

Activities:

The new visitor to Wompatuck should begin at the Visitor

Center near the Union Street entrance. Displays, lectures, and rangers. Open year-round. Free maps.

Hiking: A short self-guided nature trail begins beside the Visitor Center. Twelve miles of bicycle trails are available for walking as are another five or six miles of woodland trails. The most interesting walk in the park circles through the big trees of the Forest Sanctuary Grove. Another nice walk makes a gentle ascent of Prospect Hill. Pick up free map at the Visitor Center.

Camping: 440 developed campsites, open year-round. Five dollars a night, six dollars with electricity. Toilets and showers. Some privacy.

Swimming: None. Go to Nantasket.

Fishing: Three small ponds challenge young anglers. Perch, sunfish, catfish, and pickerel. Check with rangers about stocking.

Bicycling: Twelve miles of biketrails laid out on former military roads. Easy grades make it a great place for children, families, and older bikers, yet there's enough space for the more aggressive biker to work out.

Nature study: Climax Grove Trail, Prospect Hill, and the area south of Mount Blue Spring. Check with rangers for seasonal specialties. Interpretive programs are offered during the summer months.

Ski touring: More than twenty miles of trails along hiking and bicycle routes. No preparation. Mostly flatlands or easy grade. Better to the west of Union Street, because no snowmobiles. Visitor Center open for warming and toilets.

Horseback riding: Eight miles of well-groomed bridle trails. Horses available at Hingham Riding Stable. Telephone: 749-9734. (See Section 50, Whitney and Thayer Woods.)

Directions:

Bike: Follow Route 3A from Neponset through Quincy, turn right on Lincoln Street in Hingham, four miles to right on Free Street, then right on Union Street.

Auto: Route 3 to Route 228 in Hingham, right on Free Street, cross Lazell Street and enter park.

Parking: Plenty.

Telephone: 749-7160

52. NORTH RIVER
Pembroke, Hanover, Norwell, and Marshfield
National Natural Landmark, 1975   Scenic River, 1979

Activities: canoeing, nature study, birdwatching, historic sites

Map: free map of river between Elm Street in Pembroke and Bridge Street in Norwell with thirty-two historic sites indicated and described; send SASE to North and South Rivers Watershed Association, c/o Philip Causer, 66 Bridge Street, Norwell, MA 02161

Dip your paddle into the tranquil dark waters of the North River and move with the current past grassy marshes and wooded hills, then listen. Can you hear the roaring blast furnace and the trip-hammer of the forge? Can you hear the screeching sawmill or the thud of wood pegs being driven into solid oak planks? Or can you hear the sharp low whisper of a scythe flying through the meadow grass? These are echoes of the river's agricultural and industrial past. But now, like a good plow horse put out to pasture or a hoary professor granted the title emeritus, the North River has been retired: to honor its faithful service, it has been designated a National Natural Landmark and in 1979 it became the first official Scenic River in the state of Massachusetts.

Running through a wide valley carved by the meltwaters of the retreating glacier, the North River winds through extensive marshes, past heaps of glacial till, around drumlins and moraine deposits. The river is tidal all the way to the confluence of its two sources in Pembroke, the Herring River and the Indian River. The early settlers of the wilderness towns of Marshfield and Scituate found the cleared fields and shell heaps of a fair-sized Indian encampment along the river, but few of the native Massakeesetts. Coastal Indians had long used the river's upper reaches as a passage to the Taunton River and Narragansett Bay. It is not clear whether the river received its present name from early Plymouth Colony settlers because it flows northward or because it is the northerly of the two rivers that enter the sea together north of Plymouth.

On a journey to Plymouth Colony in 1633 Governor Winthrop had to be carried over the rain-swollen river on the back of one of his men, named Luddam, immortalizing their crossing point as Luddam's Ford (where Elm Street crosses the river). The first ferry over the river was established seven years later. Early land grants in the two towns often included four separate tracts: pasture, house site in the village, woodlot, and marsh meadow.

In the fall of each year from the 1630s to the beginning of our own century, local farmers with their oxcarts and families seasonally migrated down to the river to cut hay. The tall grasses not only fed domestic animals during the winter, but could also be thatched for roofs and stuffed into walls for insulation. In the upper meadows the cut hay was massed into great stacks with bull rakes to dry before being carted off. To reach the wetter grasses "down medder," closer to the running river, channels were cut in the marsh. Long flat-bottomed boats called gundalows, capable of carrying several tons of hay, were floated up the cuts with the tide and piled with hay when the tide receded. Then the gundalow was poled out with the incoming tide and unloaded at the nearest landing.

The marshes also filled the early settlers' table with game, particularly waterfowl; salmon, shad, and herring were found in abundance in the river. By 1644 three ferries were operating on the river; twelve years later the first bridge was erected. Sawmills and grist mills were established on many of the tributary streams and brooks.

The colonists found bog iron in the swamps that lay at the head of so many of the river's tributaries. But although there was a grant for a foundry in 1658, the first ironworks did not begin operation until 1704. The town where the iron industry was centered was named Hanover after the German iron-producing town of that name.

But the river's real glory was shipbuilding. Between 1650 when the first boatyard opened its doors and 1871 when the last boat produced on the river slid off the ways, more than a thousand boats were built along the North River. The great trees that lined the banks—oak, white pine, and hackmatack (larch)—were felled and sawn into planks or hewn into keels and fittings. The boats built in the 1660s probably were fishing boats for the active Scituate fleet, but later hundreds of two- and three-hundred-ton vessels made the North River famous in ports all over the world. In the peak years between 1794 and 1804, 178 ships were built along the river, mostly merchantmen, and whalers, and fishing boats—brigs, schooners, and barks of between 50 and 300 tons each.

The ironworks upriver had all turned to shipfitting, producing all sorts of hardware for the fleet, from tacks to anchors. The heavy anchor used by the U.S.S. *Constitution,* "Old Ironsides," was blasted, cast, and hammered into shape in Hanover.

As anyone knows who has canoed the sharply meandering river, it must have been quite difficult to float the finished boats down to the sea. Regular crews specialized in the job of getting a ship to sea, which could take several weeks and add as much as ten percent to the cost of the vessel. Dozens of oxen pulled along the banks, sometimes up to their necks in the rising tide. A line was often planted ahead and the ship hauled forward using the anchor winch.

After the Civil War the North River rapidly declined as a shipbuilding center because shipping firms demanded faster and larger boats than could be built on the river. The demise of the wooden-ship industry was accelerated by the use of the steam engine and steel hull, for none of the upriver ironworks could handle such complex or large projects. The last boat built on the river to descend to the sea was the *Helen M. Foster,* a ninety-ton schooner built at the Chittenden Yard in 1871. The Chittenden Yard had been operating almost continuously since 1690 and with its demise shipbuilding ended.

Meanwhile the mills and factories up the river had grown in size and number. Iron foundries and anchor works became tack and nail factories. Grist mills were replaced by cotton and woolen mills, sawmills by box factories. Damming of the river and its tributaries for power and dumping of industrial wastewaters caused the river's annual fish migrations to fall off. In 1794 the General Court acted to ensure that mill sluices were opened to pass fish. But apparently it was already too late, for in 1831 a local writer declared: "Formerly, it is said, salmon were taken in this river. Bass had been abundant until within a few years; they are taken chiefly in the winter. Shad and alewives are still taken, but they are gradually diminishing."

After the Portland Gale broke a new mouth for the river in 1898, the increased reach of the daily tide caused the abandonment of marsh haying. Where the marshes had once sold for an incredible seventy dollars an acre, by 1900 five dollars an acre was the going price. Steam had nearly replaced waterpower at the mills. The boatyards were no more. The working ships were displaced by the jaunty yachts and powerboats of the resort community that had developed on Humarock in the 1880s and 1890s. The river was nearly forgotten.

Slowly the North River began to regenerate itself, obliterating the vestiges of the past beneath a mantle of marsh grass and trees, though pollution remained a problem. In 1919 historic markers were placed at many of the boatyard sites. Somehow the river escaped the post-World War II wave of suburbanization, perhaps because of its reputation as polluted, but by the 1960s houses began intruding on the rare scenic beauty. Jean Foley, an attentive local birder, noticed the marshes being filled and the reforested hills being cut over again. In 1970 Foley and a group of conservation-minded citizens formed themselves into an organization to promote the river's protection, the North and South River Watershed Association. After nine years of effort and hundreds of meetings, the North River became the first Scenic River in the Commonwealth. That designation, and the fact that the river has been virtually freed of pollution, will help ensure that it will remain as beautiful tomorrow as it is today.

The upper river is lined with marshes of rice cut-grass, one of the most prized marsh hays, scattered patches of woolgrass and cattails, arrowhead, blue flag iris, and yellow iris. Green herons lurk in the thickets and kingbirds seem to occupy every overhanging branch. Farther down the river the predominant vegetation changes to black grass, also known as salt-marsh cordgrass. Marsh and red-tailed hawks are frequently seen soaring over the broad expanses of billowing grasses.

Activities:

Canoeing: To see that it is justly designated a Scenic River, take a canoe journey on the North River; this is one of the outstanding outdoor activities in the Greater Boston region. Because the river is tidal almost to Elm Street, with a strong current reversing direction twice a day, it is a good idea to consult a tide table to avoid struggling. On a one-way trip upriver toward Pembroke put in at any time after low tide; downriver, put in after high tide. On a round trip heading upriver put in an hour or two before high tide; downriver, an hour or two before low tide.

There are only a few places to stretch your legs or have a picnic along the river, the most notable being Blueberry Island, a small wooded hummock a mile below Route 3.

The lower reaches of the river often have many powerboats, but a speed limit of six miles an hour and courteous drivers keep the disturbance to a minimum. You should report speeders to the North River Commission, who support a river warden.

Canoe launching

Elm Street in Pembroke: Just below the last mill dam on the Indian Head River at Luddam's Ford. Directions: Route 3 in Hanover to Route 53 south, proceed three miles to

right on Elm Street; ramp one mile on right just beyond bridge. Plenty of parking.

Riverside Drive in Hanover: On Hanover side of Elm Street Bridge. Take left on second Riverside Drive turnoff just before bridge. Plenty of parking.

Brooks-Tilden Shipyard Canoe Ramp: Route 3 to Route 123,

through Norwell Center, right in three quarters of a mile on Bridge Street; cross bridge and ramp on right. Plenty of parking.

Canoe rentals: At King's Landing Marina in Norwell (telephone 659-7273), 8:00 A.M. to 6:00 P.M. every day; $4.50 for the first hour, $3.50 each additional hour to a maximum of $17.50; $30.00 deposit. If you arrive when the tide is headed out, they'll transport you upriver to Route 53 for $5.00 and an easy paddle downriver. Directions: Through Norwell Center on Route 123, past Bridge Street; King's Landing is a dirt road ahead on the right.

North and South River Watershed Association: Helps protect the river and inform people about it. For free map of the river and address, see Map above.

Reading:

Shipbuilding on the North River by L. Vernon Briggs is a detailed history of the river and its tributaries with voluminous accounts of all the old boatyards.

53. NORRIS RESERVATION
West Street, Norwell
100 acres   *Trustees of Reservations   1970

Activities: walking, nature study, fishing, ski touring, iceskating
Hours: dawn to dusk
Admission: no charge

John Bryant was one of the earliest settlers of South Scituate, as Norwell was known during the seventeenth century. A house carpenter, his land grant included an inland farm and this tract where the Second Herring Brook enters the North River. The brook was named for the herring that migrated up it to Black Pond (see Section 54) until dams created impossible hurdles. Bryant helped build a trail along this side of the North River, constructing a footbridge over the brook in 1658. In 1690 he erected a sawmill along the brook, perhaps to supply planks to the Chittenden shipyard, which opened in that same year just across the brook's mouth. Later the mill was converted into a grist mill. By 1829 two mill ponds had been created and enlarged, and a sawmill, two grist mills, and a box mill were operating on the little brook.

Fronting on a half mile of the North River and including a half mile of the Second Herring Brook, this tract was given to the Trustees by Mrs. Albert F. Norris in memory of her husband. Mr. and Mrs. Norris had allowed the trees to grow, cut footpaths through the property, and kept the mill-pond dams in repair, so that today this is the most pleasant landward access to the North River.

From the parking lot a woods road enters the forest of red maples, white ash, white pine, and big old hickories. The predominant shrubs are honeysuckle and sweet pepperbush and the forest floor is covered with hay-scented and interrupted ferns, meadow rue, and gill-over-the-ground. After you pass the mill pond on the way to the river, the pines along the woods road grow taller; tupelo, sassafrass, and an occasional holly appear; and the wildflowers become more interesting: Solomon's seal, false Solomon's seal, partridgeberry, cowwheat, pyrola, starflower, and Indian cucumber root may be found.

The ponds and swamps of the Reservation all provide good bird habitat and therefore good birdwatching. Marsh and red-tailed hawks prowl the river marshes; great blue herons and green herons are regularly sighted there as well. Mink and red fox are known to be among the woodland residents.

Activities:

Norris Reservation is a tranquil, exceedingly well-kept woodland preserve with fine views of the North River and an appealing diversity of flora and fauna. On quiet days when there is a storm out at sea you can hear the breakers pounding the Scituate cliffs and Humarock Beach. No facilities.

Walking: Three miles of pleasant, easy-walking trails lead past the mill pond, through the woods, and down to the lush green river meadows.

Ski touring: Track laid down by locals along side, well-maintained trails. Mostly level grade. No preparation.

Ice-skating: On mill pond.

Fishing: Good-sized bass and catfish in the mill pond: a really fine place to spend a few hours.

Directions:
Route 3 to Route 123; right on Dover Street to West Street just before Norwell Center.
Parking: Lot at trailhead.

54. BLACK POND RESERVE
Mount Blue Street, Norwell
50 acres   Nature Conservancy   1962
*Massachusetts Audubon South Shore Sanctuaries, Route 3A, Marshfield, MA 02050

Activities: nature study, walking, birdwatching
Map: in guidebook from South Shore Sanctuaries
Hours: dawn to dusk
Admission: no charge

Hope and the future for me are not in laws and cultivated fields, not in towns and cities, but in the impervious and quaking swamps. When, formerly, I have analyzed my partiality for some farm which I had contemplated purchasing, I have frequently found that I was attracted solely by a few square rods of impermeable and unfathomable bog,—a natural sink in one corner of it. That was the jewel which dazzled me.
Henry David Thoreau
"Walking," 1862

Even though few of us have quite Thoreau's love for wetlands, bogs, such as the one found here, seem to conjure up some faint archetypal Druidic memory in us. Let the boardwalk here take you into that strange country. The rich reddish-brown sphagnum nurses three insectivorous species: sundew, bladderwort, and pitcher plant, the carrion-red flowers of the last hanging ominously over the wet mat. Leatherleaf, water willow, and the sweet-scented swamp honeysuckle grow on little hummocks. If you jump lightly up and down on the boardwalk, you will feel the floating mass of vegetation "quaking." That screech you heard as you came out onto the bog was more likely to be a green heron or a kingfisher than the hex of an Indian or witch.

Black Pond was the highest point spawning alewives reached on their annual migration up Second Herring Brook, leaping over the dam at Bryant's sawmill on the way (see Section 53, Norris Reservoir). The boggy little pond was part of a 1640 land grant to Thomas Clapp and it remained in the Clapp family until it was acquired by the Nature Conservancy in 1962. By the middle of the nineteenth century the alewives had ceased coming to the pond, their way blocked by ever-larger and more numerous mill dams.

Black Pond Reserve is dedicated to William "Cap'n Bill" Vinal. Cap'n Bill was born in Norwell in 1881 and before the Portland Gale ruined the North River hay, he joined his farmer father scything and raking the river meadows. His grandfather had captained the *Helen M. Foster,* last boat built on the river at the Chittenden Yard near the mouth of the Second Herring Brook (see Section 52, North River). At the turn of the century Cap'n Bill went off to college, leaving the river's side for the next fifty years. In 1951 he retired as a university professor and returned to the North River. For the next twenty-five years he alerted people to the river's problems—loss of wildlife, pollution, and threat of development—but more than that, he served as a living reminder of the river's glorious past, its beauty, and its place in the human scheme of things.

Activities:

Because of the fragility of the bog environment and the rarity of the wildflowers found here, you should not visit this site without first calling or sending a note to the South Shore Sanctuaries. Be sure to ask for the excellent "Black Pond Nature Reserve Discovery and Information Guide," an abundantly illustrated, excellent introduction to the natural history of the Reserve.

Prohibited: No dogs, fires, or facilities.

Directions:

Contact South Shore Sanctuaries.

Telephone: 873-9400

55. AMES NOWELL STATE PARK
Linwood Street, Abington
600 acres   *State Park   1964

Activities: picnicking, fishing, birdwatching, nature study, boating

Map: ask for free map at entrance or send SASE
Hours: 10:00 A.M. to 8:00 P.M.
Admission: three dollars a car or state season pass

Schumacastacut, "beaver place always dependable": that was the Indian name for Beaver Brook, the steady stream flowing through this park, into and out of Cleve's Pond, and then on a long journey to Buzzards Bay via the Taunton River. Abington, as the area came to be called, was part of the large Bridgewater tract purchased from Massasoit and given as grants by Plymouth Colony in 1649. Lands granted to former Colonial Governors Bradford and Jonathan Belcher met at the brook, though apparently neither settled here. Peregrine White, the firstborn of the Plymouth colonists, was also granted land nearby and did apparently live there, at least for a while.

The original pond here on Beaver Brook was much smaller than the present one. A sawmill was built in 1729 on the outlet stream. From 1790 to 1830 a box mill made "chocolate, soap, candle, card, book, and hardware boxes." Fulling and shingle mills also operated here. The little pond was known as Washburn's Pond.

In the 1930s the area around the pond was acquired for use as a bird sanctuary. The pond itself was greatly enlarged to increase waterfowl habitat. The area was named Peregrine White Bird Sanctuary until the state purchased and enlarged the Park in 1964.

One of the interesting places here is the power line right-of-way at the back of the park. Hiding among the dogbane and goldenrod amidst the tall grasses, the beautiful erect orange flower of the wood lily may be found. In the shrubs the warblers compete for attention with the brilliant blue of an indigo bunting. Blueberries and black raspberries are abundant. At the bottom of the right-of-way, Cleve's Pond is lined with sphagnum, sundew, golden hedge hyssop, buttonbush, and sedges, the last providing perches for a myriad of iridescent dragonflies.

The forest of some sections of the Park is also lovely. Beech, white pine, red maple, and sassafras provide a shady environment for lush ferns, starflowers, whorled loosestrife, wintergreen, Canada mayflower, and sarsaparilla. The boulder-strewn pond shore is lined with sweet pepperbush, swamp honeysuckle, and tupelo, with fragrant water lily and pickerelweed growing on the dark water beyond. Even the burned-over hills here—sprouting sweet fern, wild indigo, and bayberry—are worth noticing.

Activities:

Leap from rock to rock across the pond's outlet stream and scramble up a little rocky ledge and you will be in Ames Nowell's back country. Running this Lilliputian obstacle course is easy for most adults and children.

Picnicking: Picnic tables and fireplaces in tall white pine grove. Bring your own wood. If you can't get here early on weekends, bring a blanket, chairs, and your own grill. Bathrooms. Very pleasant.

Fishing: Eight- and nine-pound bass are pulled out of Cleve's Pond every year, a sure lure for fisherfolk. Also pickerel, catfish, and sunfish. Lots of fishing spots around pond.

Boating: Launching ramp for canoes and cartop rowboats and sailboats.

Nature study and birdwatching: Cross the brook for excellent birding and nature study.

Hiking: Five or six miles of trails, mostly easy walking. A fine place to ramble.

Directions:
Route 3 in Weymouth to Route 18 south, right on Route 123 in South Abington, right on Rockland Street at signs to Park, to Linwood Street.
Parking: Plenty.

56. BORDERLAND STATE PARK
*Massapoag Avenue, North Easton, MA 02334
1,400 acres   State Park   1973

Activities: walking, fishing, picnicking, ski touring, jogging, nature study, ice-skating, birdwatching, boating, house tours, scenic area
Map: free at park office or send SASE
Hours: 9:00 A.M. to 5:30 P.M.
Admission: no charge

By Man's power of thought, we distinguish him from brute Creation. Unless he develops this power, he neglects the most splendid of his gifts from the supreme being. Thought leads us into channels of varying pleasure, it elevates us above the mere commonplace. Wisdom is the end of life, it takes us to the borderlands of—Truth.

Oakes Ames

Borderland is one of those special places characterized by a rare quality of scenic beauty and an equally rare feeling of tranquility. From the wide lawn spreading before the castlelike mansion of Oakes and Blanche Ames to the narrow fields bordered by great pines and oaks and shimmering ponds, Borderland invigorates spirit and body.

Although the discovery of arrowheads here indicates that Indians once frequented the area, little is known of their activities. By the early eighteenth century, residents of Sharon and Easton began to pasture cows here. The first settler of the area, Jedidiah Willis, built himself a home near Pud's Pond in 1746. After completing his house, Willis dammed the pond's outlet stream and erected a sawmill. The next resident to arrive was Captain Ebenezer Tisdale, a hero of the Revolution, who built a farmhouse here in the mid-1700s. Tisdale's house was rebuilt by his son in 1811 and still

195

stands today within the park.

The brook that ran through Poquonticut White Cedar Swamp led to Easton's Furnace Village, where as early as 1751 a blast furnace and iron foundry were operating. These ironworks manufactured cannons and cannonballs for the Revolutionary Army. The swamp itself was mined for bog iron; its white cedars were cut and sold for shingles and clapboards. In 1808 General Shepard Leach acquired the works at Furnace Village and by 1823 he was operating seven furnaces there. To ensure a constant supply of water to power his bellows and trip-hammers, Leach purchased Poquonticut Swamp, which was then excavated and dammed to make a reservoir, since known as Leach's Pond.

The Ames family became established in Easton in the 1700s when John Ames moved to the town and began to operate America's first shovel works there. His son Oliver invented and manufactured a light yet strong shovel that became the tool used by pioneers to dig the Great Plains and miners to search for California's gold. The Ames shovel became the largest-selling shovel in the world and the basis of the Ames fortune.

When Oakes Ames began in 1898 to purchase land for an estate of his own—the family already owned a dozen estates in North Easton—the property he selected (now Borderland) was divided into twenty-two separate parcels. Two years later Oakes, just beginning a career as a Harvard botanist, married Blanche Ames, a painter from an unrelated Ames family, and six years later they moved into the Tisdale house. In 1910, having acquired 1,200 acres for their estate, the couple built themselves a massive English Gothic-style mansion house designed by Blanche, constructed of fireproof concrete, and faced with native fieldstone.

Because Oakes's professorial duties took him to Cambridge only a day or two a week—he also had an outstanding botanical library in the mansion—both he and Blanche devoted themselves to Borderland. Blanche the artist and Oakes the botanist both loved nature. After consulting with some of the world's foremost foresters, they laid out their estate as a game and forest reserve, using Blanche's sensitive eyes to make it beautiful as well as ecologically sound. The two delighted in walking through the woods and fields, skating on the ponds, and riding horses.

After the death of Oakes and Blanche, the estate was sold to the state in 1971 as a State Park. The Ames family remains closely involved with Borderland, serving on its advisory board and working with the Friends of Borderland.

Activities:

This large park of woods and fields is one of the most beautiful places in the region to picnic, walk, or fly a kite.

Picnicking: Wide-open lawns, grassy fields, pondsides, and forest groves for informal picnics. No tables. Toilets provided. Bring your own charcoal grill and dispose of hot coals properly. Lots of room to stretch out.

Walking: Six or seven miles of exquisite walking paths and pasture and woodland roads.

Fishing: Pickerel, catfish, and sunfish make for good fishing here; and large bass provide a real challenge. Popular ice-fishing spot.

Jogging: Woods roads ideal for jogging: easy grades, wide, good surface.

Ski touring: Fields and woods roads make this an excellent place for ski touring. Novice to intermediate. Toilets open all winter.

Boating: Canoes and cartop rowboats permitted in ponds.

Nature study: In addition to the many ornamental trees and shrubs planted by the Ameses, there are many great white oaks, beeches, and hickories on the property. In an unusual section of the woods, Atlantic white cedars predominate. Many flowering dogwoods and a great profusion of wildflowers may be found here.

Birdwatching: A popular birding spot where ospreys, herons, warblers, and waterfowl may be sighted.

Ice-skating: On the ponds. Occasional night skating.

Friends of Borderland: Sponsors tours of the fully furnished mansion, a variety of nature walks, concerts, night skating, and kite flying. Write or call State Park for upcoming schedule.

Directions:

From Sharon Center head south on Pond Street to Massapoag Avenue. Park entrance four and a half miles on the left.

Parking: Plenty, though crowded on Sunday afternoons.

Telephone: 238-6566

FOR THE BIRDS:
THE MASSACHUSETTS AUDUBON SOCIETY
Massachusetts Audubon Society, South Great Road, Lincoln, MA 01773.

Killing birds for sport or table was once an integral part of America's rural life-style. Such bird hunting was mostly limited to supplementing a family's food supply until the urbanized nineteenth century, when market gunning became a profession. During that century ducks and geese by the millions and passenger pigeons by the billions were blasted out of the air and off the water with rifles and grapeshot from cannons. But the slaughter did not limit itself to these common birds. Bobolinks and curlews, sandpipers and herons, robins and orioles by the hundreds of thousands were all fair game for bird pies. As late as the 1880s the kitchen of Boston's Parker House was offering gunners fifty cents a bird for small lesser yellowlegs. Entire species were driven to extinction and others came so close that they have still not recovered.

Some people in Massachusetts were aware of nature's limits though—in 1818 the Legislature provided a closed season for robins and horned larks. But it was not until after the Civil War that a movement of any consequence developed in response to the rapidly dwindling flocks of nearly every species. The movement was led by William Brewster, a Cambridge native and curator of the Museum of Comparative Zoology at Harvard. In 1873 Brewster had organized and served as first president of the Nuttall Ornithological Club, a Cambridge group dedicated not only to the scientific study of birds, but also to their protection. Ten years later the nucleus of the Nuttall Club formed a national group for similar purposes, the American Ornithological Union (AOU).

It soon became apparent that much of the worst bird slaughter had nothing to do with feeding a family, which at least could be rationalized, but was simply for fashion. Late in the nineteenth century using bird feathers, wings, and even entire stuffed bodies for personal adornment, particularly hats, became "The Fashion." The AOU estimated that in a few decades five million North American birds were killed by plume hunters and turned by the millinery trade into fashionable ladies' hats. Tern and egret wings and the feathers of spoonbills, herons, and flamingos were prized ornaments. In less than twenty-five years more than a dozen species came close to being wiped out for their plumes.

In 1886 *Forest and Stream* magazine organized an Audubon

Society. Cards pledging the signer not to kill wild birds were printed in the magazine and distributed around the country. Within two years 48,000 pledge cards had been returned. But no organization grew out of the effort and by 1890 this Audubon Society had faded away.

Several years later, a small group of Beacon Hill ladies decided that the slaughter of birds for the millinery trade was outrageous. Three of the women, Harriet Hemenway, Harriet Lawrence, and Minna Hall, began to go through the Blue Book, Boston's social register, writing down the names of stylish women. Each of the women whose name was on the list was sent a circular describing the group's aims. Soon after, in 1896, the ladies and those who had responded to their letter formed themselves into the Massachusetts Audubon Society for the Protection of Birds, the first organization dedicated primarily to that purpose in America and only the third in the world. William Brewster was elected president and an office was opened at the Boston Society of Natural History (now Bonwit Teller's).

The Society's first effort was a boycott of egret feathers. At the time such feathers were worth more per ounce than gold. The millinery trade fought the boycott but within a few years a millinery buyer in Boston was forced to declare in a trade magazine: "Birds do not meet with much favor, on account of the strong prejudice aroused by the Audubon Society, which is especially active in this state."

The society lobbied successfully for the passage of state laws requiring closed seasons for migratory birds. Another of their efforts focused on recent European immigrants, who often had a taste for toothsome songbirds, and thought nothing of shooting a scarlet tanager or indigo bunting. The Alien Gun Law was passed prohibiting aliens from hunting in the state. And at the national level, Massachusetts Audubon Society led the battle for the Lacey Act, which prohibited interstate trade in bird products that violated any state law.

By 1917 the Society had grown to 30,000 members. Their birding lectures at Tremont Temple and Ford Hall drew thousands of patrons. Slowly the Society awakened to the need not only to protect birds but to provide them with nesting and resting habitat, and so in 1922 the Society acquired its first bird sanctuary at Moose Hill in Sharon (Section 57, Moose Hill Sanctuary). Sanctuaries also provided a place for birdwatching and educating the public. By the 1930s Massachusetts Audubon's awareness of ecology was growing; people were realizing that birds do not exist independent of all the complexities in both the natural and the man-made environment. Such factors as quality of air and water, chemical pollution, and recreation are important to human society as well as animal species. But the membership of Massachusetts Audubon had begun to decline after World War I, and by the early 1950s it had dropped to a mere 5,000 members.

By 1955 the Society was on its way to a dramatic renewal of both its purpose and membership, spurred on by three events: the donation of Drumlin Farm as an educational center, the publication of Rachel Carson's *Silent Spring,* and the hiring of dynamic Executive Vice-President Allan Morgan. Morgan had the courage and foresight to lead Massachusetts Audubon into battles to stop the use of DDT, conserve wetlands, and preserve habitat, while reaching out for new members and expanding the Society's educational commitments.

Today the Massachusetts Audubon Society is the largest conservation organization in New England and is recognized, as well, as one of the oldest, most respected, and most effective environmental groups in America. Membership is up nearly to the all-time high of 1917. Sanctuary holdings have grown to about 12,000 acres in twelve staffed sanctuaries and thirty-five open-space sanctuaries. Massachusetts Audubon conducts research, sponsors educational programs, and actively involves itself with state and federal environmental regulations.

Massachusetts Audubon Sanctuaries in this book: Section 101, Drumlin Farm Sanctuary; Section 74, Ipswich River Wildlife Sanctuary; Section 57, Moose Hill Sanctuary; Section 89, Stony Brook Sanctuary; Section 77B, Marblehead Neck Sanctuary.

Membership: Membership in Massachusetts Audubon Society includes free admission to the sanctuaries, ten issues a year of *Sanctuary* (Massachusetts Audubon's excellent newsletter), the opportunity to participate in adult and family birdwalks and educational activities at a discount, and the right to count yourself as a part of one of America's premier conservation organizations.

Reading:
Man's Dominion by Frank Graham, Jr., provides an account of the early days of the bird-conservation movement.

Telephone: 259-9500

57. MOOSE HILL SANCTUARY
300 Moose Hill Street, Sharon, MA 02067
227 acres   Massachusetts Audubon Society   1922

Activities: birdwatching, nature study, walking, interpretive
  programs
Map: free at entrance shelter or send SASE
Hours: 8:00 A.M. to 6:00 P.M.
Admission: adults $1.50, children .75 cents

You've come at the right time.

Moose Hill has been the site of farms since the late 1630s, and
nearly all of this currently forested tract was cleared in the past to
pasture livestock. Vegetation-overgrown cellar holes and stone
walls, and trees and herbs planted around the farmhouses, are
nearly all that remains of the old farming days on the area's glacier-
sculpted hills, eskers, and kettleholes. The Billings barn, a remnant
building of the mid-eighteenth century, now lies surrounded by
old fields in various stages of woodland succession and such pastoral domestic plants as lilacs, hollyhocks, and an assortment of
evergreens. In spite of Moose Hill's long history of use, it is one of
the lushest and most pristine woodlands in the region.

The Sanctuary had its beginnings in 1916 when Dr. Field,
former director of the state Fish and Game Department, made his
house on the side of the hill available to Audubon members. Most
of the audubon people were from Boston; that is, they were city
people, and Dr. Field's house became their outpost in the country.
They took the train from Boston, then walked through the woods
to Field's house, which was set up as a sort of museum and
clubhouse under the direction of Harry Higbee, the first Massachusetts Audubon Sanctuary employee. In 1922 Massachusetts
Audubon purchased forty-three acres on another part of Moose
Hill for $8,000 to begin the Society's first sanctuary, which, as
well, is one of the oldest bird sanctuaries in America.

On the portion of the property behind the headquarters, a
boardwalk crosses a swamp filled with tussock sedge, meadowsweet, sphagnum moss, highbush blueberry, red maple, and half a
dozen fern species. The swamp provides excellent habitat for
spring and fall migrating warblers and nesting sites for song sparrows and common yellow-throated warblers. Along the nearby

Fern Trail, the observer with an eye for detail and a great deal of patience may discern as many as twenty-two species of fern.

This Sanctuary was one of the favorite haunts of Larry Newcomb, whose *Wildflower Guide* is the standard field guide to New England's wildflowers. Newcomb not only looked at flowers, he planted them as well. A wildflower garden here is planted with giant Solomon's seal, wild columbine, Dutchman's-breeches, trillium, and doll's-eyes. The wild woods are verdant with wood anemone, wild oats, silky and flowering dogwood, Indian cucumber root, and barberry. Small wetlands are highlighted by spring's blue flag iris and summer's forget-me-not.

Nearly seventy-five tree species grow on the property, some rare or unusual for this region, some planted by former tenants. This is a good place to find holly, hornbeam, and hop hornbeam, and to compare sweet pignut, pignut, and shagbark hickory. Grand old sugar maples are still tapped each spring as part of the Sanctuary's maple sugar program.

Approximately 160 bird species have been sighted here, and the nesters include great horned and screech owls, broad-winged and red-tailed hawks, cuckoos, veeries, Canada geese, and wood ducks.

Activities:

Moose Hill is managed for the benefit of wildlife rather than active recreation: its miles of woodland trails, open fields, and streamcourses show the signs of utmost care to maintain its natural integrity. For the visitor, this care translates into beauty and serenity.

In addition to nature walks and birding, the Sanctuary offers a wide range of high-quality programs for children and adults devoted to its natural and cultural history. A natural-history day camp is run here during the summer. Contact the Sanctuary for a schedule of events and programs.

Walking: Five or six miles of gentle, well-marked trails. Many short circuits, but enough territory to stretch your legs. Free map of trails at office or entrance shelter. Sanctuary staff runs guided walks.

Prohibited: Fires, picnicking, and dogs.

Directions:

Route 1 to Route 27; first right beyond Route I-95 overpass; left on Moose Hill Street, proceed one and a half

miles to Sanctuary entrance and parking lot.
Parking: Lot holds twenty to thirty cars.

Telephone: 784-5691

58. WATSON POND STATE PARK
Bay Street, Taunton
10 acres   *State Park   1956

Activities: fishing, picnicking, swimming, boating

From the time John Gilbert began his Pond Brook Farm in 1641 until the 1950s the area around Watson Pond was almost continuously cultivated. A farmhouse and barn were still in use here when the state acquired this pleasant little family area in 1956.

Activities:
This small area by the shore of Watson's Pond is an extremely popular family picnic spot. Territory for children to explore and open fields for playing ball or Frisbee.
Picnicking: Nearly a hundred picnic tables, choice of sunny or pine-shaded. Room to lay down a blanket. Bathrooms, bubblers, and rain pavilion. Fireplaces; bring your own wood or charcoal grill.
Swimming: Clean, lifeguard-supervised freshwater beach. Pond water used as local drinking water supply, and so of very good quality. Bathhouse with showers.
Boating: Hand-carry canoe launching.
Fishing: Pickerel, catfish, and largemouth bass.
Admission: Three dollars or season pass.

Directions:
Route 138 south through Raynham; turn right on Bay Street after crossing over Route 495; continue approximately three miles. Watson Pond on right just before Dever School.
Parking: Plenty.

Telephone: 823-1523

Nearby:
Lake Sabbatia, across the street from Watson Pond. Boat-launching ramp and parking. Motorboating, fishing, waterskiing.

Telephone: 823-1523

59. MASSASOIT STATE PARK
*Middleboro Avenue, East Taunton, MA 02718
1,500 acres   State Park   1974

Activities: camping, picnicking, bicycling, fishing, walking, jogging, boating, ski touring, horseback riding, nature study, swimming, birdwatching
Map: free at park entrance or send SASE

Hours: 10:00 A.M. to 8:00 P.M.
Admission: Three dollars a car or state season pass

Named after Massasoit, sachem of the Wampanoag who maintained a fifty-year peace with the Pilgrims, this park was well brushed by the moccasin. Massasoit's winter camp was less than ten miles away in land that is now Middleboro. Assawampset village of the Titiquet Indians was nearby until they were decimated by plagues. When the park was being developed scads of arrowheads and projectile points were uncovered.

The first white men to view this neighborhood, in 1621, appear to have been Edward Winslow and Stephen Hopkins, the Plymouth colonists' explorers and informal ambassadors to the Indians. Within a few years they were followed by another adventurous Plymouth colonist, Elizabeth Pole. Pole purchased much of the land that is now Taunton for "a jackknife and a pot of beans" from one of the last surviving natives. Pole's farm was called "Littleworth Farm" after a place with a similar name she had visited in her youth in England. She dug stalls into the side of a hill, now Stall Hill, to protect her cattle in the winter. In 1643 she had a grist mill built on one of the streams that coursed across her property.

In 1724 King's Furnace, the fifth iron foundry in the Colony but the first hollowware factory, was built here, using a dammed stream to power its bellows. The nearby bogs were "mined" for lumps of bog iron that were then smelted and cast into everything from "a jobie kettle to a ten pail cauldron." In 1812 the Dean Cotton Mill began to operate on "Bare Hole Neck," and in the 1860s a boxboard sawmill was erected at the former foundry site.

The loose sandy soil of the park indicates that this land is an outwash plain, laid down as the glacier retreated northward, its meltwaters releasing millions of tons of rock dust, sand, gravel, and small boulders. All this debris spread out, creating a vast, gently rolling plain. Enormous chunks of ice, which broke off and were surrounded by the rising tide of sand before melting, left depressions known as kettleholes in the plain, several of which may be found here as ponds and bogs.

Among the flowers that bloom on the pine and oak forest floor are pinks, lady's slippers, blueberries, and blackberries. Around the turtle-filled bogs and ponds such fascinating species as boneset and the insectivorous sundew thrive. Red-tailed hawks and green herons are sighted here all summer long.

Activities:

Massasoit is a fairly large, well-tended forest and pond park. A summer interpretive program (check for information at entrance) really digs into this park's history and natural history.

Swimming: Two sandy beaches, one for day use, one for campers, both with bathhouses, toilets, and lifeguards.

Dark but clean shallow water. The state is currently deepening the swimming pond.

Walking and nature study: Five miles of trails; those around the ponds and marshes are particularly interesting.

Birding: Around the bogs and marshes.

Fishing: In all ponds, bass, pickerel, and sunfish. May be stocked in the near future. Big Bearhole Pond has some good-sized fish.

Camping: 126 campsites nicely laid out with some privacy. A few sites with electricity and sewage available. Grills and picnic tables. Six dollars a night. Fills by 11:00 A.M. on weekends.

Picnicking: Few tables but plenty of places to spread a blanket. The swimming area and the shore of Big Bearhole Pond are the popular places.

Horseback riding: Along trails. No nearby stables.

Boating: Rowboats, canoes, and small sailboats. Launching ramp and parking. No motors.

Bicycling: On park roads. Bicycle campers on the way to the Cape are welcome.

Ski touring: Excellent ski touring when enough snow, though trails not prepared. No winter facilities except parking.

Directions:
Route 24 south to Route 44 exit to Middleboro. Cross over highway and take first right, continue past airport to entrance.

Telephone: 822-7405

60. DIGHTON ROCK STATE PARK
Bay View Road, Berkley, MA 02780
85 acres   State Park   1955

Activities: picnicking, historic site, fishing
Hours: 10:00 A.M. to 6:00 P.M.
Admission: free; three-dollar parking fee or state season pass for picnickers

. . . there are very deeply Engraved, no man knows How or When, about half a score Lines, near ten Foot Long, and a foot and a half broad, filled with strange characters.
　　　　　　　Cotton Mather
　　　　　　　The Wonderful Works of God Commemorated

Although spray paint has been a great boon to the graffito artist, a visit to Dighton Rock will assure anyone that the propensity to scrawl one's initials or talisman on a flat surface transcends cultures and historical epochs. Since at least 1680 curious historians have puzzled over and tried to decipher the carvings chiseled into Dighton Rock. Many inconclusive theories have been posed about the carvers or the meaning of their carvings, and the rock remains a "Puzzle on the Taunton River."

Dighton Rock is believed to be a glacial erratic dragged to Southern Massachusetts from Canada by the ice mass. Until the early 1960s when the state raised it out of the river, Dighton Rock sat about a hundred feet from shore partially submerged by the Taunton River. Among those to whom the carvings have been attributed are Indians, Phoenicians, Norsemen, and Portuguese.

Activities:
A fine little museum has been developed around the rock. An interpretive program will help you see how the thirty-five or so theories about the rock evolved and encourage you to formulate a theory of your own.

Picnicking: A very lovely shaded picnic area has been created here along an undeveloped stretch of the Taunton River. Bathrooms and bubblers.

Fishing: Saltwater fishing along the river.

Directions:
Route 24 south to Dighton exit. Good signs lead the way from there.

Parking: Plenty

Telephone: 882-7527

61. HORSENECK BEACH RESERVATION
Westport Point, Westport, MA 02790
537 acres   State Reservation   1957

Activities: swimming, camping, boating, nature study, bird-watching, walking, picnicking, bicycling
Hours: 8:00 A.M. to dusk
Admission: three dollars a car during the summer

All cheap and childish waste gradually sinks into oblivion in the
presence of its magnificence. The high tides of Horseneck are a cleansing
and rejuvenating force for good.

Promotional brochure of 1890s

Horseneck Beach is the most extensive and beautiful state-owned
beach south of Boston. Like Plum Island and Duxbury Beach this
is a barrier beach created by the longshore drift of sands eroded off
glacial deposits. And as at other barrier beaches, a vast area of tidal
marshes has developed behind the beach, along the Westport
River. Sailboats and lobster boats pulling traps make for a lively
offshore scene.

The Indian name for the beach, Hassanegk, not its shape, gave
the beach its name. Hassanegk, "house made of stone," referred to
a dwelling the Indians had dug into the side of a dune and lined
with flat rocks to keep the sand from caving in. The Seaconnet
Indians from Little Compton made Hassanegk the site of an annual
summer encampment, fishing from the beach and clamming on the
flats behind.

In 1652 Bradford, Winslow, Standish, and other Plymouth
colonists purchased Dartmouth, which included Hassanegk, from
Massasoit. The beach served as an effective blind for American
ships hiding in Westport Harbor from British eyes during the
Revolution. In 1787 when Westport was separated from Dartmouth there were no homes or cottages on the entire beach, but
farmers and fishermen were grazing cattle and cutting firewood on
it. Occasional trips were taken to the beach to collect bayberries
for candlemaking and many of the wetlands in the dunes were
developed into cranberry bogs.

In the 1870s hunters began building "gunning shacks" on the
beach. Within a few years a number of boarding houses were built
to cater to the hundreds of duck hunters who arrived on the beach
every spring and fall along with the migrating waterfowl. The few
year-round residents, most of whom ran boarding houses in the
spring and fall, spent their winters and summers fishing and lob-
stering. Around the turn of the century vacationers began making
the twenty-mile ("all day") journey from New Bedford to Horseneck and a resort community began to blossom along the beach.
Many of the vacation homes and cottages were destroyed during
the hurricane of 1938. Not heeding nature's warning signals, many
of the homes were rebuilt, only to be destroyed again during
Hurricane Carol in 1954. Two years later the state bought the

beach to put an end to hazardous development and to ensure that the beach would be open to the public.

Gooseberry Neck, the little island reached by a causeway at the east end of the beach, had given the region its Indian name, Acoaxet, "land beyond the little land," because the island formed a natural barrier between Buzzards Bay and Narragansett Bay for the canoe-borne natives. The rocky shingle beach is a fine place to cast a line or sort through the flotsam. The little reed-filled marshes are lush with birds and at sunset flocks of unusual glossy ibis flutter over the Neck and back to the marshes. This is a fantastic place to watch the sunset and a great place for a walk during any season.

Activities:

This is a really fine beach for swimming, sunbathing, picnicking, or just wandering.

Swimming: Three miles of beautiful sandy beach. Lifeguards. Toilets, bathhouse, complete snack bar, and first aid station. Water warmer than at North Shore beaches. The waves can be quite high here, great for bodysurfing, but there may be a dangerous undertow: use caution.

Picnicking: Picnic tables scattered along the beach and in the dunes. Most people use a blanket. Complete facilities. Shady deck near bathrooms. Gooseberry Neck is also an excellent place for a picnic.

Boating: State launching ramp beside the bridge to Horseneck at Westport Point.

Birdwatching: Excellent birding in the marshes behind the beach. The marshes have the largest concentration of ospreys in the state, their nesting sites towering over the marshes. Lots of egrets and herons. The thickets on the beach itself attract a myriad of nesting and migrating warblers. Terns nest along the beach.

Camping: A hundred campsites along the beach and behind the dunes, none out of earshot of the waves. Not much privacy but friendly campers, and tern cries as an alarm clock. Each site with picnic table. Showers and bathrooms. Bring your bicycle to travel to the beach or Gooseberry Neck. Six dollars a night. Arrive in the morning during the summer if you want a campsite.

Bicycling: Bicycle trail the length of the beach behind the dunes. Also bike to Gooseberry Neck.

Directions:
Route 24 south to Route 6 east, to Route 88 south to the end.
Parking: Room for more than a thousand cars. Rarely filled.

Telephone: 636-8816

62. DEMAREST LLOYD STATE PARK
Barney's Joy Road, South Dartmouth, MA 02714
222 acres   State Park

Activities: saltwater swimming, picnicking, walking, nature study, horseback riding, birdwatching, boating
Map: free at contact station
Hours: 9:00 A.M. to 6:00 P.M.
Admission: three dollars a car or state season pass

This beach on Buzzards Bay, facing the Elizabeth Islands, is one of the least-known beautiful places for saltwater swimming or sunbathing in the region. The large oak-shaded picnic area is also one of the prettiest around.

The beach was named for Demarest Lloyd, Jr., a naval aviator killed in World War II, and his father, Demarest Lloyd, Sr., a foreign correspondent for several of the nation's leading newspapers during the first half of the century. The Lloyd family had tried to develop the tract as an exclusive resort, but after several failed attempts, they sold it to the state.

Beyond the lifeguard-patrolled portion of the beach a little neck of sand, long known as Barney's Joy Point or Deepwater Point, sticks out into the mouth of the tidal Slocum River, providing nesting habitat for least terns. These squeaky little birds flutter and dive for fish in the small harbor inside the neck. Between the beach and the woodlands song sparrow and blackbird gather amid the beach grass, roses, blue toadflax, beach heather, and bayberry. Great white swans, which nest on one side of the park and feed on the other, fly just above the picnic area's oaks and pitch pines. Ospreys are seen here in the summer and eagles have been reported in the winter.

Activities:

An incredible sandbar extending out into the bay at low tide, reaching halfway to Naushon Island, and three other sandbars make this a delightful place to sunbathe, build sand castles, and play at the water's edge. Bathrooms, showers, first aid booth, bubblers.

Swimming: Sandy beach with small pebbles. Clear water, gradual dropoff, and gentle surf. Lifeguards. Comparatively warm water.

Picnicking: About a hundred tables and fireplaces in the low shady hills near the beach. Extremely nice picnic area.

Walking and nature study: Walk along the beach to the point or use between two and three miles of trails and old roads that wind through the woods and around the marshes. A beautiful trail leads out to a forested hummock overlooking the Slocum River.

Boating: Boat-launching ramp may be used by motorboats only two hours either side of high tide. Fine for canoes, small sailboats, and flat-bottomed rowboats at any tide. Parking.

Horseback riding: Three miles of bridle trails. No nearby rentals.

Directions:

Route 24 to Route 140, to Route 195, North Dartmouth Exit. Head south from Old Westport Road, to Chase Road, to Russel's Mill Road, to Horseneck Road. Follow signs to park.

Parking: Plenty.

Telephone: 636-3848

63. FORT PHOENIX STATE RESERVATION
Green Street, Fairhaven
23 acres   *State Reservation

Activities: swimming, picnicking, walking, tennis, ballfields, fishing

Hours: 10:00 A.M. to 6:00 P.M.

Admission: three dollars a car or state season pass

This park at the head of Fairhaven Harbor consists of a sandy bathing beach and old Fort Phoenix. The fort, which looks across and protects New Bedford Harbor as well, was built in 1775 to defend Fairhaven and New Bedford against British attack. Soon after the fracas at Lexington and Concord, one of the first naval battles of the Revolution took place in these waters, when the American sloop *Success* captured two British sloops. In 1778 the British attacked and destroyed the fort. After the Revolution it was rebuilt and helped stave off a British landing party during the War of 1812. During the Civil War the battlements were enlarged and new cannons were installed.

Activities:

Close to urban New Bedford and the Fairhaven fishpiers, Fort Phoenix is a nice place to picnic or take a cool swim after visiting the Whaling Museum and other historic sites in the area. From the ramparts of the fort you may observe cormorants and the local fishing fleet steaming to and from George's Bank.

Swimming: Sandy beach approximately a third of a mile long, spangled with golden money shells. Lifeguards, bathhouse, toilets, and small snack bar. Another small undeveloped section of the beach will be found on the far side of the fort.

Picnicking: A few tables, but the best places are on the grassy sides of the fort or the rocks that overlook the water. Use the beach facilities. Children's play area.

Fishing: Surf casting from the rocks for mackerel, flounder, bass, and pollock.

Tennis: Two new asphalt courts plus a basketball court.

Directions:

Route 6 from New Bedford to Fairhaven, right on Green Street just past town hall; follow Green Street to the end.

Parking: Plenty.

Telephone: 992-4524

64. SCUSSET BEACH STATE RESERVATION
Headquarters, Scusset Beach Road, Sandwich
380 acres   State Reservation   Leased from U.S. Army
Corps of Engineers

Activities: swimming, fishing, bicycling, jogging, picnick-
ing, camping, birdwatching, nature study
Hours: 8:00 A.M. to 8:00 P.M.
Admission: three dollars a car or state season pass

This well-maintained ocean-shore Reservation provides access to
the Cape Cod Canal and Cape Cod Bay, a fine beach, a fishing pier,
and the eight-mile-long canal roadway. Although the Reservation
is on the north side of the canal, it is nonetheless on Cape Cod,
with a typical Cape Cod environment. Pitch pine, scrub oak, beach
plum, chokecherry, and staghorn sumac dominate the woods.
Among the common wildflowers are salt-spray rose, beach pea,
beach heather, yarrow, dwarf cinquefoil, and an abundance of
blueberries. Across the canal the massive oil-fired power-generat-
ing plant owned by the New Bedford Gas and Electric Company
sends out electricity to the Cape.

As early as the 1620s Pilgrim merchants were seeking to avoid
the long and dangerous sail around Cape Cod. The shoal waters,
sandbars, and tidal currents were fearsome. Before the canal was
built in 1914, as many as six thousand ships are recorded as having
sunk while making the voyage, at a cost of hundreds of lives and
millions of dollars.

To avoid the Cape circuit, early Pilgrims tried sailing up the
Scusset River, portaging their goods for three miles over the
height of land, then cruising down the Manomet River. But this
route was not only time consuming, it was simply not feasible for
goods in any quantity and was very dependent on tides, winds, and
large numbers of ships. In 1697 the Massachusetts General Court
proposed that a canal be cut connecting the two rivers, but nearly a
hundred years passed before any action was taken. After the
Revolution a seven-and-a-half-mile canal was begun across the
isthmus, but as work proceeded farther from the salt rivers, the
going became tougher—ultimately the project was abandoned as
technically unfeasible.

In 1883 the Cape Cod Ship Canal Company incorporated and
won a charter to build a canal connecting Buzzards Bay and Cape
Cod Bay, but soon failed for lack of financing. Other companies

explored the proposed project as well, while every year more ships went down off the Cape. Then in 1899 a competent group appeared on the scene; the Boston, Cape Cod, and New York Canal Company headed by DeWitt Clinton Flanagan. In 1904 Flanagan successfully interested wealthy civic-minded banker August Belmont in the project, and found a creative yet highly skilled civil engineer, William Parsons, to design the canal. After wrangling over the distribution of stock and long negotiations with local, county, state, and federal governments, work began in the summer of 1909. After five years of dredging and blasting, dealing with such unforeseen difficulties as giant boulders and the construction of bridges and breakwaters, the canal opened with a grand celebration. It was hailed as "the greatest lifesaving institution on the Atlantic."

But the canal had problems: it was only wide enough for traffic to pass one way at a time, which meant long waits at either end; the water was too shallow for large vessels; and the tolls were too high. Additional time was wasted waiting for drawbridges to open. And so despite a constant stream of steamships and the millions of tons of coal that moved through the canal, its backers were losing money. Yet there was something right about the canal and everyone agreed that it benefited the public safety.

In 1927 the canal was sold to the government, at an estimated loss of five million dollars for Belmont, and turned over to the U.S. Army Corps of Engineers. Tolls were eliminated and the bottom was dredged and deepened. In 1928, 1,312 vessels passed through the canal, but many of the problems persisted. During the 1930s the canal was doubled in width, the bridges over it were raised, and new entrance channels were dredged making the canal as we see it today—"the widest artificial waterway in the world."

Reading:

The Cape Cod Canal by Robert H. Farson tells the story of the canal in all its fascinating detail and is abundantly illustrated as well. A number of antique photographs of the canal may be viewed at the Sagamore rotary McDonald's.

Activities:

Explore the canal on foot or bicycle. Guided programs are offered during the summer by the State Park and the Army Corps of Engineers.

Swimming: Half a mile of beach with fine white sand, long enough to find privacy, if desired. Bathhouse with picnic tables under awning. Lifeguards. Play area and wading pool for kids. Large parking lot fills only on hottest summer Sundays, and then not until noon.

Fishing: A wooden fishing pier hangs out over the canal.

Cod in the spring: striped bass, flounder, pollock, blue-fish, and mackerel in the summer. Bait shop and snack bar next to pier. Bathrooms. Surf casting on the beach after the bathers clear out in the evening. Fishing also along the jetty at canal entrance.

Bicycling and jogging: The level, eight-mile-long access road along the canal is ideal for family bicycling, and joggers declare it to be "fantastic."

Walking: Trails through woods; stroll out the jetty; walk the canal at your own pace.

Picnicking: Tables at beach, pier, and elsewhere in park.

Ballfield: One softball diamond.

Birdwatching: Shorebirds, ducks, cormorants, and migrating warblers.

Camping: Ninety-eight campsites with electricity, nearby water, and adjacent bathrooms and showers. This area is primarily used by camping trailers; nearest tent camping is Shawnee Crowell State Forest, two miles beyond the bridge in Sandwich. Open year-round. Fee: Eight dollars a night.

Directions:

Bike: Route 3A south from Plymouth for fourteen miles, follow signs to entrance.

Auto: Route 3 to Sagamore traffic rotary; three quarters of the way around the rotary and then follow signs one mile to beach.

Parking: Plenty.

Telephone: 888-0859

65. PLYMOUTH BEACH
Route 3A
Jointly owned by the *Town of Plymouth and private citizens

Activities: swimming, birdwatching, walking, nature study, fishing

Hours: 9:00 A.M. to 6:00 P.M.

Admission: three dollars a car summer weekdays, five dollars weekends, free in the off-season

Plymouth Beach, a long exclamation point of sand, extends three miles into Plymouth Harbor. This narrow barrier spit, covered with American beach grass, goldenrod, and salt-spray rose, is greatly expanded with flats when the tide is out. Visitors may walk to the point along the beach, along the breakwater, or along the sand road. As a reward for the long trek, nature has provided a great view of Plymouth and an abundance of birdlife.

Sand dollars, mussel and quahog shells, rockweed, kelp, and an interesting assortment of pebbles contribute to the especially pleasant beachcombing here. The broad low-tide beach is fine for jogging, throwing Frisbees, or a long walk to the point.

Out near the point several colonies of terns nest in late spring and summer. The largest colony is composed of common terns, but least, roseate, and arctic terns are here as well. If you find yourself being dive-bombed, you know that you are too close to their nesting area. The inside of the beach is a natural bird sanctuary as well, where, with binoculars, you'll see egrets, bay ducks, black-bellied plovers, sanderlings, and even a loon or two.

Activities:

In spite of the great natural beauty of this beach, it will be unappetizing to lovers of peace and quiet during the summer because large numbers of dunebuggies are on the beach from mid-June through mid-September. This is a terrific place to visit during the off-season. Dogs must be leashed, particularly during tern nesting season. Respect private property of cottage owners.

Swimming: Good clean beach with gradual dropoff. Bath-house, bathrooms, and snack bar. Lifeguards.

Fishing: Surf fishing on the beach. Bait shops on road out of Plymouth.

Birding: Outstanding birding in all four seasons. More information about birds of the beach may be had with a call to Manomet Bird Observatory.

Directions:

One mile south of Plymouth Center on Route 3A. Entrance next to Bert's Restaurant.

Nearby:

Plimouth Plantation: A re-creation of the Pilgrim settlement of the 1620s, first permanent colony in New England. The "natives" of the little town have each adopted not only the dress but the personality and history of an individual early settler. Three miles south of Plymouth Center on Route 3A. Adults three dollars, children a dollar and a quarter.

White Horse Beach: a developed beach lined with summer homes and resorts but open to the public. If you can find a parking place you will enjoy the powdery white sand and rocky tidepools of this two-mile beach. Beach access paths marked with signs. No public facilities. Several resorts are open to the public and offer cool drinks on shady piazzas overlooking the beach. No lifeguards but light surf and gentle dropoff. Follow signs from Route 3A south of Plymouth.

Cleft Rock: This little undeveloped park was a favorite lookout of the Indians of Patuxet, the Indian village where the Pilgrims settled. From the viewpoint, the visitor looks down on White Horse Beach and out across Massachusetts Bay. The Pilgrim Monument, seventeen miles away in Provincetown, is visible on clear days. The cool breezy hill is strewn with large boulders left by the retreating glacier. Merchant ships and smaller boats are constantly streaming to and from the entrance to Cape Cod Canal to the south. A recent fire has made the hill a gold mine for blueberry picking from mid- to late summer. No facilities.

Pilgrim Shorefront: This little park, built by Boston Edison, is next to the company's Pilgrim I nuclear generating station. Take a look at "our" nuclear plant. Bathrooms.

66. MYLES STANDISH STATE FOREST
P.O. Box 66, Cranberry Road, South Carver, MA 02366
16,000 acres   State Forest   1916

Activities: camping, fishing, swimming, boating, bicycling, horseback riding, hiking, ski touring, birding, nature study

Map: free map from Headquarters or send SASE

Hours: 8:00 A.M. to dusk

Admission: free

This vast tract of pitch pine and scrub oak was named after the military leader of the Pilgrims. The park originated in 1916 as the second State Forest in Massachusetts when the newly created State Forest Commission purchased 5,700 acres of burned-over land for less than five dollars an acre. Dotted with ten ponds and laced with fifty-five miles of dirt roads and trails, this area provides the most abundant outdoor recreational opportunities of any park in the region.

Little is known of Indian habitation here, but as soon as the Pilgrims arrived in Plymouth in 1620 they turned to the native forest for firewood and building materials. Because fifteen to twenty cords of wood a year were needed to supply each household's open-hearth fireplace, and tall pines and oaks were needed for masts and timbers of locally built ships and the king's navy, soon few big trees were left. During the eighteenth and nineteenth centuries, the gentle sandy hills were logged repeatedly to fuel salt-boiling works and the furnaces of the iron industry. The wetlands of the region were "mined" for bog iron. All this logging and the fires that then raged through the brush depleted the soil, turning the area into a virtual wasteland by the Civil War.

During the 1930s, the CCC planted millions of trees here, developed campsites, erected recreational buildings, and built many miles of fire roads. It is nearly twenty years since a major fire roared through the park.

The rolling landscape is molded of glacial deposits laid down by the melting glacier whose long moraine parallels Route 3, forming a north–south spine through Plymouth. A few stands of mature white oak and plantations of white, red, and scotch pine grace the park. Blueberries grow profusely in the fire-scarred wastes, and wild cranberries, prime for picking after the first frost, grow in the low-lying bogs. In the spring, the forest floor is speckled with Canada mayflower, lady's slipper, and other wildflowers. The scrub growth is a natural shelter for the area's deer, fox, grouse, and raccoon, and the endangered red-bellied turtle has been sighted in the ponds. By day, hawks search the low brush for prey, to be replaced after dark by several species of owl. The scrub also attracts spring and fall warbler migrations, and the ponds provide habitat for ducks, geese, and kingfishers.

Activities:

Camping: The 475 campsites, each with picnic table and fireplace, are at twelve areas around ponds. Nearby bathrooms and showers; no utilities. No reservations, but two-week maximum stay; six dollars a campsite per night. Five group campsites, reservations required. Winter camping at Barrett's Pond.

Swimming: Fearing's Pond and College Pond have nice sandy beaches, clear water, lifeguards, and bathhouses.

Picnicking: Hundreds of picnic tables and fireplaces at Fearing's and College ponds. Nearby swimming, bathrooms, and drinking water.

Fishing: Fearing's Pond is so massively stocked with trout that even a kid can catch 'em. Bass, hornpout, perch, and an occasional trout at other ponds.

Boating: On all ponds. No boat ramps or gasoline motors. Good for a canoe or sailing dinghy.

Bicycling and jogging: 15.5 miles of asphalt trails wind through the woodlands and open areas of the park. Excellent, well graded, few steep hills. Ride it all or just a portion. Spectacular. Free map at Headquarters.

Hiking: Beautiful three-mile hiking trail begins near Headquarters. Also feel free to walk the many woods roads and the bicycle trails (give bikers the right-of-way).

Horseback riding: Fifteen miles of well-maintained trails. No nearby rentals. Free map at Headquarters.

Nature study: Daily ranger-guided walks; check at Headquarters. Storytelling around the evening campfire. Lots of territory to explore.

Ski touring: 15 miles of bridle trails used for ski touring in winter if there's snow on the ground. Uncrowded. Free map.

Directions:

Auto: Route 3, Exit 3, Long Pond Road four miles to park entrance on right. Follow signs to Headquarters for information, maps, or check-in. Plenty of parking.

Telephone: 866-2526

67. DUXBURY BEACH
*Gurnet Road, Duxbury, MA 02332
Duxbury Beach Association   1929

Activities: swimming, hiking, nature study, birdwatching, fishing, jogging

Between Crane's Beach and Cape Cod, Duxbury Beach is the longest and least-developed beach open to the public. This extensive barrier beach, sandy on the Atlantic side and rocky on the harbor side, is strung between the mainland and a glacial deposit known as the Gurnet. From the Gurnet the beach has been angled sharply to the west by tidal currents flowing in and out of Plymouth Harbor, before reaching another glacial deposit, Saquish. The little wooded island hummock nestled in the long arm of the beach is Clark's Island.

Provincetown, first landing place of the Pilgrims in November 1620, lacked freshwater or cultivable land, and so on a chilly December day a group of colonists set out in their recently reassembled shallop to look for a better site for their colony. Caught in a storm just before entering Plymouth Harbor, they spent a rough night in the lee of Clark's Island. The next day they awoke to beautiful sunshine. After a rest for the Sabbath, "they sounded the harbor . . . found diverse cornfields, and little running brooks." They felt it was the best place they could find with winter coming on, and so returned to the Mayflower in Provincetown; soon the "Pilgrims and strangers" sailed for Plymouth.

Duxbury may well have been the first informal summer resort in North America. After Plymouth Colony was on an even keel, the leaders of the Pilgrims, including Myles Standish and elder Brewster, built themselves summer homes along the mainland shore of Duxbury. Frustrated by the dangerous and time-consuming sail around the Gurnet, the people had a canal cut through the marshes behind Duxbury Beach to make it a harbor ride all the way, among the first canals in the colonies.

During the eighteenth century and early in the nineteenth the beach was lined with salt evaporation pools. It was known as Salt House Beach, after a cottage on the beach in which sacks of salt were stored for shipment. During the late nineteenth century the son of one of Duxbury's wealthiest shipbuilding families purchased the beach to develop it as a resort and built several houses on it. Soon it became obvious that storms damaged any houses along the beach, and it was abandoned and the buildings were floated over to the mainland. Still hoping to see his beach settled, the developer used his influence to have the state, the county, and the town build a pile bridge across the harbor. That bridge, rebuilt and restored many times, is the longest wood pile bridge in America.

As automobile use grew, the neighbors of the beach grew tired of beachgoers parking, changing, and worse on their front lawns. To deal with this problem and at the same time ensure both the environmental quality of the beach and public access to it, a group of wealthy Duxbury citizens formed themselves into the nonprofit Duxbury Beach Association, purchased the beach as far as the Gurnet lighthouse, and built parking lots for the townspeople and the public. Today the Association encourages people to use the beach while maintaining a strict conservation policy to protect its fragile ecology.

The harbor side of the beach is covered with tan, white, olive, pink, and green rounded and skippable beach stones. Among the common plants above high water are banks of salt-spray rose, dusty miller, goldenrod, and sea rocket. The dunes are covered with beach grass. About a mile and half from the bridge a lively colony of terns nest on the shingle beach.

The marsh along the harborside parking lot, through which the canal was dug, is the summer home of a sizable colony of snowy egrets and a good place to see marsh hawks or even an occasional glossy ibis. Cormorants, sanderlings, swallows, and ducks also congregate along this shore.

Activities:

The long beach itself is composed of fine gray sand with a scattering of pebbles. Because the second half of the beach is open to dunebuggies, if you want a peaceful walk out to the Gurnet, make it a spring or fall trip—that's when you'll find the best birdwatching, anyway. Just make sure you stay away from tern nesting areas—they'll let you know by dive-bombing when you approach too close. The rocky backshore is quiet and pleasant even in the summer.
Swimming: Crystal-clear water, gentle dropoff, and fair-sized waves at this beautiful beach. Lifeguards patrol the first mile of beach. Bathhouse with showers, bathrooms, and complete snack bar. Plenty of room on the beach for large groups or spreading out.
Fishing: Catch flounder and pollock off the pile bridge.

Surf casting from the beach in the evening.

Hiking: Walk to the Gurnet along the beach or, during the summer, up the rocky backshore.

Birdwatching: Good at all times of year.

Jogging: Along the beach or the gravel road to the Gurnet.

Nature study: Typical barrier-beach ecology.

Bicycling: Plenty of bike parking racks.

Directions:

Bike: Route 3A south through Marshfield, left on Route 139, follow signs.

Auto: First Duxbury exit, Route 139, on Route 3. Continue toward Duxbury, bearing left at the fork; follow signs to beach on Gurnet Road.

Parking: Summer season four dollars weekends, two dollars weekdays. Large parking lot rarely fills even on summer Sundays.

Telephone: 837-3112

68. MALACHI BROOK WILDLIFE SANCTUARY
c/o South Shore Sanctuaries, Route 3A, Marshfield
135 acres   Massachusetts Audubon Society   1978

Activities: walking, hiking, birdwatching, nature study, ski touring, picnicking

Map: free from South Shore Sanctuaries, send SASE

Hours: dawn to dusk

Admission: no charge

Malachi Brook Sanctuary is composed primarily of a large sparkling pond set in a thousand-acre Duxbury "wilderness." Out beyond the bowed swamp loosestrife and fragrant waterlilies a pair of multihued wood ducks tend their fluffy young brood. Two squabbling kingbirds shatter the silence as they loudly debate property lines on a high branch overlooking the pond. A kestrel sitting on a nearby limb glances disdainfully at the raucous little birds, as the clouds billow across the sky.

In the old days the area around the pond was used as woodlots by neighboring farmers and many of the swamps were dug out and converted into cranberry bogs. Around 1920 Joe Lund and three of his friends, avid hunters all, purchased the property as a private hunting reserve. In the 1930s the four hunters enlarged the dam at the north end of their pond to increase the area's wildfowl habitat and to hold more water for local cranberry bogs. As the years went by the four friends became worried about the increasing numbers of hunters they saw in the field and the loss of open space in the region. Their approach to wildlife and land use gradually changed until in the late 1960s they gave Malachi Brook to Massachusetts Audubon Society.

During the spring and fall the pond is a favored migratory stop for sizable flocks of freshwater and bay ducks, including buffleheads, goldeneyes, and ringnecks. The area also is an important stopping place for thousands of tree swallows. In the pine and oak woods that surround the pond, the forest floor is carpeted with pipsissewa, Canada mayflower, starflower, and huckleberry.

Activities:

Plans are under way for the development of the thousand-acre tract that surrounds the pond as a conservation and passive-recreation area. No facilities. You should call or write to South Shore Sanctuaries before visiting here.

Walking: Three miles of trails and old woods roads. Easy walking. Very lovely trail skirts much of the west shore of the pond.

Picnicking: Beautiful pine grove for pack-it-in/pack-it-out picnics on the southwest shore of the pond.

Ski touring: Wide, gently graded woods roads are very good when there is snow. No preparation.

No dogs, fires, or vehicles.

Directions:
Contact South Shore Sanctuaries.

Telephone: 837-9500

NORTH PARKS

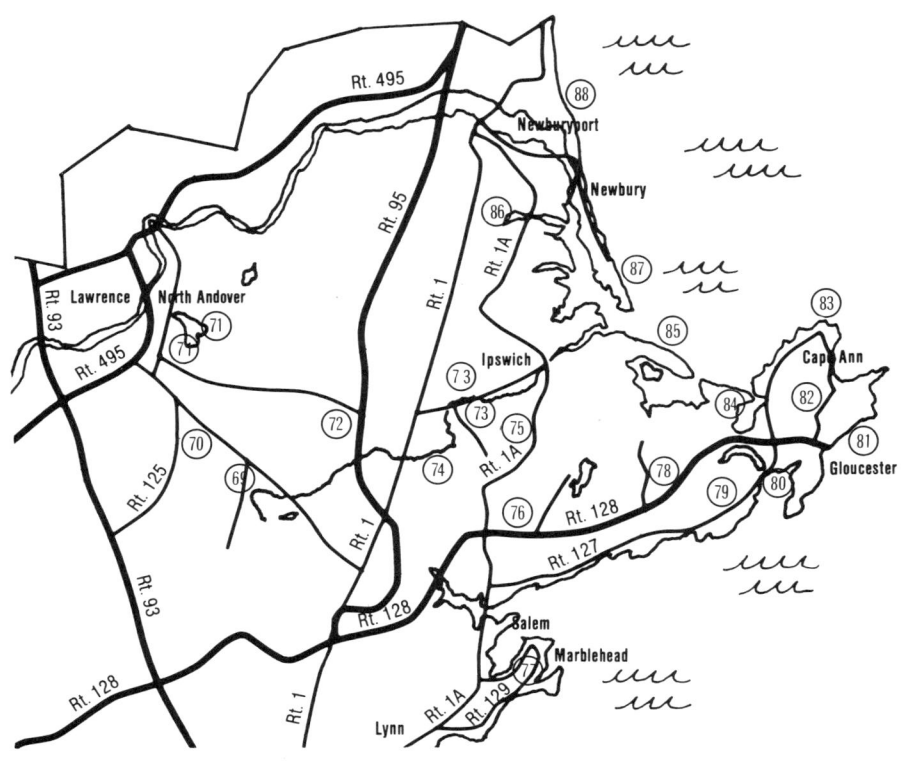

North Parks
Quick Guide to Outdoor Activities

	WALKING	PICNICKING	SWIMMING	JOGGING	NATURE STUDY	SKI TOURING	FISHING	BIRDWATCHING	HIKING	CANOEING & BOATING	ICE-SKATING	PROGRAMS	CAMPING	HORSEBACK RIDING	TOWERS, ZOOS, ETC.	HISTORIC SITES	BALLFIELDS	TOT-LOTS	BIKE TRAILS	TENNIS
69. Harold Parker State Forest	•	•	•	•	•	•	•	•	•	•			•	•					•	
70. Ward Reservation	•	•			•	•			•	•										
71. Weir Hill Reservation	•	•			•	•	•		•	•										
71A. Stevens-Coolidge Place					•											•				
72. John C. Phillips Wildlife Sanctuary	•	•			•	•	•		•	•										
73. Bradley W. Palmer State Park	•	•			•	•	•	•	•	•				•						
73A. Willowdale State Forest	•	•			•	•	•		•	•										
74. Ipswich River Wildlife Sanctuary	•	•			•		•		•	•		•			•					
75. Appleton Farms Grass Rides	•				•				•	•						•				
76. Long Hill	•				•											•				
77. Marblehead																				
77A. Devereux Beach		•	•																	
77B. Marblehead Neck Wildlife Sanctuary	•				•			•												
77C. Chandler Hovey Park	•	•					•													
77D. Fort Sewell Park		•														•				
78. Agassiz Rock	•	•			•				•											
79. Ravenswood Park	•	•		•	•	•			•	•										
80. Stage Fort Park	•	•	•				•			•						•				
81. Good Harbor Beach		•	•		•		•	•												
82. Dogtown	•	•		•	•	•			•	•						•				
83. Halibut Point Reservation	•	•			•		•	•												
84. Wingaersheek Beach	•	•	•																	
84A. Long Wharf	•				•		•			•										
85. Crane Beach Reservation	•	•	•	•	•		•	•	•											
85A. Cornelius and Miné S. Crane Wildlife Refuge					•			•		•		•				•				
86. Old Town Hill	•	•			•	•			•	•										
87. Plum Island	•	•	•	•	•	•	•	•	•	•										
88. Salisbury Beach State Reservation	•	•	•	•			•			•			•							

69. HAROLD PARKER STATE FOREST
Middleton Road, North Reading, MA 01864
3,400 acres   State Park   1916

Activities: camping, fishing, swimming, horseback riding, picnicking, jogging, ski touring
Map: free at campground and picnic-area contact station or send SASE
Hours: sunrise to sunset; overnight camping
Admission: free except at camping area and Stearns Pond; the latter costs three dollars a car or state season pass

The picnickers flock to Stearns Pond and the campers to Frye Pond, but the bulk of this large tract is quiet woodland and still ponds. Beyond the road and parking lot is a deep oak and pine forest, more like Maine than suburban Boston, entered through old fire roads and mossy trails. Rockrose, blue toadflax, indigobush, sessile-leaved bellwort, sweet fern, and honeysuckles line the margin between the pathway and the wilderness, where pink lady's slippers, lambkill, Canada mayflowers, starflowers, and hay-scented ferns take over.

Harold Parker was a descendant of Puritans, his family arriving in Massachusetts Bay around 1635. A distinguished civil engineer and builder of roads and railroads with offices in Worcester and New York, Parker served as chairman of both the State Highway Commission and the Wachusett Mountain State Reservation Commission before becoming chairman of the State Forest Commission in 1912. Although the Commission had been authorized in 1904, it was only under Parker that forest land was first acquired in 1914. To honor this civic-minded lover of nature and protector of forests, this park was named after him when it was purchased in 1916, the year of his death.

Like so many other state forests, the land was bought cheaply, after being cut repeatedly and ravaged by forest fires. Between 1916 and 1933 a small crew maintained the fire roads, set out a twenty-five-acre pine plantation, and built a small picnic area. Then the Civilian Conservation Corps arrived with two camps of two hundred men each. Over the next seven years they planted 225 acres of trees; thinned, weeded, and pruned 1,015 acres; and constructed eight miles of roads, seven dams and ponds, three picnic areas, and several buildings, including the present headquarters. Though some of the facilities have been allowed to decline in recent years, there is much that is good here and a backcountry that grows finer every year.

Activities:

Heavily used and crowded on weekends, this place is really just about what a state forest should be: woods.

Picnicking and swimming: Stearns Pond has shaded tables, grills, portable toilets, a snack bar, and a CCC-built changing house. A nice sandy beach on a large pond with clean, translucent brownish water. Lifeguards. Great for kids. Admission: three dollars a car or state season pass.

Camping: Large, pleasant campsites set in a pine grove along or near Frye Pond. Each site has a picnic table and grill; bring your own charcoal or wood; check at contact station about possible firewood. Small campers' beach. Camper fishing in pond. Bathrooms with showers. No electrical hookups. If you want a quiet site, ask for it. Campground fills early on weekends. Six dollars a site.

Walking and nature study: Eleven miles of unmarked trails; obtain the free map. Nice walks around Brackett and Stearns ponds and in the north-central portion of the forest.

Fishing: Berry Pond is stocked with trout and is much used for ice-fishing. Sudden, Salem, and Stearns ponds have catfish, sunfish, perch, and pickerel. The ponds in the eastern part of the forest, Brackett, Collins, and Field ponds, are used as fish hatcheries and so are absolutely closed to all fishing.

Horseback riding: Eleven miles of bridle trails. Check at Headquarters for rental status at nearby stables.

Jogging: Along the many miles of fire roads and trails. Very good surface for woodland jogging.

Ski touring: Along the unmarked trails and fire roads. Snowmobiles also use this state forest. Ski rentals a possibility in the near future; check with Headquarters.

Directions:

Rutherford Avenue in Charlestown to Broadway in Everett, to Main Street in Malden, Melrose, and Wakefield, to Haverhill Street in Reading, North Reading, and Andover.

Parking: Plenty, though Stearns Pond lot is filled by 11:00 A.M. on Sunday

Telephone: 686-3391

70. WARD RESERVATION
*c/o Stevens-Coolidge Place, 139 Andover Street, North Andover, MA 01845
610 acres   Trustees of Reservations   1940

Activities: hiking, nature study, picnicking, ski touring
Map: send SASE to address above or drop by
Hours: closes at sunset
Admission: free

Surmounted by the drumlins Boston Hill and Holt Hill, the latter at 420 feet the highest point in Essex County, the Ward Reservation is one of the most beautiful and interesting outdoor spaces in the Boston region. For two hundred and fifty years the land on and around these two large drumlins was farmed by the Holt family, descendants of Nicholas Holt, who first settled here in 1646. Thousands of glacial rocks were cleared from the cultivated fields and pastures and piled into mounds or strung out as stone walls by generations of farmers.

Nine miles of trails lead past hillsides covered with pyrola, starflower, lady's slipper, and numbers of spring violets, to the summit fields. Though the area has been farmed and logged, many sections of the Reservation are overspread with tall maples, white pines, and ash and carpeted with hay-scented fern so that the wanderer feels it is like walking through a forest primeval.

The partially cleared summits of both hills provide a view of the distant skyscrapers of Boston through a notch in the Middlesex Fells and of what appears to be solid forest between the hills and the city. To the north the isolated Monadnocks of southern New Hampshire lead hazily to the White Mountains. At the start of the Revolution the local citizenry stood on Holt Hill and watched the smoke rising when the British torched Charlestown during the Battle of Bunker Hill. Boston Hill is crowned by antennas and Holt Hill by a fire tower and reservoirs, but the open fields around

these structures make for the best views in the region north of Boston.

On the summit of Holt Hill a series of granite megaliths has been druidically arranged around an old mill wheel to indicate the cardinal points of the compass and the direction of the sunrise and sunset on the longest and shortest days of the year. An outer circle of stones, collected from the property, is described in a little booklet, "The Geology of the Charles W. Ward Reservation."

Beginning in 1917 Charles W. Ward began purchasing the former Holt lands around Holt Hill. His wife donated this land to the Trustees after his death in 1940 and also kept on purchasing land and adding it to the Reservation. It was Mrs. Ward who placed the solstice stones at Holt Hill's summit.

One of the most naturally intriguing places in the Reservation is Pine Hole Bog, an exotic three-dimensional tapestry of nature, woven of subtle shadings of red and green vegetation. This "quaking" sphagnum bog, made accessible by a long boardwalk, is a fantasyland of wild calla, insect-eating sundews and pitcher plants, prehistoric-looking horsetails, marsh saint-john's-wort, and a half-dozen varieties of fern. Among the unusual trees found on the bog, which though spindly may be fifty years or more old, are black spruce and eastern larch. A guide to the bog is available for purchase from the address above. Please don't pick any flowers.

Activities:

This Reservation is a sheer pleasure for walkers, skiers, naturalists, and connoisseurs of the "long view."

Hiking: Nine miles of trails over a diversity of terrain. Be sure to send SASE for excellent map.

Nature study: The Pine Hole Bog trail is one of the most unusual sites in the region. Easy walking, but be prepared to get your shoes wet or wear boots. Send one dollar plus fifty cents postage for excellent bog interpretive booklet.

Picnicking: The summits of Holt and Boston Hills are fantastic places to picnic.

Ski touring: This is an exceptionally good place for ski touring. The trails are wide and maintained for this use. Novice to intermediate. Be sure to obtain the property's trail map, which is marked with contour lines.

Directions:

North on Route 125 in Andover, right on Prospect Street, just before North Andover border.

Parking: Fair-sized parking lot on Prospect Street.

71. WEIR HILL RESERVATION
6 Stevens-Coolidge Place, 139 Andover Street, North Andover, MA 01845
183 acres   Trustees of Reservations   1968

Activities: hiking, nature study, skiing, picnicking, toboganing

Map: free, send SASE or drop by Stevens-Coolidge Place

Hours: closes at sunset

Admission: no charge

From the cleared field on a peak of Weir Hill, the viewer looks out over urban Lawrence and the Merrimack Valley to the mountains of New Hampshire rising on the horizon. On the hill across a narrow valley sits a hilltop farm more reminiscent of Vermont than of the industrialized Merrimack. The mowed fields slope sharply away from the forested summit, providing a fertile habitat for yellow and orange hawkweed, wild indigobush, wild rose, yarrow, and gnarled apple trees.

For the hundreds if not thousands of years before the white man arrived in the area, the local Indians wove sticks and vines together and placed them across the nearby brook, an outlet of Lake Cochichewick, to trap spawning alewives. This fish weir, which gave the hill its name, filled the bellies of the Indians and fertilized their corn; the practice was later adopted by the area's first white settlers. Those settlers also logged the hill and then used it for a sheep pasture.

Today several miles of quiet trails wind to the hilltops of this Reservation, past old stone boundary walls, beneath a forest of shagbark hickory, white ash, white pine, and oak. The area is habitat for Solomon's seal, bedstraw, speedwell, and starflower. A particularly beautiful trail weaves its way along the quiet shore of Lake Cochichewick, now a reservoir. Lush highbush blueberries line the water's edge, groves of yellow stargrass poke up from the partridgeberry groundcover, and red-osier dogwoods bloom dramatically along this trail.

Activities:

This is an undeveloped woodland, hilltop, and lakeshore reservation.

Picnicking: The grassy summit of the hilltop or the shady shores of Lake Cochichewick are fine places for a blanket-borne picnic. No facilities.

Hiking: Six or seven miles of trails along lakeshore and to summits.

Skiing: Trails very good for ski touring, well maintained though not prepared.

Directions:

One mile from North Andover Center, off Route 125/133, on Stevens Street.

Parking: Along Stevens Street, just before Osgood Street.

71A. *STEVENS-COOLIDGE PLACE
139 Andover Street, North Andover, MA 01845
91 acres   Trustees of Reservations   1962

This garden estate, once known as Ashdale Farm for the giant ash trees that grow here, was owned by the Stevens family from the time that Captain James Stevens acquired the land in 1728 until it was bequeathed to the Trustees in 1962. The main house, part of which was built in 1730, was enlarged and restored in the Colonial Revival style over the years.

The family farm became the summer residence of Helen Stevens Coolidge and her husband in 1914 and Mrs. Coolidge lived here until her death in 1962. The house is filled with the Coolidges' collection of Chinese porcelain, antique American furniture, Irish and English glassware, and oriental carpets.

Behind the house are several delightful formal gardens and tree plantings. Shaped hedges, false cypress and cedar trees, flowering dogwoods, and dawn redwoods frame the pastel iris and peony blossoms of the central garden, which is primarily planted with the flowers that would have been found in a colonial flower garden. A walled rose garden is being restored. Plantings along a serpentine brick wall, one of only two in New England, are sheltered from the sun by a sky-reaching stand of Alberta spruce.

Activities:
The grounds and gardens are open every day. Guided tours of the elaborate house are conducted every Sunday from April 15 through October 30, 1:00 P.M. to 5:00 P.M. Group tours may be arranged for other days by calling 682-3580. Small admission fee for tours.

Directions:
A quarter of a mile from North Andover Center on Andover Street.
Parking: Along Andover Street.

72. JOHN C. PHILLIPS WILDLIFE SANCTUARY
Middleton Road, Boxford
335 acres   *Division of Fisheries and Wildlife   1929

Activities: walking and hiking, birdwatching, nature study, picnicking

Map: map in *Wildlife Sanctuaries* by Marilyn Komins; available for fifty cents plus forty cents postage from Massachusetts Division of Fisheries and Wildlife, Westborough, MA 01581

Hours: dawn to dusk

Admission: no charge

Phillips Wildlife Sanctuary was the first state-owned sanctuary in Massachusetts. Donated to the state by John C. Phillips, a sportsman and ornithologist, and the New England Federation of Bird Clubs in 1929, it is a quiet woodland area crossed by meandering trails and old woods roads. This is one of the only places in the region where you are likely to hear the loud rasping call of the pileated woodpecker, largest woodpecker in New England and, with the exception of the nearly extinct ivory-billed woodpecker of the South, the largest woodpecker in North America. If you are lucky, you might catch a glimpse of the great birds fluttering through the treetops.

The forested hills here are covered with a mature growth of white pine, hemlock, and oak. Pipsissewa, pyrola, blueberry, and lady's slipper are among the common plants of the forest floor. Whole hillsides are covered with a lush growth of ferns, often in mixed stands of Christmas, lady, hay-scented, and bracken ferns. The swamps here are also quite attractive with their wealth of royal and marsh ferns, sweet pepperbush, and buttonbush. In addition to the pileated woodpecker, this is a likely place to sight owls, warblers, grouse, and the Louisiana water thrush.

Activities:

This is a very pleasant woodland, surrounded on three sides by Boxford State Forest, for leisurely strolling, birdwatching, or a pack-it-in/pack-it-out picnic. The birds and other wildlife are abundant, and the opportunity to see the pileated woodpecker is alone worth the trip. No fires. No facilities.

Directions:

Route I-95 north. Take Topsfield Road exit toward Boxford. Go through Boxford Center bearing left on Depot Road. Continue on Depot Road crossing Main Street to

Middleton Road. Proceed south for two miles to a blocked-off woods road and sanctuary entrance sign. *Parking:* For two or three cars.

73. BRADLEY W. PALMER STATE PARK
*Asbury Street, Topsfield, MA 01983
721 acres   State Park   1948

Activities: hiking and walking, fishing, boating, picnicking, wading pool, ski touring, bicycling, nature study, birding
Map: free at the Headquarters or send SASE
Hours: 8:00 A.M. to dusk
Admission: three dollars a car to developed picnic area; free to rest of park

Given to the people of Massachusetts as a place to enjoy the peace and beauty of river, woods, fields, and hills.
                                                                    Bradley W. Palmer

Bradley Palmer was fabulously wealthy, and as his fortune grew during the first forty years of this century he kept buying more and more land in the towns of Hamilton, Topsfield, Ipswich, Boxford, Georgetown, and Rowley to enlarge his country estate, "Willowdale." He wanted to freely indulge his passion for genteel horsemanship and the hunt. Although the area within this state park included his manor house and received his greatest devotion, his property included: 780 acres now in Boxford State Forest; 1,112 acres, now in Georgetown-Rowley State Forest; and 2,400 acres, now in Willowdale State Forest.

Palmer was a graduate of Harvard and Harvard Law who became lawyer for and partner in the greatest Boston-based corporations of the pre-World War II days. He served as counsel and director of United Fruit Company, which just about owned Central America. He worked with Gillette to make it the biggest razor company in the world. He was a partner in the monopolies that owned nearly all the railroads south of the Rio Grande. He was a principal of International Telephone and Telegraph, which controlled communications over half the world. Often accused of manipulating world markets and owning governments, he loved the North Shore sporting life.

His house overlooking the Ipswich River, now the state's Civil Defense Training Academy, is filled with ornate woodcarvings, walnut paneling, and stained and leaded glass windows. He imported Italian stonecarvers to sculpt half a dozen marble mantlepieces and mouldings. He built a private chapel in the house, and he also had a "theater," where he threw wild parties for his friends with "imported" women.

Italian and Scottish gardeners laid out, planted, and groomed the area around the house. Many species of European trees and shrubs were planted at Palmer's direction, including his favorite trees, black spruce and oriental pine. Large tracts around the house and throughout the reaches of the estate were planted with rhododendron and mountain laurel. Today, the woods wanderer will discover impenetrable walls of cascading pink and white blossoms deep in the forest. Palmer's head gardener, ninety-six years old, was still living on the estate in 1982.

Behind the house, Palmer had his workers erect brick stables, workshops, and tack houses, but growing displeased with the brick, he paid for the difficult job of shingling all the buildings over. Water for the entire estate was supplied by gravity from a cistern on a hill. Palmer was a real believer in self-sufficiency; his estate had its own electricity-generating system as well.

In 1913 Myopia Hunt Club held its annual steeplechase here and the state park is still used for races, riding events, and fox hunts.

On the banks of the Ipswich River or around one of the lily-pad-covered ponds, nesting wood ducks, geese, and mallards drift by blue flag iris and marsh primrose on their way to a bread handout; herons, bitterns, and kingfishers lurk here as well. Blueberry Hill, a gold mine of highbush blueberries, and the mown summit of Willowdale Hill are good places to see red-tailed hawks, goshawks, cedar waxwings, goldfinches, cardinals, and scarlet tanagers, and even an immature bald eagle has been sighted here. In the parklike woods, in addition to exotic plants, you may find jack-in-the-pulpit, wild geranium, lambkill, gentian, and yellow lady's slipper, the last two flowers unusual in the eastern part of the state.

Activities:
Still a much-frequented haunt of the North Shore eques-

trian crowd, Bradley Palmer State Park's primary summer use is for quiet family picnicking.

Hiking: Ten miles of fine, gentle trails and many acres of open fields. Walk along the Ipswich River and to the summits of Blueberry and Willowdale hills. Self-guiding nature trail near Headquarters.

Picnicking: Pleasant picnic area under tall white pines. Lots of tables and grills; bring your own wood. Wading pool for children. Bathrooms and bubblers. Open fields nearby for sunbathing, running around, or playing catch. Duck-feeding at ponds.

Fishing: From banks of Ipswich River; stocked with rainbow trout.

Boating: Canoe launch from bridge near park entrance.

Nature study: Diverse woodlands and wetlands with abundant plant and animal species. Self-guiding nature trail begins behind Headquarters; tour map and key to numbered sites available at picnic area or Headquarters.

Ski touring: Many miles of well-laid-out trails through woods and fields. Beautiful, very popular, and enough territory to find quiet out-of-the-way places. Beginner to intermediate.

Birding: Many nesting birds around ponds and in the margins between woods and fields.

Bicycling: On park roads.

Canoe rentals: At Foote's Boat Livery, Topsfield Road, Ipswich, MA 01938, telephone 356-9771. A half mile beyond Hamilton Road on Topsfield (Ipswich) Road, five dollars an hour for first hour, three dollars each additional hour; ten to twelve dollars a day. For fifteen dollars they will truck you and a canoe upriver for a four- to five-hour, twenty-two-mile leisurely ride back down the river.

Directions:

Route 1 north to Topsfield, right on Ipswich Road, approximately three miles to right on Hamilton Road to park entrance. Signs from Route 1.

Parking: Just beyond entrance and at picnic area.

Telephone: 887-5931

73A. WILLOWDALE STATE FOREST
c/o Bradley W. Palmer State Park, Asbury Street, Topsfield, MA 01983
2,400 acres   State Forest   1948

Activities: hiking, birdwatching, nature study, ski touring, picnicking
Map: free at Bradley Palmer Headquarters or send SASE
Hours: 8:00 A.M. to dusk
Admission: no charge

This vast tract of woodlands and wetlands was part of Bradley Palmer's Willowdale estate. Crossed by many miles of wide horse-trails that wind over low glacial hills and eskers and by streams, Willowdale State Forest is managed as a wildlife preserve. White pines and red oaks predominate on the hills; red maples predominate in the swamps. The forest floor is carpeted with club mosses, lady's slipper, starflower, partridgeberry, wild lily-of-the-valley, and spring violets.

Activities:
This is a fine place for a long walk in the wilds or a pack-it-in/pack-it-out picnic. Recently closed to snowmobiles, it is an excellent place for quiet ski touring. The mosquitos are fierce here in the summer; be sure to carry repellent. Pick up a map at Bradley Palmer State Park.

Directions:
Route 1 north to Topsfield, right on Ipswich Road. Continue three and a half miles. Trailhead on left just beyond Hamilton Road on the right.
Parking: Limited but satisfactory.

74. IPSWICH RIVER WILDLIFE SANCTUARY
Perkins Row, Topsfield, MA 01983
2,000 acres   Massachusetts Audubon Society   1951

Activities: birdwatching, hiking and walking, nature study, picnicking, interpretive programs, canoeing, ski touring

Map: available at office or send SASE
Hours: dawn to dusk
Admission: one dollar and a half adults; seventy-five cents children

In the spring of the year the meadows on the banks of the river were overflowed, so that hundreds of acres were covered with water, making a veritable sea where wild geese and ducks abounded to the delight of sportsmen. Early in the spring the waters would recede and pass out into the ocean through the mouth of the river at Ipswich. There would soon grow up a luxuriant crop of grass on the meadow which, when mature, was harvested.

Nathaniel Bradstreet

In 1643 the first white settlers of these lands were Simon Bradstreet, assistant governor of Massachusetts Bay Colony, and his wife, Anne, America's first poetess. Topsfield was known to the Indians as Shenwendy, "Pleasant place by the waters," before being sold by Masconomet to Governor Winthrop. Though Simon and Anne moved to Andover in 1658, this beautiful farm remained in the Bradstreet family until 1900. Generations of Bradstreets mowed the river hay, raised corn, cows, and chickens, planted gardens and orchards, and hunted along the river. Bradstreet Lane, which ran by the farmhouse, was used as a public way between Ipswich Center and the river ford at the hill's base.

In 1900 the land was purchased and occupied by Thomas B. Proctor, a wealthy young Bostonian with a hunger for land so insatiable that within a few years he had acquired 4,000 of Topsfield's 8,400 acres. Proctor was a very active horticulturist, admirer of Sargent and the Arnold Arboretum, and underwriter of several of "Chinese" Wilson's Far Eastern expeditions. He wanted his estate on Bradstreet Hill to be a private arboretum.

Using the Arboretum staff as advisers, Proctor began his self-appointed task. He hired crews of recently immigrated Italians to do the planting, grading, and road building. In 1902 he hired Shintare Anamete, a Japanese landscape architect, to direct the project. For the next nine years Proctor focused his attention and that of his staff on the construction and planting of a huge rock garden, The Rockery. Because there were few massive boulders on the property, or in Ipswich or Topsfield for that matter, Proctor had his men cart rocks from as far away as Byfield and Rowley. Greenhouses were built. Trees arrived on flatcars at the railroad station from all over the country and the world, then were carted to the estate and planted. Once the work was complete, Proctor opened his estate to the public on Sundays. Proctor lost a great deal of his fortune during the Depression and was forced to sell his lands.

In 1951 Massachusetts Audubon began acquiring this sanctuary with funds from the sale of their sanctuary on Plum Island to the federal government. Another five hundred acres in Hamilton were added to this sanctuary as a donation from Peter Higginson.

The two most significant geological features of the sanctuary are the Bradstreet Hill drumlin and two eskers—both types of hill deposited by glacial activity. The eskers, formed by streams running through or beneath the melting glacier, are parts of the longest esker in New England, extending from East Groveland to the ocean in Beverly.

Few tracts of land in Eastern Massachusetts have as many different habitats, making the Ipswich River Wildlife Sanctuary a natural wonderland, spiked with Mr. Proctor's exotic plantings. A little causeway across a large pond filled with pinkish-white water lilies, blue-stalked pickerelweed, and purple loosestrife, and lined with daisies and asters, leads out to a beech-covered island. Wide and exceedingly lovely trails run across the eskers and snake through a forest of mixed hardwoods and tall white pines. Starflower, partridgeberry, periwinkle, wintergreen, stands of Indian pipe, and Canada mayflower carpet the forest floor. Redwing blackbirds and kingbirds rule over cattail, buttonbush, swamp azalea, and great masses of blue flag iris in the marshes. Old fields are being taken over by buckthorn, dogwood, steeplebush, red cedar, and sumac. And there are still fields covered with grasses, rough-fruited cinquefoil, clovers, and hawkweeds.

Scattered throughout the grounds, though concentrated along the Arboretum Trail and at The Rockery, are an amazing assortment of exotic trees. Rhododendrons, magnolias, laurels, azaleas, cork trees, hop trees, Korean pines, and sawara cypress are just a few of the exotic specimens to be found here. Something is always blooming during the warm half of the year.

Activities:

Although spring and fall are the most exquisite times here, this largest of Massachusetts Audubon's sanctuaries is a fine place to visit during any season and deserves regular revisitation to see what each month brings and to explore the different habitats and special places. Among

other things, be sure to climb the observation tower over-looking Bunker Meadow, peek into the wildflower garden, contemplate The Rockery, and walk the eskers. Bring your camera and binoculars and don't forget your mosquito repellent from June through August.

Walking and hiking: More than ten miles of beautiful trails wind throughout the sanctuary. There are many short, easy circuit walks from the parking lot yet enough country to spend the whole day wandering. Most trails are

wide, well graded, and laid out for constant little surprises. A well-thought-out self-guided nature trail can be
toured in an hour. Most trails are blazed, but the free map
is very helpful.

Picnicking: Pack-it-in/pack-it-out picnics at parking lot and
Arbor only.

Interpretive programs: For all ages. Call or write for current
listing. Day camp in the summer.

Ski touring: Along the ten miles of trails. Extremely beau-

tiful place in the winter. Trails marked. Novice to intermediate.

Prohibited: Fires and dogs.

Directions:

Route 1 north to Topsfield; right on Route 97; first left on
Perkins Row; continue one mile to sanctuary entrance.

Parking: Plenty.

Telephone: 887-9264

75. APPLETON FARMS GRASS RIDES
Cutler Road, Hamilton
164 acres   *Trustees of Reservations   1970

Activities: walking, hiking, nature study
Hours: closes at sunset
Admission: no charge

When Samuel Appleton settled in Ipswich in 1638 he was granted
a house lot in the village and a large farm on the outskirts "contain-
ing, four hundred and sixty acres, more or less, meadow and
upland as it lyeth. . . ." Appleton was active in the community's
affairs, signing a petition to keep John Winthrop, Jr., a resident in
the town; building a cart bridge over a swamp; and malting the
town's surplus corn. His son, Major Samuel Appleton, a leading
officer during King Philip's War, inherited the farm and built a
sawmill along one of its streams. That farm is still in the Appleton
family today, 350 years later, making it "the oldest farm in continuous operation in the United States." Appleton Farms Grass Rides,
the only portion of the farm now open to the public, was given to
the Trustees by Colonel and Mrs. Francis R. Appleton in 1970.

Long years of continuous yet conservative (in the best sense) use
have resulted in an unusual landscape: open grass strips, once used
for horseback riding, run like grandes allées through a red maple
swamp, upland woods, and tree plantations. Among the wildflowers blossoming in the tall grassed rides are common saint-john's-
wort, dogbane, meadowsweet, bluets, yellow stargrass, wild
indigo, and anemones. A closer inspection reveals as well spring
violets, spotted cowbane, water horehound, and white beard-

tongue. Along the edges of the rides silky dogwood and black cherry provide shade for a garden of ferns: New York, sensitive, lady cinnamon, and interrupted. Lady's slipper, Canada mayflower, and starflower carpet the woods, shaded by big old red and white oaks, red and white pines, and shagbark hickories.

One of the most interesting features of this tract is the grassy-spoked rustic merry-go-round used by the Appletons for hayrides. At Round Point, in the hub of the spokes, a gray granite pinnacle stands as silent sentinel, one of twenty similar pinnacles that once stood high on the buttresses of Gore Hall, Harvard's library built in 1838. Francis R. Appleton, chairman of the University's Library Committee, received four of the pinnacles when Gore Hall was torn down and replaced by the Widener Library in 1913. This pinnacle, inscribed with uplifting words by Appleton's sister, Ruth Appleton Tuckerman, was placed at Round Point in 1914 on the occasion of Appleton's sixtieth birthday.

Activities:

Crossed by five or six miles of sylvan grass rides, Appleton Farms Grass Rides is quiet, yet the beauty of the place and its unusual display of flora and fauna make it deserving of visits in every season. No facilities.

Walking: Tranquil grassy trails wind over low hills, by swamps, and along pastures. Abundant wildflowers and birds.

Directions:

Route 1A through Hamilton Center; left in a mile or so on Cutler Road. Parking lot at very end of Cutler Road.

Parking: For ten or twelve cars.

76. LONG HILL
572 Essex Street, Beverly, MA 01915
114 acres   Trustees of Reservations   1979

Activities: strolling, nature study, historic building
Hours: closes at sunset
Admission: one dollar each adult, two dollars an adult for garden tour

In 1916 Mabel and Ellery Sedgwick purchased the former fields of Long Hill as a site for their summer home. Mr. Sedgwick was editor of *Atlantic Monthly* from 1909 to 1938; his wife was an accomplished horticulturist and author of *The Garden Month by Month*. The two main features of Long Hill are the house they had built and the landscaped grounds.

In the year that Long Hill was purchased, Mr. Sedgwick had discovered Ball House in Charleston, South Carolina. Built in 1802, this old house was run-down and about to be converted into laborers' quarters by the railroad that owned it. Noticing its exquisite interior woodwork, Sedgwick contacted the railroad president and purchased the dwelling's insides. The woodwork was carefully removed and shipped to Beverly, where it was installed in a house designed by architect Philip Richardson and built of bricks from an early Ipswich mill.

Mrs. Sedgwick devoted herself to the gardens around the house, planting both native and exotic shrubs and trees, and developing a large cutting garden to supply the inside of the house with flowers. After Mrs. Sedgwick died in 1937, Ellery Sedgwick married Marjorie Russell, a native of England and a "distinguished gardener and propagator of rare plants." The second Mrs. Sedgwick took over where the first left off, growing tree peonies from seed, planting dozens of different rhododendrons, installing two lotus pools, and planting hundreds of other ornamental trees and shrubs with as much thought for fall foliage as for spring blossoms. When Mrs. Sedgwick died in 1978 she left the property and an endowment for its maintenance to the Trustees.

Activities:

The gardens and grounds here are of outstanding beauty, an exotic pageant of color artistically laid out, and an elegant place to stroll around. The plants put on their most spectacular display during the month of May, and June is also a bright month. But the garden is worth visiting from April through October, when the fall foliage provides another show.

House tours: The interior of the house equals the garden in elegance, but is not regularly open to the public. Tours are occasionally given: if you are interested, write to the property or call 922-1536.

Reading:
A Guide to Sedgwick Gardens indicates the common and Latin names, source, blossom time, location, and date of planting for several hundred individual flowers, plantings, shrubs, and trees. Includes map of the estate. Available from Long Hill superintendent.

Directions:
Route 128 north to Beverly, Essex Street exit north, one and a half miles to entrance on left.

77. MARBLEHEAD

77A. DEVEREUX BEACH
Beach Street, Marblehead
*Marblehead Park Department

Activities: swimming
Hours: 9:00 A.M. to 6:00 P.M.
Admission: two dollars a car; more on weekends

This beach, just south of the causeway leading out to Marblehead Neck, was once a favorite summer encampment of the Naumkeag Indians. As many as 2,000 Indians may have spent the season here, visiting the Neck to quarry rock for their projectile points, having clambakes, and escaping the inland mosquitoes. The first white settler along the beach was Hugh Peter, who was granted a large tract running from the beach inland in 1636. Peter was an especially active Puritan, and while raising money for the cause in England at the time of the Restoration, he was captured and beheaded. His land was sold to John Devereux, who lived here and farmed his land for fifty-nine years. During the witch scares of the 1670s, a young woman accused of witchcraft leapt into the surf off the beach and drowned herself. The land remained in the Devereux family until 1837, when a depression forced them to sell it.

After 1870 when the railroad was driven through nearby, the land behind the beach was subdivided as a resort development. Mansion houses and boarding houses were built, the beach being a principal attraction. The resort thrived until the 1930s.

Activities:

This is a small but beautiful beach with a distant view of Nahant ahead; behind is Marblehead Harbor filled with what appear to be thousands of sailboats. It is a pleasant place, though somewhat crowded on weekends.

Swimming: Half-mile-long curve of beach, partly white sand and partly gravel. Lifeguards. Bathhouse, toilets, and snack bar. Long row of shaded benches and a dozen picnic tables. Easy dropoff and gentle surf. Well-equipped children's play area.

Directions:

Route 129 to Marblehead, right on Beach Street; beach on right half a mile ahead.

Parking: Plenty, but plan on arriving by 11:00 on weekends.

77B. MARBLEHEAD NECK WILDLIFE SANCTUARY
Risley Road, Marblehead Neck
15 acres   *Massachusetts Audubon Society   1953

Activities: birdwatching and walking
Hours: dawn to dusk
Admission: no charge

By the late 1940s the citizens of Marblehead Neck, settled three hundred years earlier, were becoming aware that their rocky retreat was in danger of becoming completely overlain with private residences. Old-timers sad about a fading quality of life, newcomers who had learned to appreciate the Neck's ambience, and birders combined forces to preserve this fifteen-acre tract, the last bit of inland wild land on the Neck. With contributions and land donations, the tract was acquired and turned over to Massachusetts Audubon Society in 1953.

This is a small quiet woodland dotted with rock outcroppings and a man-made pond and laced with trails. Big old maples and white birches fill the swampy woods. Wild roses, blueberries, and juneberries thrive around the open ledges. Wintergreen, sweet pepperbush, and elderberry are among the common flowering plants and many more will be found in the spring.

More than 235 bird species have been sighted in this small sanctuary. The spring and fall warbler migrations are outstanding here, with thirty-eight species recorded. Every flycatcher listed for the state has been seen here, as have eighteen species of sparrow— if you have the patience to differentiate them. Don't forget your binoculars.

Activities:
This is also a nice place for a quiet walk, an hour's exploration, or a pack-it-in/pack-it-out picnic. No facilities.

Directions:
From Devereux Beach proceed out the causeway to Ocean Avenue, second left on Risley Road to end.
Parking: Limited to a few cars. Easy walk from Devereux Beach if lot is filled.

77C. CHANDLER HOVEY PARK
Marblehead Town Park   1948

Activities: walking, picnicking, scenic area, skindiving
Hours: 9:00 A.M. to dusk
Admission: Free

Located on Point o' Neck, a rocky headland hanging seventy feet above the entrance to Marblehead Harbor, this is a fine place to watch sailboat races or relax in the sun. When Marblehead was at its peak as a port, thousands of vessels cruising to and from the ports and seas of the globe sailed majestically by the point. During the War of 1812 locals standing here saw their favorite, the *Chesapeake,* defeated by the British. In the next year they had something to cheer about when the *Constitution* slipped around the Point, escaping a superior British force.

In 1835 a lighthouse was constructed on the point, actually a white stone tower, which burned lard or whale oil to warn vessels away from the rocky point. The first keeper was a veteran seaman from the *Constitution.* The second keeper, a woman, was the only female lighthouse keeper on the coast—she had learned the job from her father, keeper of Baker's Island Light. In 1895 the old light was torn down and the present spidery structure was erected. Keepers continued to maintain the light until 1920, when it was automated.

After World War II the government sold Point o' Neck. Fortu-

nately it was purchased by Chandler Hovey, a wealthy resident of
Marblehead Neck and yachtsman, who then donated it to the town
as a park.

Activities:

This is a beautiful place for a picnic. Watch the sailboats
and the cormorants, and look across the head of the
harbor to Fort Sewell. A few shaded benches, but most
people lay their blankets on the rocks. Tidepools and a
tiny unsupervised beach below. A favorite of artists and
skindivers. Toilets.

Directions:

Ocean Avenue to the end.
Parking: Space for forty cars.

77D. FORT SEWELL PARK
*Marblehead Park Department   1922

Activities: picnicking, scenic, sitting, strolling
Hours: 9:00 A.M. to 6:00 P.M.
Admission: free

Marblehead's first fort was built here of wood on Gale's Head in
1644 for a total of thirty-nine pounds. Constructed to defend
against marauding Dutchmen, Frenchmen, and pirates, the site had
been previously used by Ambrose Gale as a place to dry fish, and
his name stuck. Over the next hundred years, as England and
France continued their "little wars," the town and the colony
argued repeatedly about who should pay for the fort's maintenance. Finally in 1742 the province allocated money to replace the
run-down battlements. The fort was rapidly upgraded at the beginning of the Revolution but saw no action, perhaps by its mere
presence keeping the British out of the harbor. After the Revolution much of the fort was dismantled and sold to pay the debt
incurred in its construction.

In 1794 Gale's Head was turned over to the new federal
government, which rebuilt the fort following plans drawn up by
Rochfontaine, the country's foremost military engineer. During
the Civil War the fort was enlarged. It was last manned during the
Spanish-American War, when it was officially named Fort Sewell.

After more than 230 years as a military reservation, its guns never having been fired in battle, the fort was given to the town.

Activities:

Today the battlements are lined with benches rather than twenty-four pounders on this breezy point overlooking the entrance to Marblehead Harbor. From the shade of a huge old maple there is a grand view of the bustling harbor. This is a very pleasant place to sit and relax or have a picnic while wandering about the town. The old muster ground is fine for tossing a Frisbee or playing catch. Bathrooms.

Directions:

Park near the Old Town House on Beacon Street, and walk out to the end of Front Street.

Reading:

Marblehead by Priscilla Sawyer Lord and Virginia Clegg Gamage is an excellent history of the town.

78. AGASSIZ ROCK
School Street, Manchester
104 acres   *Trustees of Reservations   1957

Activities: walking, nature study, picnicking, scenic area

No individual did more to awaken America to the value of natural-history studies than Louis Agassiz, the man who brought the techniques of modern science from Europe in the middle of the nineteenth century. Born in Switzerland, educated in his native land, in Germany, and in France, a professor at the University of Neufchâtel, Agassiz's work on the glaciers of the Alps was the beginning of our understanding of the great Ice Ages. In 1848 he emigrated to America and became Professor of Natural History at Harvard, a position he held almost continuously until his death in 1873, teaching two generations of scholars the scientific method.

Although the rocks on top of Manchester's Beaverdam Hill (elevation 180 feet) had long been known by the locals as the Sunset Rocks, it was Agassiz who shortly before his death identified them as glacial erratics. That is, these large granite boulders sitting on the hilltop are of rock different from that of the hill itself. Noticing this, Agassiz realized that the huge rocks had been dragged there. Notice that the boulders have a different grain and color than the rock they stand on, and may have been plucked from rocky New Hampshire hills or nearby Cape Ann.

The path to the summit passes beneath hemlocks, beeches, maples, and birches. Boulders clothed with mosses and rock tripe lichen lay everywhere; from their crevices spring mats of polypody ferns. On the mostly bare summit of the hill, where Agassiz Rock sits, blueberries, huckleberries, bearberries, and juneberries grow in the shallow soil. In the steep ravine beyond the summit, a little trail leads a short distance down to Swamp Agassiz Rock, another erratic.

Activities:
This is a quiet, undeveloped tract with a single trail through it. From the summit of Beaverdam Hill you can see the church spires of Manchester in the distance and the sea beyond. A pleasant place to stop on your way home from the beach, it is only a mile from Route 128.

Walking: The trail to the summit is short—less than half a mile—but a fairly steep ten-minute hike.

Picnicking: The summit is a good spot for a pack-it-in/ pack-it-out picnic. No facilities.

Directions:

Route 128 to School Street, Exit 15, in Manchester. Head north for approximately a mile, turnout on the right.

Parking: For five or six cars.

79. RAVENSWOOD PARK
Route 127, Gloucester
500 acres   *Gloucester Park Department   1889

Activities: hiking and walking, picnicking, nature study, birdwatching, jogging, ski touring
Hours: dawn to dusk
Admission: no charge

. . . for the benefit of all who want to walk and enjoy the woods.
Samuel Sawyer

In the 1880s Samuel Sawyer, a native of Gloucester who had made a fortune in Boston, began to acquire woodlots back from the water of his native Kettle Cove. In 1886 he donated the land to Gloucester for use as a park and provided funds to lay out scenic roads and trails and for tree plantings. The park was superlatively landscaped: gracefully twisting trails, lined with innumerable small rocks, lead to the prettiest places in the prettiest ways. Woods roads were laid out beneath the tallest trees and lined with thousands of boulders. The roads and trails have mellowed for nearly a hundred years as lichens colonized the rocks and pine needles filled the crevices. Mellow yourself: take a walk in Ravenswood Park.

Although swamps usually receive bad press, the one that girdles the western border of this park is a green fantasyland filled with wildflowers. The most northerly stand of native magnolias in New England, discovered in 1806, grows here, the treelike shrubs bedecked with large white blossoms in June. Before the area became a park, local estate owners and gardeners dug up many of the magnolias to enliven their homes, nearly eliminating the stand. During July the air of the swamp is laced with the musky lavender scent of swamp azalea, like an older woman's floral perfume. The sphagnum-carpeted swamp floor supports round-leaved sundew, horsetail, blue flag iris, cinnamon and royal ferns, and such shrubs as sweet pepperbush and highbush blueberries. A trail running along the base of a hill on the far side of the magnolia swamp, beneath some of the North Shore's biggest hemlocks, is lined with Indian cucumber root, bunchberries, lady's slipper, and Indian pipe.

Dense stands of mountain laurel cloud the mature upland woods with pinkish-white blossoms for much of July. Beech, black and white birch, hemlock, oak, and tall white pines shade boulder fields luxuriantly overgrown with sarsaparilla and polygala. Crouching in the woods, sphinxlike glacial boulders lie covered with rock tripe, a lichen used in the old days to thicken soups and stews. From the wooded summit of Ledge Hill, a view is maintained of Eastern Point and the sea beyond.

The area had long been used by man as woodlot, pasture, quarry, and homesite. One woods road follows the winding route of the old Salem Road, which connected Salem and Cape Ann until around 1800. Many a teamster drove his oxcart fully laden with hay, salt cod, vegetables, and fuelwood to the Salem markets along this route. Old quarries dimple the rocky hills. Two noteworthy cellar holes along the woods roads belong to a 1777 "Pest House," around which smallpox victims were interred, and the cottage of a hermit named Walton. Walton moved to Ravenswood in 1884 and remained twenty years, curing himself of several ailments and befriending the wildlife.

Activities:

This park is a beautiful, seemingly undeveloped woodland crossed by many miles of roads and trails. Please don't pick any flowers.

Hiking and walking: The trails and roads are gently graded for easy walking and laid out for the saunterer's aesthetic pleasure. Be sure to visit the swamp (with mosquito repellent handy). The trail over Ledge Hill is especially lovely.

Birdwatching: The swamp is filled with birds.

Jogging: Some of the best woodland jogging in the region along the well-graded and well-tended old roads.

Picnicking: Many fine woodland sites for a pack-it-in/pack-it-out picnic. No facilities.

Ski touring: Some of the best ski touring on the North Shore using the old roads. Not prepared or blazed but glorious. Parking lot usually plowed.

Directions:

Route 127 a mile and a half north of Manchester. Entrance just beyond Heperus Road behind Ravenswood Community Church.

Parking: For twenty cars.

80. STAGE FORT PARK
Western Avenue (Route 127), Gloucester
45 acres   *Gloucester Park Department   1930

Activities: picnicking, walking, swimming, ballfields, boating, historic sites
Hours: 8:00 A.M. to dusk
Admission: free

When in 1624 a group of fishermen from Plymouth Colony arrived off Cape Ann to pursue the Almighty Cod, they found that a small band of early Massachusetts Bay Colony fishermen had settled on Cape Ann the year before. Nonetheless, the Plymouth colonists set up fishing stages here to dry their catch. The stages, also known as flakes, were long open rows of branches or slats upon which the gutted fish were salted and laid in the sun to dry. On the low area behind the beach, the fishermen set up salt pans to sun-dry salt for their fish curing. When the Massachusetts Bay colonists set up fortifications on the heights here overlooking Gloucester Harbor, the place became known as Stage Fort.

The fort was occupied during King Philip's and King George's wars and two companies of militia were garrisoned here during the Revolution. The fort was enlarged during the War of 1812, but British raiders nonetheless invaded Gloucester. During both the Civil and Spanish-American wars the fort was again mobilized, then it was allowed to decline. In 1930 the fort was turned over to the town, restored, and turned into a park.

257

Activities:

Old fortifications and cannons, granite crags, and cliffs with a commanding view of Gloucester Harbor, two small beaches, and a playground: this is one of the nicest family shoreside parks in the region.

Picnicking: Picnic tables along the beach and among the rocks, some shaded. Lots of places to toss down a blanket or set up chairs. Well-equipped children's play area. Grassy fields and a softball diamond. Bathrooms, bubbler, nearby snack bars.

Swimming: Two small, reasonably clean beaches are fine for kids. The larger beach has lifeguards and a diving float.

Walking: Along beach by Fishermen's Memorial or clamber over the rocks. Surprising amount of territory to explore for a small park.

Boating: Small launching ramp for canoes or cartop boats at end of beach.

Directions:

On Western Avenue (Route 127) just before it jogs right to enter the town of Gloucester.

Parking: Plenty except on the very busiest weekends; Gloucester residents may have priority.

81. GOOD HARBOR BEACH
Thatcher Road (Route 127) Gloucester
*Gloucester Park Department

Activities: swimming, picnicking, birdwatching
Hours: 10:00 A.M. to 8:00 P.M.
Admission: three dollars a car

This long crescent of satiny, light-gray sand is the finest beach open to the public on the "island" of Cape Ann. Nearly a mile long, the beach fronts on Little Good Harbor and Salt Island. According to Copeland and Rogers's *The Saga of Cape Ann,* legend had it that the harbor was named Little Good by an Indian who wanted to indicate that it was not a good anchorage. But Copeland and Rogers found that a basin had once existed on the tidal stream behind the beach, and that early Gloucester fishermen probably tied up their boats there, making it a little, good harbor.

Good Harbor Beach is a bay-mouth barrier beach, a long spit of sand strung across the mouth of an indentation in the shoreline. Sand pounded off glacial headlands was sent streaming parallel to the shoreline by wind- and water-created currents. In the quiet protected waters behind the beach, silt running off the land and entering with the tide settled in the protected bay and built up, preparing the way for a tall, waving salt marsh such as we see here. This is just the sort of place for some good birdwatching.

Activities:

This is a very popular beach, much used by the locals. To avoid the weekend crowds, why not walk around Dogtown, then come here in the afternoon?
Swimming: Plenty of room to toss down a blanket or chairs. Clean, fairly wide beach, though parts are rocky. Fair-sized waves but a gradual dropoff make this a good beach for children. Lifeguards. Bathrooms, bathhouse, snack bar.

Directions:

North of East Gloucester on Thatcher Road (Route 127A).
Parking: Plenty except on weekends, so arrive early then.

82. DOGTOWN
Gloucester and Rockport
More than 2,000 acres   Gloucester Water Reserve
*Rockport Town Forest   *Gloucester Conservation Commission

Activities: nature study, walking and hiking, birdwatching, historic sites, berrypicking, ski touring, jogging, picnicking
Hours: dawn to dusk
Admission: free

Old cellar holes, paths that peter out in a tangle of overgrown shrubbery, and carved granite boulders: these are merely the outward signs of the legends and old stories haunting the former Cape Ann Commons. This vast area of old fields, rocky woodlands, and wetlands is the nearest thing in Eastern Massachusetts to a genuine ghost town and a beautiful place to wander in and explore.

The earliest settlers of Cape Ann were farmers rather than fishermen, and so they built their first meetinghouse in 1642 on the Green along the Annisquam River rather than by Gloucester Harbor. As a community grew around the Green's meetinghouse, it soon became apparent that there was a shortage of tillable land. To meet this deficiency the low plateau in the center of Cape Ann was designated a common. Each settler of the Green was allowed rights to cut fuel and building wood, and graze cattle and sheep there. By 1646 a road had developed between the Green and the Commons for herding animals and trucking out wood; that road was improved in 1707 to provide access to a sawmill along the Mill River. The original road between the Green and the settlement at Annisquam also ran through the Commons.

In 1719 the Commons was divided among individual residents of the Green, a number of whom began to move to the logged-off tract. Twenty-five years later there were twenty-five houses in the little settlement and at its peak before the Revolution there may have been upward of a hundred houses, a schoolhouse, grocery store, and blacksmith shop. But the soil quality was poor and barely able to support gardens, never mind farms. The opening of a new road to Annisquam reduced through traffic. The growth of the fishing industry along the shore attracted many Commons settlers to its more abundant life-style. By 1830 the Commons village was no more, there having been only a handful of residents over the previous twenty years. Only a few abandoned pet dogs remained to lord it over the husks of the settlement, leading the locals to call the former Commons Dogtown.

Yet it was the declining years of the Commons that inspired the most tantalizing legends. During the Revolution and again during the War of 1812, shoreside residents of Cape Ann, including some of the wealthiest citizens, fled to the Commons, but few remained once hostilities ended. After the Revolution, as the village's long-time residents moved out, poor widows—many of whom had lost their husbands in the war—moved into the slowly degenerating houses. To survive, they took in washing, supplied the more prosperous Gloucester townspeople with berries, herbs, and tonics, and told fortunes. Because there was little to do for entertainment in the shoreside towns, young people often came to the Commons for picnics, and the old widows sold them johnnycakes and told their fortunes with coffee grounds. The last resident of the Commons was "Black Neil," an old black man who lived in a cellar until he was taken to the poorhouse in 1830, where he died just a week later.

The former village no longer had any residents, but the people of Gloucester and Annisquam continued to pasture sheep, cattle, and horses in the open fields. As a boy, Roger Babson, born in 1875, took the family cows to pasture on a corner of Dogtown. After making a fortune as a financier, founding Babson College, and running for president on the Prohibitionist ticket, Babson returned to Gloucester and Dogtown became one of his leading interests. He wrote a little book about the ancient Commons. He purchased 1,100 acres of Dogtown and donated it to Gloucester as park and watershed-protection land in the late 1920s. He supervised the carving of large glacial erratics with numbers designating cellar holes and with didactic mottos. While wandering through the woods, one comes upon a high granite rock that says "Help Mother," and another that says "Prosperity Follows Service," and another, "Save."

Until World War II the locals returned to Dogtown to cut firewood and graze a horse or two. Over the years another thousand acres of Dogtown have been acquired by the town and public and private conservation agencies to protect the two artificial reservoirs and to preserve this huge chunk of open space for future generations and the public's enjoyment.

Once completely wooded, in its heyday Dogtown's central area, a sand and gravel moraine laid down by the glacier, was a patchwork of pastureland crossed by stone walls constructed of boulders wrested from the fields. Though some old fields remain, most of the former pastureland and the house sites have been taken over by red cedar, juniper, black cherry, white birch, raspberry, huckleberry, sumac, and blueberry. Around the rocky hills and great lichen-covered boulder fields and boulder mounds, oaks and beeches grow anew. Most of the low spots are submerged in swamps with sweet pepperbush and red maple predominating and such unusual wildflowers as pitcher plants and sundews also growing. The southeast shore of Briar Swamp, once mined for bog iron, shelters a fine grove of old-growth hemlocks and the densest stand of mountain laurels in the region, filling the air with pink blossoms in June.

Activities:

Dogtown is certainly one of the most interesting places to explore on the North Shore as well as being quite beautiful and naturally diverse. The blueberries and blackberries are just about the most abundant in the entire region, though mosquitoes are thick in the late July and August picking season; be sure to bring insect repellent. *The AMC Massachusetts and Rhode Island Trail Guide* and *The Wilds of Cape Ann* include maps that are notably helpful here. All the maps currently available leave off minor trails, and so a wandering expedition here can be very confusing: therefore, be sure to bring your compass and a canteen. No facilities.

Hiking and walking: At least fifteen miles of old roads and trails course through remnant fields, skirt wetlands, and wind over rocky hills. Some of the trails have been blazed by friends of the local conservation commission: red dots lead from the northeast side of Babson Reservoir to Dogtown Square; green-over-orange dots lead from Dogtown Square to Whale's Jaw, a great fractured glacial erratic; orange dots mark the trail around the south shore of Briar Swamp to Poole's Hill; and blue dots lead south from the Briar Swamp dam.

Dogtown Road, Wharf Road, and Commons Road provide easy walking through the most interesting part of the tract. The trails from Briar Swamp south and Babson Reservoir north are fairly rugged.

Picnicking: Plenty of fine sites for pack-it-in/pack-it-out picnics. No facilities.

Nature study: See *Wilds of Cape Ann* in "Reading" below.

Birdwatching: Thickets, berries, and wetlands make for an abundance of birdlife here during all seasons. In spring and fall large flocks of migrating warblers fill the upland shrubbery.

Historic sites: The Dogtown map in *The Saga of Cape Ann* is a must for anyone searching for old cellar holes; see "Reading" below.

Jogging: Dogtown is a favorite jogging place for the local people. Squam Road, Dogtown Road, Commons Road, and portions of Wharf Road are wide and open old woods roads with gravelly surfaces.

Ski touring: Excellent. Use the same trails as in jogging because other trails are steep or narrow in many places. No grooming but good track established by locals. Map a must.

Reading:

A good account of the history of Dogtown appears in *The Saga of Cape Ann,* available at most libraries and in Cape Ann bookstores. *The Wilds of Cape Ann* includes an excellent guide to the natural history of Dogtown and provides three detailed walks; available at local bookstores or from Resources for Cape Ann, 159 Main Street, Gloucester, MA 01930.

Directions:

Second Route 128 rotary to Blackburn Industrial Park; park on dirt road beyond pavement and walk back to pathway leading to Babson Reservoir by carved boulders. Lots of parking. Red-dot trail leads north to Dogtown Square just across railroad tracks on right.

Or: First Route 128 rotary, north on Route 127, right on Reynard Street to end, left on Cherry Street, then right on unmarked Dogtown Road. Park across from gravel pit. Most direct route to Dogtown Square.

Or: Route 127 through Rockport, left on Squam Road. Park along road after pavement ends. Shortest route to Whale's Jaw.

83. HALIBUT POINT RESERVATION
Gott Avenue, Rockport
12.5 acres   *Trustees of Reservations   1934
52 acres   *State Reservation   1982

Activities: picnicking, nature study, fishing, scenic area, birdwatching

Hours: half hour before sunrise to half hour after sunset
Admission: one dollar each adult weekdays, two dollars
weekends

Out on the northern tip of rocky Cape Ann, this granite headland
soars fifty and more feet above the crashing Atlantic surf and is one
of the outstanding scenic areas of the Massachusetts coastline. The
country lane that leads out to the reservation is walled by a lush
green catbrier jungle, winding its way up black cherry, locust, lilac,
and shagbark hickory trees. Gray-barked juneberry trees, with the
first white blossoms of spring, are laden in June with deep purple
berries that make a luscious pie. At the head of the lane is the
home of Samuel Gott, a weaver from Wenham who built the first
home on the point in 1702.

No one knows for sure how Halibut Point received its name,
but historians believe it was given because this is the place where
coastal sailing vessels "hauled about" to tack into Ipswich Bay. In
1934 Dr. John C. Phillips and the Village Improvement Society of
Pigeon Cove raised $1,500, purchased 12.5 acres of Halibut Point,
and donated it to the Trustees.

Near the water, steplike pink slabs of Cape Ann granite are
flaking off, the result of water seeping into tiny cracks, freezing,
and expanding. Some slabs were quarried, and to the left of the
Reservation in the new state park is an impressive nineteenth-
century site known as Babson's Quarry. Along the shore are two
towering heaps of quarry tailings probably used as piers to load
rock onto sailing vessels below. Back from the shore is the main
quarry site, a shimmering emerald pool today.

Among the cliffs grow bayberry, arrowwood, and blackberry, as
well as such wildflowers as wood lily, violet, wild aster, and
goldenrod. Down by the water's edge extensive tide pools filled
with rockweed, hermit crabs, and starfish are a natural attraction
for explorative children.

From the cliffs, the visitor looks east to Europe, west to Plum
Island and Salisbury, and northwest to the coasts of Maine and
New Hampshire and the hazy blue dome of Mount Agamenticus.

Activities:

Outstanding scenic viewing. Great place to visit in the off-
season to watch crashing surf, particularly after a storm,
but dress warmly. Use caution on the wet rocks; they can
be quite slippery.

Picnicking: Great spot to picnic; lots of places to look around. Fires permitted on the rocks with permit from Rockport Fire Department. No facilities.

Fishing: From rocky shore. Mackerel, striped bass, pollock.

Birding: Hundreds of cormorants. Migrating hawks in fall, woodland birds in the interior. Winter sea ducks and occasional gannets.

Directions:

Route 27, two and a half miles north of Rockport Center, turn right on Gott Avenue (sign at Old Farm Inn), proceed to parking lots.

Parking: If the first lot is filled, there is a private lot beyond the Gott House.

84. WINGAERSHEEK BEACH
Atlantic Street, Gloucester
50 acres   *Gloucester Park Department

Activities: saltwater swimming, picnicking, nature study, winter birding, and walking
Hours: 9:00 A.M. to 6:00 P.M.
Admission: four dollars a car weekdays; five dollars weekends and holidays

I still remember the feeling of delight when of a hot Sunday my folks would say: "Let's go to Wingaersheek." Of all the beaches in the region perhaps none is more favored by kids. There are great pink granite rocks to clamber over; sandy tide pools filled with glass shrimp and fish stranded by the outgoing tide; and a fabulous sandbar along the entrance to the Annisquam River. Wandering through the shallows along the beach side of the sandbar, which extends out nearly half a mile, we always found sand dollars, hermit and horseshoe crabs, moon snail shells, and occasionally a sea urchin. The beachgrass-covered dunes behind the beach are enlivened by seaside goldenrod, pink blossoms of salt-spray rose, and the red-fruited staghorn sumac—not to mention abundant poison ivy. Behind the beach is an extensive salt marsh.

Wingaersheek Beach is actually only a part of the longer Coffin's Beach, which extends to the northwest and is privately owned. Large mounds of clamshells found here by the early settlers of Cape Ann tell us that this was a summer resort of the local Indians. Settled around 1635 by English colonists, the area passed through several hands before being purchased by Tristam Coffin in 1688. It was developed by his son and grandson into one of the largest farms in Gloucester, totaling around five hundred acres. The Coffins sold the fine sand from their beach to householders from Boston to Portsmouth for use as a wood-floor cleaner and for winter insulation. During the Revolution, Major Coffin and his friends drove away a marauding group of British raiders seeking to steal his mutton sheep pastured here. In 1882 the land was subdivided and sold as lots for resort homes, a proceeding greatly accelerated after World War II.

How the portion of the beach known as Wingaersheek received its name is not clear. There are legends that this was a landing place of Norse explorers and that they named it. Another theory has it that the "hoek" was the Dutch form of "hook" and referred to the hook-shaped beach with its sandbar, early settlers having been exiled in Holland before emigrating to New England.

Activities:

This is an extremely nice beach for children of all ages. It is very crowded on Sundays, and so come early or during the week if you can.

Swimming: The beach is composed of very fine gray sand, excellent for building sandcastles. The surf is gentle, the dropoff gradual, and though the water is shallow at low tide, you can walk out to the sandbar then. Lifeguards. Crystal-clear water that, though cool, is about the warmest for a North Shore Beach.

Picnicking: Plenty of room to spread blankets or beach chairs. Complete snack bar, bathrooms, bathhouse, and first aid station. Please don't litter or bring glass containers.

Walking: This is a nice beach to wander in the winter, particularly when the tide is out. Good winter birding.

Directions:

Route 128 north to exit 13; follow signs to beach, continuously bearing right.

Parking: Plan on arriving by 11:00 A.M. at the latest on weekends.

84A. LONG WHARF
Atlantic Street, Gloucester
25 acres   *Gloucester Conservation Commission   1977–1979

Activities: walking, birdwatching, nature study
Hours: dawn to dusk
Admission: free

Long Wharf is a granite pier built in 1880 to load stone quarried across the street into boats, though the quarry failed before it ever got going. Smugglers supposedly used the wharf during Prohibition days. The wharf sticks out into a marsh dominated by salt-marsh cordgrass and ends at the tidal Jones River. A trail on the left leads out to Boynton Island, a low mound of glacial deposits covered with a forest of oak, sassafras, beech, and pitch pine, with a few stands of shadbush and tupelo. On a summer afternoon you are likely to find snowy egrets, greater yellowlegs, semipalmated sandpipers, and a kingfisher or two along the wharf or over the marshes.

Activities:

This is a nice place to take a walk on your way home from Wingaersheek. You can stroll out to the end of the wharf and around the island in an hour or less. The private property at the far end of the island should be respected.

Directions:

A mile from the beach, headed back to Boston, on the left, just before a snack bar.
Parking: Plenty.

85. CRANE BEACH RESERVATION
Richard T. Crane Reservation, Argilla Road, Ipswich, MA 01938
1,400 acres   Trustees of Reservations   1945

Activities: swimming, nature study, birdwatching, walking and hiking, fishing
Hours: closes at sunset
Admission: four dollars a car weekdays; six dollars weekends for parking during summer; lower rates off-season

In 1634 the Ipswich town fathers voted "That the Neck of Land whereupon the great Hill standeth, which is known by the name of the Castle Hill, lying on the other side of the river towards the sea, shall remayne unto the comon use of the Towne forever." The four-and-a-half-mile Castle Neck had once served as a summer resort and clamming and fishing ground of the Agawam Indians and one prehistoric campsite on the neck has been carbon-14 dated as 9,000 years old, making it one of the earliest Indian sites identified in New England. Most of the local Indians were wiped out by plague and smallpox epidemics that preceded the first white settlers.

In 1637, in an effort to keep John Winthrop, Jr., one of the founders of the Ipswich settlement, from moving to Connecticut, Ipswich granted him Castle Hill and the neck in contradiction to their earlier "forever" commons regulation. Though the land was granted with the condition that Winthrop live there, he apparently never did; in 1644 the town unsuccessfully contested his right to sell the land he had never occupied. That year Winthrop did sell a portion of his lands to Samuel Symonds, a farmer; the rest of Winthrop's lands were sold in 1660 to another farmer, Daniel Epes.

In spite of these transactions, the neck was used as a commons. By 1646 Ipswich had become a principal supplier of beef to Boston, and every day the herds were driven out to graze the beach grass of the neck. Regulations were passed controlling this grazing and forbidding the cutting of trees without the written permission of the town. All timber cutting was prohibited in 1650 because of the blowing sands set free by the destruction of the groundcover. Finally in 1664 the neck, along with other common lands, was divided among private proprietors.

A group of destitute Indians from Lake Winnipesaukee settled for a year on one of the neck's hills beginning in 1669, causing it to be named Wigwam Hill. Occasionally carpenters were given permission to cut timber on the neck and Ipswich's blacksmiths were granted the right to cut pitch pines on the neck, and nowhere else—for charcoal for their forges. During the Revolution a watchtower was erected on Castle Hill and equipped with a flagpole, tar, and other combustibles to give an alarm if the British were sighted.

Castle Hill was purchased in 1843 by Manasseh Brown, who began landscaping the grounds with ornamental trees and shrubs, a beautification still going on in our own day. Around the turn of the century the property passed to John B. Brown, a wealthy Chicagoan. Although Castle Neck had been privately owned, it had nonetheless been treated for 250 years as semipublic commons land, the locals digging clams on the mudflats, hunting in the marshes, and fishing from the beaches. When Brown fenced off the neck with barbed wire in 1903, believing in the ultimate right of private property, the locals were outraged. Town officials themselves snipped the wire and entered the neck, thumbing their noses at Brown, and forcing him to subordinate his "sacred rights" to those of the townspeople. In 1910 he sold his property to Richard T. Crane.

Crane, also a wealthy Chicagoan, a manufacturer of plumbing fixtures, built a magnificent Italian villa on Castle Hill, only to tear it down in 1925. Work was immediately begun on a huge new Georgian mansion, designed by architect David Adler. The thirty-five-room "great house" has elaborate woodcarvings, massive fireplaces, and all the other amenities of the age of elegance. The grounds were landscaped on designs by the Olmsted firm and Arthur Shurcliff, designer of Franklin Park Zoo. After Crane's death, his wife donated Castle Hill and Neck to the Trustees as a memorial to her husband.

The neck is a long barrier spit, punctuated by two drumlins, Castle Hill and Wigwam Hill. The excellent "Pine Hollow Interpretive Trail" booklet, available at the beach office or entrance station, provides thorough discussions of the geological evolution of the beach as well as the flora and fauna that may be found there. Several maps and cross-sections of the beach make the booklet an outstanding introduction to all the barrier beaches of the region.

Activities:

Crane Beach is one of the most popular and beautiful beaches on the North Shore. Though the beach is very crowded on weekends, it is long enough so that if you walk a way, you will find all the privacy you desire. Make your day at the beach a learning experience by picking up the Pine Hollow Guide booklet. Try visiting in April when the shadbush is in bloom or in early September when the shorebirds are migrating. Heed all erosion-control signs; the dunes at Castle Neck are very fragile.

Swimming: Beautiful white sand beach, gentle dropoff, and varying surf. Lifeguards along most heavily used section. Toilets, bathhouses, and complete snack bar. Delightful.

Walking and hiking: Along four miles of beach and through dunes. Begin with Pine Hollow walk. Stay off posted dunes. Best walking in the spring and fall, when the sands are not shimmering hot.

Nature study: Take the Pine Hollow walk. Booklet at office.

Fishing: Surf fishing beyond swimming area and around dusk when the beach is clear of bathers. Striped bass, bluefish, flounder.

Castle Hill: The Great House is open for occasional tours: call Reservation for times and more information: 356-4351. An outstanding classical music concert series is held each summer on the "grande allée" looking over the neck, the marshes, and the distant hills of southern Maine.

Directions:

Route 1A north to Ipswich, right on Argilla Road at sign to beach.

Parking: Plenty.

Telephone: 356-4351

85A. CORNELIUS AND MINÉ S. CRANE WILDLIFE REFUGE
Essex and Ipswich
700 acres   *Trustees of Reservations   1974

Activities: nature study, birdwatching, historic site, walking
Admission: adults two dollars; children one dollar

Nestled between Castle Neck and the mainland, this refuge, donated to the Trustees by Mrs. Cornelius Crane, is a green wonderland of marshes and five islands at the mouth of the Essex River. Hog Island (also called Choate Island), a drumlin and the largest of the islands, was farmed by the Choate family for more than two hundred years. The farmhouse on Hog Island was built by Thomas Choate in 1725 and adds great cultural interest to the island's landscape. Senator Rufus Choate was born here in 1799. The former summer cottage of Mrs. Crane, also on Hog Island, is now a visitor center with displays of the Reservation's natural history. Rising 177 feet above the marshes, the island is covered with woodlands and old fields, and boasts a spectacular view of the neck and marshes and a substantial population of white-tailed deer. Migratory waterfowl and shorebirds are of special interest in the fall.

The island is accessible by boat only; a canoe will do at any tide. Launching ramp at end of Island Street in Essex. A naturalist-historian conducts tours of the island. This is a very special place to visit.

Friends of Hog Island, P.O. Box 228, Ipswich, MA 01938, holds an annual field day on the island, providing transportation and activities. A map of the island and self-guiding tour appear in *The Wilds of Cape Ann.*

86. OLD TOWN HILL
Newman Road, Newbury
293 acres   *Trustees of Reservations   1952

Activities: hiking, views, ski touring, nature study
House: dawn to dusk
Admission: no charge

From the top of this huge, gently rounded drumlin, surrounded by the marshes of the Parker River and Newbury's horsefields, we look east on the two long sandspits of Plum Island and Castle Neck and to the sparkling Atlantic beyond; north to blue Mount Agamenticus and the low Isles of Shoals, and south to rocky Cape Ann. A pastureland nearly devoid of trees at the beginning of this century, today portions of the hill, 168 feet above sea level, are again covered with woodlands. On several slopes the old fields are maintained by annual mowing; thus at least a part of the hill has been constantly farmed for close to 350 years.

Old Town Hill was first settled by John Kelly in the early 1600s and used by him as a sheep pasture. A contemporary record tells that he killed a wolf there that was attacking his sheep. "A huge and ancient elm" that stood on the summit of the hill served as a landmark to generations of coasting mariners.

The old timothy field at the beginning of the summit trail has been invaded by common saint-john's-wort, Queen Anne's lace, Virginia creeper, deptford pink, rough-fruited cinquefoil, raspberry, and the flaming orange hawkweed. In the woods beyond, the fields have been completely obliterated by crabapples, red cedar, buckthorn, red oak, and white pine. Dense thickets of pasture rose, honeysuckle, quaking aspen, staghorn sumac, and arrowwood crowd the unmown sections of the summit. Where the fields have been mown and the vistas maintained, innumerable asters and daisies add a dash of color in season to the beige and green grasses. Ah, it is very peaceful here listening to a catbird or watching a red-tail hawk sailing over the slopes and marshes below.

Activities:

Stop here on your way back from Plum Island; it's only a ten-minute jaunt to the summit and the view is great. Don't forget your binoculars or your mosquito repel-lent—the mosquitos can be extremely annoying here in July and August. Tall-grass fields are great to tumble around in the fall.

Walking: Trail to summit is ten-minute walk. Continue over the summit and down the far side of the hill to the road and then walk back to your car for a one-and-a-half-mile circuit.

Ski touring: Fields around the summit particularly suitable for ski touring.

Directions:

Route 1A north through Rowley. After crossing Parker River, Newbury Common is on your left with Newman Street on its far side. Entrance on right a few hundred yards up Newman Street.

Parking: Along road. Limited.

87. PLUM ISLAND

*Parker River Wildlife Refuge Northern Boulevard, Plum Island, Newburyport, MA 01950
4,650 acres   U.S. Department of the Interior   1942
80 plus acres   Plum Island State Park   Circa 1960

Activities: birdwatching, nature study, picnicking, swim-ming, fishing, walking and hiking, ski touring
Map: free at entrance (ask for it) or send SASE
Hours: dawn to dusk
Admission: no charge

Plum Island is unquestionably the most spectacular birdwatching site in New England. From March, when the impoundments are flush with tens of thousands of ducks and geese, to the following January, when your chances of seeing a snowy owl are as good here as anywhere, there is always some avian action—more than 300 bird species have been sighted here.

Built up in the last ten thousand years as sand pounded off glacial headlands and pouring out the mouth of the Merrimack River was formed into a sandbar by longshore currents, Plum Island is one of the largest and least-developed barrier islands on the Atlantic seaboard. Like Duxbury Beach or the Outer Banks of North Carolina, this long stretch of sand forms a barrier between the pounding ocean surf and the mainland.

Barrier beaches, like Plum Island and many of the other ocean beaches in the state, are "colonized" by beach grass, particles of which wash ashore and take root. Beach grass—*Ammophila arenaria* in Latin, the first meaning "sand-loving"—captures windblown sand and slowly builds up a dune, which in turn captures even more sand. As the long roots of the beach grass stabilize the beach, dusty miller, seaside goldenrod, beach pea, and seabeach sandwort, all plants tolerant of salt spray, begin to grow beyond the reach of the waves. Dunes continue to build higher, providing protection from the wind and salt spray, allowing bayberry, beach plum, and salt-spray rose to take hold just over the dune crest. As the dunes continue to grow and the beach grows wider, pitch pine, juneberry, scrub oak, and black cherry begin to appear singly and in thickets behind. In the sheltered embayment between the beach and the mainland, where silt can settle, a salt marsh develops. This complex construction has occurred here over the last several thousand years, resulting in seven-mile-long Plum Island.

Complicating the geological story of Plum Island are four mounds of glacial deposits embedded within the beach. These deposits provide a habitat different from that of the beach and likewise a different flora and fauna. The rounded hill at the southern end of the island, within the state park, is such a drumlin.

In 1639 Plum Island was included in the towns of Newbury, Ipswich, and Rowley, and managed as a common. While cows grazed the dunes and men hayed the marshes, the ownership of the island was a source of dispute between the towns. In 1664 the island was divided among those private individuals with commonage rights there and so entered private ownership—though each fishing boat out of Ipswich was allowed to graze one cow in the tall grasses. By 1679 the people of Ipswich were becoming disturbed that cattle grazing the beach grass was permitting sand to blow

away, thus "damnifying" the beach. Even back then people could see that barrier beaches were fragile: in 1739 the General Court finally put an end to horse and cattle grazing on the island, at least temporarily.

The towns around Plum Island all became great seaports during the eighteenth century and it became necessary to isolate sailors arriving from foreign ports suspected of being disease carriers, and so in 1769 the towns combined efforts and built a small quarantine hospital on the island. During the 1776 smallpox epidemic, a guard was stationed on Old Town Bridge to prevent the hospital inmates from leaving the island.

At the start of the Revolution batteries were erected at the northern end of the island to protect Newburyport from British attack. The cannons installed were a monstrous forty-two pounder and two twenty-four or eighteen pounders. The battery was reestablished during the War of 1812, and though it saw no action, there was a skirmish on the island. A British crew, hungry for meat rather than battle, put ashore some distance from the guns and killed a cow. They began to carve it up, but before they could finish the job, the Americans drove them off. In 1816 the fort was dismantled and sold at auction.

In 1807 landward access to the island was facilitated by the completion of the Plum Island Turnpike, a long causeway through the marshes with a substantial bridge over the Plum Island River. Soon the first of many resort hotels opened, fetching a clientele of sport hunters. By the middle of the century though, hundreds of market hunters were shooting thousands of birds a day to supply the serving boards of Newburyport and Boston, with little regard for species. The little village on the northern end of the island started to grow after 1897 when the Plum Island Electric Street Railway began to provide regular summer service between the island and downtown Newburyport.

After the Migratory Bird Treaty was passed, stopping the market hunters and protecting dozens of species that had been driven to the verge of extinction, birders and scientists realized that something more was needed to ensure regeneration of depleted bird populations. Birds needed places to rest and nest on their long migratory journeys, and Plum Island was the ideal sort of site. In the 1930s Massachusetts Audubon Society began to buy land here for a sanctuary. In 1942 the U.S. Fish and Wildlife Service purchased the Audubon Society's 1,600 acres and 3,050 additional acres of the island, thus beginning the refuge as we know it today.

Beach grass and trees were planted to stabilize the eroding dunes. Fires were controlled. Two long dikes were built, forming 262 acres of freshwater impoundments to provide habitat for freshwater-seeking birds. More than 300 bird species have been sighted on the refuge. The more common ducks of the marshes are still hunted, but now they are ably managed for a sustained yield. America's National Wildlife Refuges are in large measure purchased and sustained by the sale of annual duck-hunting stamps required for all duck hunters.

No matter at what season you visit here, no matter what the state of your birding skills, if you own a pair of binoculars you are going to see birds. If you bring along a field guide, you will probably expand your bird list. Summer's swimmers are never far from wheeling and crying terns. As many as seven hundred snowy egrets have their annual convention here in August, just when thousands of tree swallows are filling the air and warblers are beginning to gather for the trip south. From spring to fall the shallow marsh ponds, known as salt pans, attract dowitchers, rails, knots, a half-dozen species each of sandpipers, sanderlings, and plovers, and great blue, black-crowned night, and green herons. Fall brings more warblers, a myriad of ducks, and an abundant hawk migration. The bay serves as winter home for mergansers, buffleheads, oldsquaws, goldeneyes, and loons, while off the beach gannets dive-bomb into the waves. Each spring the ducks wintering farther south return and those which don't pass on northward settle in: by June the impoundments are swarming with quietly peeping ducklings and goslings.

Activities:

Greenhead flies can be a real problem here during July and August, though the numbers of these vicious little biters has sharply declined since the introduction into the marshes of the mysterious black-box traps. Though there are flyless days even during the height of the greenhead season, and some people just don't get bitten, be prepared to leave unless you've remembered your insect repellent.

On weekends you should arrive here by 9:00 A.M. at the latest: the parking lots fill up and the gates may therefore be closed. If the gates are closed, they will reopen at 3:00 P.M. Fall is a good time for a beach-plum or cranberry-picking excursion.

Restrooms at entrance (beach) and Hellcat Swamp parking lots.

Swimming: One of the most spectacular beaches in Massachusetts, six and a half miles of clean white sand, dunes, sun, and waves. No lifeguards—be careful. Surf may be heavy and undertows may be a problem. The water is cold until pretty late in the summer; that's the best time to swim here anyway, because the greenheads have declined, if not disappeared, by then. Miles of room to spread out, though dunebuggies use the end of the island. Bathhouse and toilets.

Walking: Walk the long beach to your heart's content at any season. It is always fabulous. You can also walk down the refuge road, but passing cars raise a lot of dust.

There are two self-guiding nature trails on Plum Island, each less than an hour's walk and each equipped with its own small parking lot. Hellcat Swamp Trail is a good tour of a birdy freshwater swamp, glacial deposits, and the marshes; observation tower. Plum Island State Park at the tip of the island has a well-thought-out trail over the drumlin that is the island's terminus; outstanding views of Ipswich Bay, Crane Beach, and Plum Island itself. Free interpretive brochures are available at Hellcat Swamp and state park trails.

Fishing: Outstanding surf casting for saltwater sport fish. Ask for free fishing brochure when you arrive or send SASE. Night fishing by permit.

Birdwatching: Free bird list at entrance station.

Ski touring: Although the snow doesn't last long here because the air is warmed by the ocean and salt spray is always blowing, when there is snow Plum Island becomes a wonderland of beauty and an exceptional place to ski. Two trails have been laid out, beginning at parking lots 3 and 5. Obtain map at the entrance or Refuge Headquarters and come when the snow is fresh.

Reading:

Barrier islands and beaches not only grow, they migrate toward shore as the sea level rises. The geology and natural history of barrier formations is a fascinating story, expertly told in Stephen P. Leatherman's *Barrier Island Handbook,* available from Cape Cod National Seashore, South Wellfleet, MA 02663.

Directions:

North on Route 1 in Danvers, turn right on Route 133 in Rowley, then left on Route 1A. North on 1A through Newbury. Follow signs to Parker River Refuge.

Telephone: 465-5753

88. SALISBURY BEACH STATE RESERVATION
Beach Road, Salisbury, MA 01950
520 acres   State Reservation

Activities: swimming, camping, fishing, picnicking, boating, walking, birdwatching
Hours: 8:00 A.M. to dusk
Admission: three dollars a car or state season pass

Salisbury Beach State Reservation is the southern tip of the long Salisbury barrier beach. To the north of the Reservation are the developed resort community and a popular amusement park. The Reservation itself is developed but very attractive, jutting out into the entrance to Newburyport Harbor and looking out toward Plum Island.

Activities:
Swimming: Three miles of clean white sand and clear cold water. Bathhouse, bathrooms, and snack bar. Lifeguards and first aid station. Fairly steep dropoff and heavy surf.
Camping: 481 campsites with grills, picnic tables, showers, and electrical connections. Little privacy, but pleasant atmosphere. Six dollars a night.
Fishing: Surf casting for striped bass, bluefish, pollock, and flounder. Jetty at end of beach particularly popular.
Picnicking: On the beach or at a few shaded picnic tables. Nearby children's play area, beach, snack bar, and bathrooms.
Boating: Launching ramp for motorboats at end of Reservation. Plenty of car and trailer parking.
Walking: Walk along the beach or out the long jetty at the end of the beach. Good birding and you may even see a seal.

Directions:
Routes 95, 1, or 1A north to Salisbury. Follow signs to beach.
Parking: Abundant.

Telephone: 462-4481

WEST PARKS

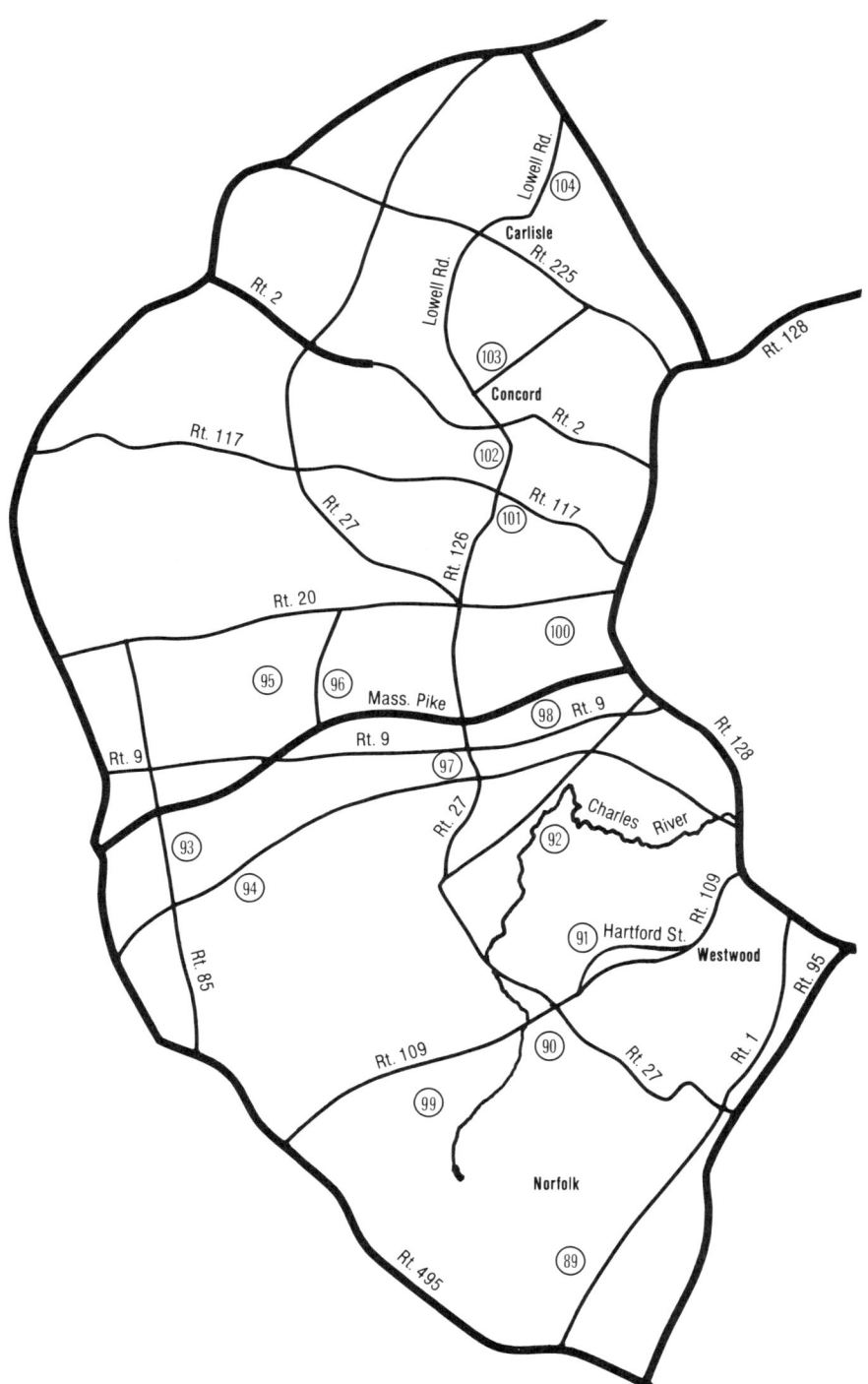

West Parks
Quick Guide to Outdoor Activities

	WALKING	PICNICKING	SWIMMING	JOGGING	NATURE STUDY	SKI TOURING	FISHING	BIRDWATCHING	HIKING	CANOEING & BOATING	ICE-SKATING	PROGRAMS	CAMPING	HORSEBACK RIDING	TOWERS, ZOOS, ETC	HISTORIC SITES	BALLFIELDS	TOT-LOTS	BIKE TRAILS	TENNIS
89. Stony Brook and Bristol-Blake State Reservation	•				•			•				•				•				
90. South Medfield																				
90A. Noon Hill	•	•			•	•			•											
90B. Shattuck Reservation	•				•			•												
90C. Medfield Rhododendrons	•				•															
90D. Stop River Bridge							•	•												
91. Rocky Woods Reservation	•	•		•	•	•	•	•	•											
92. South Natick																				
92A. Pegan Hill	•				•			•												
92B. South Natick Dam		•					•			•						•				
93. Hopkinton State Park	•	•	•	•			•	•		•										
94. Ashland State Park	•	•	•				•	•	•	•										
95. Callahan State Park	•	•			•	•	•		•	•										
96. Garden in the Woods	•				•							•								
97. Lake Cochituate State Park		•	•				•			•						•				
98. Wellesley																				
98A. Kelly Park/Boulder Brook Reservation, Rocky Ledges	•				•			•	•											
98B. Cochituate Aqueduct	•				•											•				
98C. Hunnewell Park	•	•			•			•												
99. Upper Charles River					•		•	•		•										
100. Case Estates	•				•			•												
101. Drumlin Farm Sanctuary	•				•	•		•				•								
102. Walden Pond State Reservation	•	•	•	•	•	•	•	•	•	•	•		•			•				
103. Great Meadows National Wildlife Refuge	•	•			•	•		•				•			•					
103A. Concord River					•		•			•										
104. Great Brook Farm State Park	•	•		•	•		•	•	•											

89. STONY BROOK SANCTUARY AND BRISTOL-BLAKE STATE RESERVATION
North Street, Norfolk, MA 02056
200 acres   State Reservation   1959
102 acres   Massachusetts Audubon Society   1963

Activities: nature study, birdwatching, walking, educational
   programs
Hours: sunrise to sunset
Admission: donations welcome

*Have you stopped lately to sit and meditate? If not, isn't this a good time
and a good place? How fast the world turns.*
"Stony Brook Self-Guiding Trail"

Even though less than a mile of trail comprises all the public access,
a rare, almost tangible quality of peacefulness here will quiet even
the most agitated city soul. This atmosphere is in sharp contrast to
the shrill command of the mill whistle and the roar of machinery
that filled the air for more than a hundred and fifty years along the
shallow valley of Stony Brook, a tributary of the Charles. Lost in
summer's rich atmosphere of roses and swamp honeysuckles, ears
tuned to the pleasingly grating squawk of a green heron, eyes
resting on the shimmering ponds, it is difficult to imagine the scale
of the industry that once ruled this place.

Norfolk was part of the huge Dedham Grant that was opened
up to settlers from Watertown in 1637 by the Great and General
Court. The Dedham Grant, which included the present towns of
Bellingham, Dedham, Dover, Franklin, Medfield, Natick, Needham, Norfolk, Norwood, Walpole, Wellesley, Westwood, and
Wrentham, was slow in attracting new settlers, in part because of
trouble with the dispossessed Indians. To encourage farming and
occupation of the area along the Stony Brook, an offer of free land,
haying rights in the marshes, and possession of the brook was made
to anyone who would build a "good and sufficient corn mill at
Stony Brook"—corn being the staple crop of the colonists and a
mill being an attractant to farmers.

Although a corn mill may have been erected, early records
speak only of a sawmill, owned by John Blake, Jr., and his son
James early in the 1700s. In 1762 Solomon Blake, a successful
farmer as well as a miller, and son of James, built a home for
himself nearby. The Blake family remained in this house until

1825, when it was sold. Then, in the 1920s, the house was repurchased by a descendant of the Blakes and has been occupied by the family ever since.

The area became industrialized, along with much of the rest of New England, when British trade restrictions and embargos after 1800 forced the region's shipping magnates to look to mills as an investment. The first major mill along the Stony Brook was the Cook, Blake, and Company cotton works, built in 1814. Along the outlet stream of the constantly expanded mill pond over the next fifty years the sawmill was enlarged, another cotton mill was built, and a box factory and a clothes-washing wringer factory were operated. In 1862 a shoddy mill was established that reclaimed wool to make a reprocessed fabric known as shoddy. Under the name Norfolk Woolen Company the mill grew larger and larger until just after the turn of the century. The earlier mills were all torn down and replaced by two new large woolen mills. Norfolk Woolen finally went out of business in 1932.

After several decades in limbo, the mill ponds and surrounding land were purchased by Mrs. Bennet Bristol, a descendant of the Blakes. In 1959 she donated 200 acres to the state as Bristol-Blake Reservation. Four years later she gave Massachusetts Audubon a house and land to build the Nature Center. Over the next ten years gifts of land increased Massachusetts Audubon's holdings to 102 acres. Mrs. Bristol was a lover of wildlife and an ardent conservationist, and so according to her deeded instructions, the property is strictly managed, there being no fishing, no vehicles, and no picnicking. Her continued involvement and the high quality of Massachusetts Audubon's management have made the area into a real "sea" of tranquility.

Kingfisher Pond and its surrounding wetlands, which make up most of the Reservation, attract nearly 200 bird species as migrants, nesters, and year-round residents, everything from the pied-billed grebe to the Blackburnian warbler. During the spring and fall the marshes fill with blue- and green-winged teal and geese, while the upland shrubs provide bed and breakfast to as many as seventeen warbler species. Numerous birds may be sighted here even during the relative quiet of summer.

A delightful boardwalk crosses the open marshes past highbush blueberry, blue-stalked pickerelweed, swamp azalea, sweet gale, forget-me-not, marsh skullcap, roses, and the ever-present purple loosestrife. The boardwalk leads to a beech-oak-witch hazel-covered little island where a shaded bench looks out over the extensive lily-pad marshes teeming with turtles, frogs, and birdlife.

The trail actually begins between two lichen-splotched pasture walls along which lacy ferns, dogwoods, violets, and blue-eyed grass thrive. After skirting another island, the trail goes past the cascading outlet stream and foundations which are all that remains of the Stony Brook's industrial past.

Activities:

If you want to see birds or just need a few moments to collect your thoughts, come to Stony Brook. The trail may be walked in an hour, though it's easy to stay longer. The self-guided nature-trail booklet is among the best written and the most informative of any in the region, and a good introduction to wetland ecology. Bathroom at Nature Center. Don't forget your binoculars, field guides, and camera.

Stony Brook Nature Center, which so ably manages the area, offers a truly intriguing diversity of programs to the public. Recent activities have included a 3:00 A.M. owl prowl, a tour of the Quabbin, an evening of searching for salamanders, orienteering sessions, and, of course, bird walks. The Center's offerings include seminars on environmental issues.

The Nature Center also offers a range of children's programs, discovery sessions for mothers with very young children, and a summer day camp.

Call or write for upcoming Center listings. Small fees are charged for some activities.

A bird club and photography club both meet here regularly.

Reading:

Stony Brook's Past, available for one dollar at Nature Center, is an excellent history of the human habitation of the Stony Brook Valley and Norfolk Basin.

Directions:

Route 1A south through Walpole, right on Route 115 in Norfolk, 1.5 miles to left on North Street.

Telephone: 528-3140

90. SOUTH MEDFIELD

90A. NOON HILL
Noon Hill Street, South Medfield
52 acres   *Trustees of Reservations and Town of Medfield   1959

Activities: walking and hiking, nature study, birdwatching, picnicking, ski touring
Hours: closes at dusk
Admission: no charge

Noon Hill, at 396 feet, is one of the highest hills southeast of Boston. A view has been cleared on the summit looking south across the valley of the Stop River to the long spinelike ridge that runs through Walpole. The summit of the hill, a fine place for a pack-it-in/pack-it-out picnic, is a lichen-covered rock garden of blackberries and blueberries with pink corydalis and sheep sorrel growing on mossy outcroppings. The quiet trails are lined with sweet fern, bracken fern, dwarf cinquefoil, and several species of violets. The extensive sloping woods are comprised primarily of red and white oak with scattered beech, white pine, and red cedar.

Noon Hill received its name from colonial inhabitants of the area "who marked the middle of the day as the sun rose above its ridge." During the Indian wars of the 1670s, King Philip reputedly camped on Noon Hill before swooping down to attack Medfield's farmsteads.

Three trails ascend the summit from Noon Hill Street, reached by heading south from Route 109 on Spring Street (Route 27) one mile to right on South Street, one mile to right on Noon Hill Street. A pleasant trail makes an easy ascent to the summit from the gravel pit on the left after crossing the Stop River. Another trailhead with parking place is across the street from the sportsmen's club. And another begins at little Holt Pond, a former mill site, though the parking's limited at this trailhead.

No facilities.

90B. SHATTUCK RESERVATION
Causeway Street, South Medfield
283 acres   *Trustees of Reservations   1970

This property of the Trustees protects nearly a mile and a quarter of river frontage along the Charles River south of the confluence of the Stop River. A dirt causeway, with parking for only one or two cars, leads out to the river through grapevine-shrouded trees. The trail runs south along the river through recently logged uplands between the river's marshes and the road. Route 109 to Causeway Street (first left beyond Route 27 in Medfield Center), property begins one-third mile beyond Stop River Bridge at causeway. Very limited parking. Park at sportsmen's club or Holt Pond and walk.

No charge. No facilities. Open year-round.

90C. MEDFIELD RHODODENDRONS
Spring Street, South Medfield
196 acres   *Trustees of Reservations   1934

This undeveloped area, whose main attraction is one of the few stands of native rosebay rhododendrons in New England, will be particularly interesting to lovers of wildflowers and wetlands. A cool hemlock-shaded woods road leads through the property, which was originally granted in 1663 to John Wilson, Medfield's first minister and a member of Harvard's first graduating class. Along the path sarsaparilla, lesser switchwort, inkberry, and other wildflowers may be found. At the end of the trail the dense thicket of evergreen rhododendrons forms a pink cloud of blossoms in early July. The boggy sphagnum swamp just beyond is populated with cinnamon and sensitive ferns and numerous jack-in-the-pulpits.

There is presently (early 1983) no public access; call 359-6333 for current status.

90D. STOP RIVER BRIDGE

This little bridge on Causeway Street sits in the middle of the Charles and Stop river marshes and is almost a sure place to sight a marsh hawk. Tall grasses, tussock sedge, blue flag irises, red maples, and royal and sensitive ferns line the roadway. Though parking is limited, this is a good place for kids to catch perch, sunfish, and catfish.

Route 109 to Causeway Street.

91. ROCKY WOODS RESERVATION
Hartford Street, Medfield, MA 02052
473 acres   Trustees of Reservations   1942

Activities: hiking, nature study, ski touring, fishing, picnicking
Map: available from Visitor Center
Hours: 9:00 A.M. to 6:00 P.M.
Admission: spring, summer, fall: $1.00 a person over 16
   Winter: weekends—under seventeen, $2.25; adult, $2.75
   weekdays—under seventeen, $1.75; adult, $2.25

Aptly named, Rocky Woods is a lovely pine and oak forest covering glacially scarred rocky outcroppings and glacial rubble. Given to the Trustees in 1942 by the former owner, Dr. Joel Goldthwait, the Reservation has been nicely laid out to provide an abundance of opportunities for peaceful recreation. Nine miles of trails, mostly easy walking, wind beneath white and red oaks, shagbark hickories, hemlocks, and white pines, as well as a profusion of chestnut sprouts and spindly sassafras trees. Flowering dogwoods here are especially attractive in late April. Mapleleaf viburnum, yellow star grass, royal fern, and pipsissewa are among the many wildflowers seen along the trails.

Four artificial ponds provide sanctuary for bellowing bullfrogs, green herons, and kingfishers. Echo Lake is covered by pink-blossomed lilies and the yellow flowers of the bladderwort, a carnivorous plant whose underwater bladders trap tiny water creatures. Because Rocky Woods is the divide between the Charles and Neponset River watersheds, Notch and June ponds send their waters tumbling to the Charles River, and Chickering and Echo lakes flow into the Neponset.

The igneous rock of the Reservation includes both Dedham Granodiorite and Salem Gabbro-diorite. The area was quarried as recently as the 1920s to provide blocks for the Norfolk County Courthouse in Dedham.

Activities:
Hiking: Twelve miles of shady trails, most with easy grades.
Nature study: Many wildflowers, interesting geology, decent birding. Hemlock Knoll Nature Trail (guidebook available at Rocky Woods Visitor Center) is one of the

finest and most informative self-guiding nature walks west of Boston.

Ski touring: Seven miles of excellently maintained, clearly marked trails. Reasonably priced equipment rentals. Beginner to expert. Visitor Center with fieldstone fireplace and woodstove.

Fishing: Fair-sized bass and pickerel as well as perch and sunfish. Best at Echo Lake.

Picnicking: Plenty of shady picnic tables around Chickering Lake, many with charcoal grills. Small ballfield and horseshoe-pitching area. Bathrooms. Swings and seesaws for kids. Several rain shelters. Large shelter available for group outings.

Directions:
VFW Parkway or Route 128 to Route 109 south; just beyond Westwood Center bear right on Hartford Street; Reservation entrance three miles on right.

Parking: Plenty.

Telephone: 359-6333

92. SOUTH NATICK

In 1651 the "praying Indians," who had been converted to the Christian faith by Reverend John Eliot, were granted 2,000 acres as a reservation in Natick, an Indian word meaning "Place of the Hills." Natick was laid out with farms and a church but the little community was not destined to survive. During King Philip's War fear of hostile tribes spilled over even to the Christian Indians. Eliot's charges were rounded up and interned under the most brutal conditions on Deer Island in Boston Harbor. Only one old squaw is believed to have returned to South Natick.

92A. PEGAN HILL
Pegan Lane, South Natick
32 acres   *Trustees of Reservations   1956

Activities: walking, nature study, picnicking

Hours: dawn to dusk
Admission: no charge

This 410-foot glacial drumlin was allotted to Thomas Pegan, one of Eliot's "praying Indians," when South Natick was divided. The hill served as pasture and farmland until the beginning of our own century, when it was allowed to revert to its present wild state. Red cedars, old stone walls, spring holes, and old-field plant species are indicative of the hill's agricultural past.

A quiet trail leads to the wooded summit where a viewpoint is maintained of Great Blue Hill. The trail is lined with highbush cranberries, mapleleaf viburnum, young ash and hickory, and white pine. The forest floor is covered with wild lily-of-the-valley, mouse-eared chickweed, common cinquefoil, lowbush blueberry, club mosses, and pink lady's slipper.

Activities:
A nice place for a quiet woodland walk. The shady summit has a grassy area fine for pack-it-in/pack-it-out picnics.

Directions:
Pleasant Street south from South Natick, right on Pegan Lane.
Parking: For one or two cars.

92B. SOUTH NATICK DAM (OLD TOWN PARK)
Pleasant Street and Route 16, South Natick
*Natick Park Department   1905

Activities: picnicking, fishing, canoe-launch ramp, historic sites
Hours: 8:00 A.M. to dusk
Admission: no charge

There have been dams across the Charles River here since 1722, when Thomas Sawin began his sawmill. Over the years, fulling mills have felted cloth, grist mills have ground corn, and paper mills have chopped rags at various dams here. Often the dam owners and millers were in conflict with the farmers upstream, for the latter's hay marshes were permanently flooded by the long mill pond. In 1890 the Eliot Falls Electric Company attempted to use the falls to generate a local supply of electricity, but the water supply proved inadequate. In 1933 ice broke the privately owned dam and two years later the town replaced it, with the addition of a fishway, the first on any dam along the Charles.

Old Town Park is pleasantly situated on both sides of the dam. Big old white pines shade picnic tables and yellow irises on the south side, and benches and grass on the other side make a fine place to sit and listen to the roaring Charles. Nearby are the old Eliot Church and other antiquarian buildings of the John Eliot Historic District.

Activities:

In addition to being a popular picnic site and romantic place to sit or stroll, the dam is a favorite of kids stalking the river's giant carp with their fishing rods. Duck feeding. Canoe launching either up- or downriver.

Directions:

Route 16 to South Natick, left on Pleasant Street; park entrance in two hundred yards.
Parking: Plenty.

93. HOPKINTON STATE PARK
Cedar Street, Hopkinton, MA 01748
960 acres   State Park   1948 (transferred from MDC)

Activities: swimming, boating, fishing, picnicking, ski touring, horseback riding, fields, walking
Map: free at entrance
Hours: 9:00 A.M. to dusk
Admission: three dollars a car or state season pass

This extensive recreation area is centered on the Hopkinton Dam, built in the late 1880s of earth and granite as Dam 6 of the Sudbury waterworks. The dam itself is open for walking and provides a fine view of the islands and low oak- and ash-covered hills that nestle the reservoir. Among the wildflowers scattered around the edges of the area's open fields are ajuga, raspberry, and tall buttercup.

Activities:

Now that the state has cracked down on teen-age drinking, Hopkinton State Park is an outstanding family picnic and recreation area.

Swimming: Two pebbly and sandy beaches, both with lifeguards, bathhouses, and shady pavilions nearby. Water brownish but clean, cool, and very refreshing. Access for the handicapped.

Picnicking: Hundreds of picnic tables, many with charcoal grills, scattered in pine groves and placed under sun and rain pavilions. Plenty of bathrooms and drinking fountains. Snack bar. Easy walk to the beaches. Plenty of room for group picnics.

Boating: Boat-launching ramps for canoes, rowboats, and sailboats, with plenty of parking. Canoe rentals at boathouse for $5.50 first hour, $3.50 each additional hour. Islands and shore of large reservoir to explore. No motorboats.

Hiking: A long trail skirts the northern boundary of the park.

Fishing: From shore or boat. Stocked with rainbow trout. Bass and hornpout of good size also caught here.

Bicycling: On five miles of park roads.

Fields: One softball field. Many open fields for Frisbees and so on.

Ski touring: Five miles of park roads and trails. Some maintenance. Snowmobiles separate.

Directions:

Route 9 to Southboro, left on Route 85 (Cordaville Road), continue three miles to park entrance on the right.

Parking: Plenty, but fills up by 11:00 A.M. on hot summer weekends.

94. ASHLAND STATE PARK
Union Street, Ashland, MA 01721
470 acres   State Park   1948

Activities: freshwater swimming, picnicking, boating, hiking, fishing, birding, ski touring

Ashland State Park surrounds and includes a former reservoir built by Boston as part of its Sudbury water supply in 1878. The earth and masonry dam is nearly a hundred feet high, holding back 155 acres of water. Today the area is a popular yet quiet favorite for family picnics and fishing.

Activities:

Lots of territory to explore and a very pleasant place for a picnic.

Swimming: 3,000-foot sandy beach, bathhouse, lifeguards. Fresh cool water.

Picnicking: 75 tables beneath grand old oaks and white pines. Charcoal grills allowed and fireplaces provided (bring your own wood). Bathrooms.

Boating: Good for sailing, canoeing, or trolling; 12 miles an hour limit for motor boats; 10 horsepower maximum. Boat-launching ramp: bear left just beyond park entrance on to Olive Street; one mile to left on Spring Street; half mile to ramp. Not much parking at ramp.

Fishing: Stocked with trout. Trophy-size largemouth bass, plus smallmouth bass, perch, and sunfish. The gatehouse on the dam overlooks the deepest portion of the reservoir, 47 feet down.

Hiking: Five miles of trails. Terrific three-mile circuit trail around the shore of the reservoir.

Birding: Herons, kingfishers, geese, ducks, egrets, hawks, and an occasional osprey.

Ski touring: Along hiking trails. Long trail around reservoir. Some maintenance. Lovely spot with gentle grades. Park at entrance and ski in the park road.

Directions:

Route 135 from Ashland Center, one mile to sign at entrance on left.

Parking: Plenty.

Telephone: 881-2019

95. CALLAHAN STATE PARK
Millwood Street, Framingham
425 acres   *State Park   1970

Activities: walking and hiking, picnicking, birdwatching, horseback riding, ski touring, nature study
Map: free by sending SASE to or dropping by Cochituate State Park
Hours: dawn to dusk
Admission: free

This extensive tract of old farmland, surrounded by low hills, is a fine place to escape the roar of the city and recall our region's rural heritage. The first farmer to cultivate these grounds was Joseph Buckminster, who settled nearby in 1699. Buckminster's son constructed a grist mill on the banks of Baiting Brook. He dammed the little waterway to create Packard's Pond, thus assuring himself of a steady supply of water for his animals and power for his mill.

The farm was purchased in 1742 by Francis Brinley. In 1776 it was confiscated by town authorities because Brinley's son, the owner then, was a British sympathizer. One of Brinley's farmhands was Daniel Shays, leader of the populist Shays' Rebellion after the war. In 1812 the land was bought by Major Benjamin Wheeler.

In 1860 the farm was purchased by a wealthy gentleman farmer, Ebenezer Bowditch. Bowditch planted the latest breeds of grass and bred the newest European livestock species on his estate. In 1866 he also helped form the Millwood Hunt Club, the first hunt club in the Northeast. For nearly a hundred years the baying of hounds and the clatter of hooves reigned over these fields and woods. Much of the land was sold in 1941 to Constance Fiske, who in 1969 sold the farm to the state. The state park was named after Raymond J. Callahan, a prominent civic-minded resident of Framingham.

Miles of horsetrails and old roads wind through the former fields and into the woodlands above. The many old walls indicate that the entire tract was once pasture or under cultivation. The broad, open lower fields are verdant with tall grasses such as timothy, and the wildflowers include purple, white, and yellow clover, milkweed, and evening primrose. Morning and evening the air is filled with the sound of nesting whippoorwills and bobolinks and the occasional cry of a red-tailed or marsh hawk searching the fields for prey. The upper fields, further on their way to becoming forest again, are filled with hawkweed, cypress spurge, arrow-wood, juniper, buckthorn, speedwell, and small white pines. The white pine forest at the upper portion of the land was also fields once. Thus walking around the park can be an open education in old-field succession.

Baiting Brook, which courses through the center of the park, is overgrown with big old basswood, buckthorn, grapevines, honey-suckles, and anemones. During the hot summer months, this streamcourse is a natural hideaway for a dozen or more bird species.

Activities:
Wide old farm roads blushing with yellow camomile lead through the fields and into the woods beyond. From the upper fields the visitor can look out over much of the park and the surrounding farms. This is a fun place to explore.
Picnicking: Many quiet places along the brook, in mowed portions of the fields, and in the open woods for pack-it-in/pack-it-out picnics. No facilities.
Walking and hiking: Five or six miles of clean open trails, mostly fairly easy walking, make this a fine place for an afternoon's stroll.
Jogging: Excellent along the grassy former farm roads.
Ski touring: One of the finer places for ski touring in the region. Trails marked for novice to intermediate. Limited winter parking.

Directions:
Route 30 to Framingham Center, right on Edgell Road, left on Belnap Street, half mile to right on Millwood Road: entrance less than a half mile ahead on left.
Parking: Small lot along road.

Telephone: 653-9641.

96. GARDEN IN THE WOODS
Hemenway Road, Framingham MA 01701
45 acres   New England Wildflower Society   1965

Activities: walking, nature study, scenic area

Map: free with admission
Hours: 9:00 A.M. to 5:00 P.M. Monday through Saturday
(1984: Tuesday–Sunday)
Admission: two dollars adults, one dollar children, a dollar
fifty senior citizens

The loveliest naturalistic garden in North America

Will Curtis had a dream: to develop a naturalistic wildflower
garden where every flowering plant that could grow in New
England's temperate climate would be planted. In 1930 he acquired thirty acres of hilly, glacier-sculpted land in Framingham
and set to work. Howard Stiles, an amateur botanist and gardener,
joined Curtis at the task in 1933, and the work of landscaping and
planting began in earnest. A small propagating greenhouse was
built and the two men began to search around the country and
around the world for cuttings and seeds.

Paths were cleared, gardens laid out, and a pond excavated.
With permission to search for and collect wildflowers from the
state and many private landholders, the collection grew. New
England plants were traded for exotic wildflower species from
botanic gardens on every continent. Wildflower displays were
exhibited at the annual Boston Flower Show. All this work paid off
in the early 1940s when the Garden received international recognition with an official designation as a Botanic Garden.

As the garden grew larger, the two men grew older; by the
1960s they needed help and the knowledge that the garden's
future would be secure. The New England Wildflower Society,
founded in 1922, was informed of the situation and soon became
involved. After it successfully raised a $225,000 endowment fund,
the land was transferred to the Society in 1965. Curtis and Stiles
were both retained, the former as director and the latter as curator
of the Garden in the Woods.

Today more than fifteen hundred species of flowering plants
grow in the Garden, probably the largest collection of wildflowers
in the Northeast. Walking here gives the feeling that the Creator,
the great evolutionist-in-the-sky, was an artist: the range of flower
colors, shapes, and habitats is amazing. The incredibly beautiful
plants are a glowing illustration of nature's creative power—the
garden itself is a sign that the same force can flow through us:
gravel paths course gracefully along steep-sloped eskers, down into
glorious little bogs and cul-de-sacs, and along lush green stream-

banks. At each turn of the paths, the wanderer is surprised by a new floral scene painted as if by the loving brush of a Dutch master.

To enable the great diversity of flowers to grow successfully here, a series of mini-environments have been created by controlling amounts of shade, soil acidity, and wetness. In addition to re-creating nearly every New England habitat, the gardeners here have replicated the conditions of Southern Appalachia, New Jersey pine barrens, western scree, and southeastern woodland, each area planted with the appropriate flowers.

On any day from early spring until fall several dozen species may be found blooming in the garden. Mid-April to early July is the most colorful time; blooms include the showy but rare oconee bells, trailing arbutus (our state flower), innumerable pink lady's slippers, Dutchman's breeches, unusual yellow lady's slipper, shooting star, anemone, and much more. June brings out the trillium, showy lady's slipper, galax, a rainbow of irises, flame and torch azalea, and blossoms of the fringe tree. Prickly pear, Turk's-cap lily, and sweet pepperbush garland July. In August and September the brilliant red hummingbird-pollinated cardinal flower is sure to catch one's eye, as will the gentian, rattlesnake plantain orchid, rose mallow, turtlehead, and the franklinia. From the last frost of spring to the first frost of fall plants may be found flowering.

Activities:

Garden in the Woods is not only one of the prettiest spots in Greater Boston, but it has been called "the loveliest naturalistic garden in North America." A walk here, where it is always peaceful, and where most flowers are labeled, is like a visit to a botanical Museum of Fine Arts. Because many of the flowers are small and fragile, there is no picnicking and visitors must stay on the pathways amid the plantings. Leave dogs home. There are bathrooms, displays, and a botanical bookstore and library. No baby carriages are allowed but free backpacks are provided for carrying small children. No flower picking of any kind, of course. This is a place that deserves repeat visits to enjoy each season's unfolding blooms.

Walking: The Curtis Nature Trail is a one-hour, self-guiding introduction to the garden (booklet available for a dollar and a quarter includes map) and wildflowers in general. Another two or three miles of trails wind over ridges covered with oak, pine, larch, and hemlock.

Directions:
Route 20 to South Sudbury, left on Raymond Road beyond railroad tracks, to Hemenway Road.
Or: Route 9 in Framingham to Edgell Road north. Proceed two and a half miles to Water Street on right, left on Hemenway Road.
Parking: Plenty.

Telephone: 877-6574

97. LAKE COCHITUATE STATE PARK
*Commonwealth Avenue (Route 30), Cochituate, MA 01778
1,126 acres   State Park   1947

Activities: swimming, boating, picnicking
Map: free from Lake Cochituate Watershed Association (see below)
Hours: 9:00 A.M. to dusk
Admission: three dollars a car or state season pass

In 1834 Laommi Baldwin, "Father of American Civil Engineering," proposed that Long Pond be used as Boston's first public water supply. The pond was situated in a rural district of farms and pastures fifteen miles from the city in the towns of Framingham, Wayland, and Natick. On Knight's Flume, the pond's outlet to the Sudbury River, several cotton mills were operating. Baldwin thought that, because the pond was 130 feet above sea level, it could supply Boston's water by gravity through an aqueduct. Scientific studies found the water to be of excellent quality. But because there were as yet no waterworks in America as large as the one Baldwin proposed and the expense of constructing such a system would be great, no action was taken by the tightfisted Yankee government.

Long Pond was the largest natural pond or lake within twenty-five miles of Boston. Before the English arrived, the region around the pond had been occupied by at least one Indian village. It also served as an important link in the canoe route between the Charles and Sudbury rivers. Paddlers came up Indian Brook from the south, aided by the many beaver ponds, entered Dug Pond, and then after a few short portages reached the southern end of Long Pond. After exiting from the pond through its outlet, the Indian canoeist entered the Sudbury, which in turn entered the Merrimack, providing the Indians of Massachusetts Bay and Southern New England with access to the game-rich mountains of New Hampshire. A series of waterfalls on Long Pond's outlet stream gave the region its Indian name, Cochituate, "place of falling waters."

On a beautiful summer day in 1846, Mayor Josiah Quincy of Boston rechristened Long Pond as Lake Cochituate—after twenty years of debate, Boston and the state Legislature had agreed that the pond was the best place for Boston to obtain its water. James B. Jervis, builder of New York City's Croton Aqueduct, the largest public water supply built since the days of Rome, was hired as principal engineer of the Boston-Cochituate Waterworks. The mill owners along Knight's Flume were bought out and a masonry dam was erected at the outlet, raising the lake's water level nine feet. On the east shore of the lake a Greek Revival gatehouse of gray granite was constructed as the headwork of the aqueduct. Water entered the aqueduct at the base of the building, sixteen feet below the lake's surface. Between Cochituate and the receiving reservoir on Cory Hill in Brookline (see Section 42, Brookline Reservoir), a distance of 14.3 miles, the aqueduct descended a mere 3.81 feet. In mid-1848 the system was essentially complete and the water was turned on at a fountain on Boston Common in the greatest celebration Boston had ever held.

In 1859 a second dam was built, increasing the lake's capacity and raising the water level four feet. The gatehouse was dismantled at that time and moved thirty feet out from shore. The Cochituate was used as a water supply until the 1930s when it was taken out of service. If you stand by the gatehouse you will still hear water flowing, for Cochituate water is conducted to the Charles to increase that river's flow and help purge pollutants.

Activities:

Lake Cochituate is the largest and most complete freshwater recreation area in the region. The lake itself is divided into North, Middle, and South ponds by bridges, narrows, and highways. Although most of the shoreline is within the park, town beaches, camps, and the Army labs are definitely off-limits. Other than the 900-acre water surface, the primary public-use area is the beach-picnic area-marina site. Be sure to take a closer look at the old gatehouse off Route 30.

Boating: The best freshwater boating in the region with the best boat-launching ramp, built in 1955 as an adjunct of the Massachusetts Turnpike. Trailered sailboats and larger motorboats are confined to the middle pond by the low bridges that connect to the other sections. Speed limit of 22 miles an hour except on all Saturdays, Sundays, and holidays—then maximum speed is 5 miles an hour. Water-skiing is confined to South Pond's specially designated waterski area; maximum speed is 42 miles an hour. On weekends and holidays the north pond is closed to all powerboats and a small-boat launching ramp is opened for canoes, cartop sailboats, and rowboats.

The marina beside the boat-launching ramp rents canoes at five dollars for the first hour and three fifty for each additional hour. A number of piers along the marina make loading and unloading boats convenient.

Fishing: The lake is sixty-nine feet deep at its deepest point and is stocked with rainbow, lake, and brook trout. Other fish caught here include large- and smallmouth bass, pickerel, catfish, and sunfish. The fishing is best from a boat, but shore fishing can also be rewarding here. Check with the rangers at the contact station for permissible shore fishing areas.

Picnicking: Around a hundred pine-shaded picnic tables with fireplaces (bring your own wood); grills permitted. Open grassy fields for running around, playing, or erecting a volleyball net. One softball diamond. Bathrooms and snack bar. A very popular but well-kept picnic spot.

Swimming: Several hundred yards of clean sandy beach. Water clean and fresh, as befits a former drinking-water supply—in fact the water quality has noticeably improved in recent years. Lifeguards. Picnic area and marina nearby.

Lake Cochituate Watershed Association: This group promotes the improvement of the water quality and environment of Lake Cochituate and its watershed. They publish an outstanding free map of the lake and its surroundings, complete with water depths, historic sites, and information about the lake's fish and plants. Lake Cochituate Watershed Association, Box 1291, Framingham, MA 01701.

Directions:
Route 30 (Commonwealth Avenue) all the way. Or Route 9 to Speen Street, then right on Route 30. Or Exit 13 on the Massachusetts Turnpike, then right on Route 30.
Parking: Plenty, but come early on summer weekends.

Telephone: 653-9641

98. WELLESLEY

98A. KELLY PARK, BOULDER BROOK RESERVATION, ROCKY LEDGES
Elmwood Road, Wellesley
66 acres in all   *Wellesley Park Department   1942–1966

Activities: walking, nature study, birdwatching, picnicking
Hours: dawn to dusk
Admission: no charge

These three adjoining parks form a large tract of woods, brooks, open fields, and rocky crags. A series of quiet interconnected trails runs from Elmwood Street to the summit of Rocky Ledges, providing an unusually pleasant walk through a great diversity of habitats.

The trail begins at the Kelly Park parking lot on Elmwood Road (see "Directions" below). A beautiful little marsh on the left supports thousands of blue flag iris as well as blue-eyed grass, stitchwort, and sensitive fern. Follow the path along Boulder Brook, passing Fairy Rock, the glacial erratic from which the brook received its name. Among the plants found along the brook are multiflora rose, black cherry, quaking aspen, yarrow, and sweet fern. Cross the bridge and follow the paved path between houses to an opening with a trailhead.

The trail makes an easy ascent through a fine old hayfield before reaching a pristine woods with a little stream running through it. White ash, hickory, maple, and oak, as well as numerous flowering dogwoods, comprise the forest trees. In addition to the Canada mayflower and pipsissewa that carpet the forest floor, pyrola and trillium may be found here. Follow the trail into the woods, past a large glacial erratic known as Elephant Rock, to the base of a steep ledge.

Climb Rocky Ledges to the summit, where there is a fine view across the Charles River Valley, particularly when the leaves are off the trees in the early spring and late fall. It is estimated that the rock of the summit is 550 million years old, making it among the most ancient rocks in the region. Red cedar, mountain ash, hickory, dwarf dandelion, Venus's looking-glass, false Solomon's seal, and raspberry are among the plant species that thrive on the ledges. This is a fine place for a pack-it-in/pack-it-out picnic. No fires. Please don't litter or disturb the vegetation.

Directions:

Route 9 west, through Wellesley Hills to Weston exit. Exit right, then take third right on Elmwood Road. Parking lot a half mile ahead on the left.

98B. COCHITUATE AQUEDUCT

*MDC 1846
Activities: walking, bicycling, nature study, jogging

This flat-topped ridge, the embanked aqueduct of Boston's first public water supply (see Section 97, Lake Cochituate State Park and Section 37, Brookline Reservoir), forms a seven-mile linear park through Wellesley. Dropping only inches a mile on its way to Boston, the aqueduct twists around hills and vales to maintain the hydraulic gradient. The grassy paths along the top of the embankment are perfect for walking, bicycling, or jogging. The aqueduct and its protective buffer have remained undisturbed for the last 125 years, resulting in unusually fine trees along the way. Parts of the aqueduct run through residential areas, so that a map is necessary (see below). Respect private property.

98C. HUNNEWELL PARK

Activities: duck feeding, nature study

This little park around the Wellesley Town Hall was donated to the town by H. H. Hunnewell in 1887. Exotic and ornamental trees planted over the years include an enormous European beech, a Kentucky yellowwood, a ginkgo, magnolias, catalpas, and a tall Douglas fir. A very nice duck pond has been created in the park by damming Cold Spring Brook.

Directions:

Route 9 west to Route 16 south. Park on right where road bears right into Wellesley Square.

Information:

Wellesley Conservation Council: This nonprofit organization publishes several aids for exploring Wellesley's parks and natural areas: a good map, fifty cents; an excellent *Walks in Wellesley* booklet, fifty cents; and a geologic guide, seventy-five cents. Membership in the group is five dollars. Wellesley Conservation Council, Wellesley, MA 02181.

99. UPPER CHARLES RIVER

Activities: canoeing, fishing, nature study, birdwatching, picnicking

From its sources at Echo Lake in Hopkinton to its mouth on Boston Harbor, the Charles River, known to the Indians as Quinobequin, "meandering," twists and turns to make a trip of thirty-one air miles into an eighty-mile odyssey. The river drains a watershed of 307 square miles that includes all or part of five cities and thirty towns. Twenty-three of these municipalities have frontage on the river, ranging from 11.9 miles in Needham to .06 mile in Westwood. Seventy-eight tributary streams enter the river along its course. The river is interrupted by twenty-one dams and crossed by some ninety-three bridges.

The early Massachusetts Bay colonists found that the river was not navigable above the first falls at Watertown as they had hoped it would be. Nevertheless, many of the Colony's first settlements were founded along the river. Farmers and husbandmen were attracted by the tall grasses growing in the river's marshes, which could provide winter fodder for their domestic animals. Other settlers were attracted by the river's abundant fisheries: shad, smelt, salmon, and alewife. Entrepreneurs were attracted by the river's potential as a power source for sawmills and grist mills.

All along the river, new towns split off from the older, larger towns—Waltham and Weston from Watertown, Newton from Cambridge—and each new town always made sure that it had access to the river and its marshes. When the huge Dedham Grant of 1643 was divided into the towns of Bellingham, Dedham, Dover, Franklin, Medfield, Natick, Needham, Norfolk, Norwood, Walpole, Wellesley, and Wrentham, each town's boundaries included frontage on the river.

Prior to 1700 dams were built to operate sawmills and grist mills at Charles River Village in Needham and along the Upper and Lower Falls in Newton. Many small mills operated on the river's tributaries. During the next century three dams were built in Waltham, two were added in Newton, one in Natick, four in Medway, and one each in West Medway, Bellingham, and Milford. The new dams accompanied the growth of new industries along the river as fulling mills beat a nap into rough cloth, snuff mills ground tobacco, leather mills scraped and pounded hides, ironworks blasted and hammered iron, and scythe mills heated and sharpened blades. But along with new dams came conflicts with other river users: the dams flooded valuable hay meadows and blocked annual fish migrations. Conflicts also arose among the various mill owners because water held back for an upstream mill might leave a downstream mill high and dry, without water for power. The conflicts grew worse after 1815 as dozens of new mills were built along the river during the Industrial Revolution.

The river was not only a source of power for industry, it also provided process water to wash and dye cloth, churn paper, and scald leather. Towns along the river also began to derive their public water supplies from the river's wetlands if not the river itself. By the end of the century the profusion of dams with conflicting water rights and a series of droughts caused many of the industries along the river to convert to steam power to drive machinery.

By 1900 the Charles seemed to be on the verge of dying: too many dams, wastewater pouring in from towns and industries, and a lack of public interest had allowed the river to become polluted. But as the industries began to abandon the river in the 1920s, its banks began to regenerate themselves. With the last twenty years, a concerted effort has been made to clean up the river. Environmental regulations have improved the river's water quality. The Army Corps of Engineers has protected nine thousand acres of the river's marshes as a flood-control measure, known as the Charles River Natural Valley Storage Program. State and federal controls have also protected the river's wetlands from filling. Fish ladders are being installed on dams. As the result of all this attention, led by the Charles River Watershed Association, the recreational potential on the river has been restored almost to the point where we can swim in its muddy waters again.

Between Hopkinton and Waltham the river wanders through broad freshwater marshes with reed canary grass the dominant species. Flowers and shrubs growing in the marshes include blue flag iris, buttonbush, reeds and sedges, arrowhead, pickerelweed, and fragrant water lily. Other sections of the river run by wooded banks lined with chestnut and red oak, tupelo, elm, willow, red maple, and silky dogwood. Painted turtles sun themselves on floating logs. Kingbirds, catbirds, marsh hawks, bitterns, and herons are just a few of the bird species that may be sighted along the river.

Activities:

Between Medway and Newton much of the Charles has had its natural beauty restored and protected, making for thirty or so miles of riverine ecstasy. There are many canoe-launching sites. If you want to canoe the Charles, purchase the *Charles River Canoe Guide,* which includes detailed maps of the river, descriptions of each stretch of the river, a complete listing of launching ramps, and other information about canoeing the river. In one of the most interesting sections of the *Guide* the authors discuss canoeing on the river's tributaries, several of which lead to lakes and several of which are wild and beautiful.

Charles River Canoe Guide is available for a dollar fifty from the Charles River Watershed Association, 2391 Commonwealth Avenue, Auburndale, MA 02166. Telephone: 527-2799. Also ask for the *Charles River Profile.*

Fishing: According to the Division of Fisheries and Wildlife, fish caught on the Charles are edible. Among the species are sunfish, perch, bass, pickerel, carp, and pike. Several of the river's tributary streams are stocked with trout. For more information about the river's fish, send

SASE to the Charles River Watershed Association for the free leaflet: "Fish Facts."

100. CASE ESTATES
135 Wellesley Street, Weston, MA 02193
112 acres   Arnold Arboretum   1944

Activities: walking, nature study
Map: free self-guiding tour map
Hours: 9:00 A.M. to 5:00 P.M.
Admission: no charge

At Case Estates in Weston, Boston's glorious Arnold Arboretum maintains nurseries, special collections of shrubs, flowers, and trees, experimental and display plantings, and demonstration plots. The air of this former farm seems always filled with the warm colors and sweet fragrance of blossoms: magnolias in April; wild-flowers and blooming crabapples in May; peonies, irises, dog-woods, azaleas, and rhododendrons in June; lilies, clematis, and perennial flowers in July and August; and gaily colored crabapples and holly fruits in the fall.

From 1909 to 1942 this was the site of Mary and Louisa Case's Hillcrest Gardens, a horticultural school for boys using the most advanced techniques available to produce fruit and vegetables. The Case's ultra-modern barn, schoolhouse, and ash fertilizer incinera-tor are still standing.

One of the primary purposes of Case Estates is to provide examples of different ornamental trees and shrubs that the home gardener might want to plant. The iris collection is a collage of hundreds of varieties with huge pastel blooms in every color of the rainbow. The exquisite perennial garden contains healthy exam-ples of unusual flowering plants suitable for home planting. Sever-al rock gardens are likewise constantly abloom.

The "back-forty" woods is a natural wildflower garden where trout lily, trillium, spring beauty, and lady's slipper abound. War-blers, orioles, and finches make good use of the many orchard trees.

Activities:

In addition to being a real learning experience for the home gardener, the Case Estates is a fine place just to stroll around for an hour or two.

Walking: Interesting and informative self-guiding walk along short, mostly level pathways. Free descriptive pamphlet with map at parking lot.

Directions:

Route 20 west to Weston, left on Wellesley Street, bear right at the fork and entrance just ahead.

Parking: Small but ample lot.

Telephone: 524-1717

101. DRUMLIN FARM SANCTUARY
South Great Road (Route 117), Lincoln, MA 01773
220 acres   Massachusetts Audubon Society   1955

Activities: birdwatching, nature study, domestic and wildlife zoo, walking, educational programs
Map: available at visitor entrance
Hours: dawn to dusk
Admission: three dollars adults, two dollars children

Drumlin Farm is not only a beautiful natural area, bird refuge, and working farm, but also one of the best places to introduce children or adults to the natural world. Its outstanding programs received U.S. Department of the Interior recognition in 1971 when it was designated a National Environmental Education Landmark. Come and stroll through woods, fields, and pastures; visit the red-tailed hawk and woodchuck; climb the drumlin and gaze over green forests to the hazy blue hills of the north.

Drumlin Farm had its beginning in 1904 when Mr. and Mrs. Donald Gordon first summered in Lincoln. Initially renters, the Gordons soon purchased a home and adjoining land, and in 1914 they had a Georgian mansion built for themselves. By 1920 they owned 175 acres including Hager's Hill, a large drumlin on the north of the property after which they named their farm. The

Gordons ran a model farm, selling their surplus to such exclusive stores as S. S. Pierce.

After Mr. Gordon died, his wife married Conrad Perkins Hatheway. Mr. Hatheway took the same pleasure in country life that his new wife did. Mrs. Hatheway not only delighted in domestic animals but also loved wildlife: she covered the hills, lawns, and gardens of the estate with bird feeders, and in 1934 became a life member of Massachusetts Audubon. The Hatheways wanted to share their farm, and so in 1940 they began inviting city children for tours. In 1950, starting with the Arlington Public Schools, scheduled tours of the farm became a yearly event for many Boston-area school children. When Mrs. Hatheway died in 1955, she left the farm and an endowment for its operation to Massachusetts Audubon Society. In the following year Massachusetts Audubon moved their headquarters to Lincoln, opened the Hatheway School of Environmental Education in the former gatehouse, and started developing programs.

Several species of hawks and owls and an enormous golden eagle are displayed in open pens providing us an opportunity to examine these soaring birds close-up (while they examine us). Like most of the farm's wild animals, these are injured or orphaned birds that could not survive on their own. Three duck ponds bring visitors close to Canada geese and both wild migrating ducks and farmyard ducks. Among the most interesting display areas is the burrowing animal house, which allows us to enter the underground homes of a fox and a woodchuck.

The farm has a working chickencoop with a colorful assortment of domestic layers, and the incubators, egg washers, and other equipment behind our morning's scrambled eggs. Horses, cows, sheep, and goats are here, in their farm environment, as well as being within patting distance. Near most of the animals informative displays describe their life cycle and role in farm life. The displays appeal to both children and adults.

The grounds of Drumlin Farm attract nearly two hundred bird species. Among the many wildflowers that may be found here are jack-in-the-pulpit, trillium, wild columbine, bearberry, and spring violet. Shrub species include honeysuckle, wild raisin, juneberry, swamp azalea, mountain laurel, sweet pepperbush, and highbush blueberry. The former pastures of the drumlin are being invaded by buckthorn, crabapple, arrowwood, and bittersweet vine. Pines and oaks predominate in the woodlands.

Activities:

In addition to just strolling around the farm or taking a guided tour, be sure to look into the many excellent programs offered by Drumlin Farm. An extensive series of special programs is designed to introduce children from four to fourteen to wild and domestic nature. Other programs are geared to families. Adult offerings in natural history include introductory and advanced birding trips, canoe excursions on the Sudbury River, and nature photography. Still other programs run the gamut from solar greenhouses to raising chickens in the backyard. Modest fees are charged for the programs, which usually meet once a week for eight weeks.

Special programs include such activities as hayrides and ski touring.

For more information on programs write to Drumlin Farm (address above) for current schedule.

The Drumlin Farm gift shop has the best selection of nature-oriented books, gifts, and study aids to be found in New England. Guided tours by reservation. Summer natural-history day camp for children four to fourteen. Bathrooms. No picnicking, but Walden Pond is nearby.

Directions:

Route 117 in Waltham (Main Street) northwest, over Route 128 (exit 49), to Route 117 in Weston and then Lincoln (South Great Road).

Telephone: 259-9807

102. WALDEN POND STATE RESERVATION
*Route 126, Concord, MA 01742
411 acres   State Reservation   1922

Activities: walking, swimming, nature study, historic site, fishing, hiking, ski touring, boating
Hours: 8:30 A.M. to 7:00 P.M.
Map: free for the asking at the Contact Station
Admission: three dollars a car or state season pass

I went to the woods because I wished to live deliberately, to front the
essential facts of life, and see if I could not learn what it had to teach,
and not, when I came to die, discover that I had not lived.

Henry David Thoreau
Walden

Walden Pond: in all the world there are few natural areas so
sanctified by the short tenancy of a lone individual. Much as
Thoreau made pilgrimages to trees, swamps, and rivers, nature
lovers, individualists, poets, social activists, and *Walden*-readers
make pilgrimages to the shores of Walden Pond to taste the air
Thoreau breathed and walk the ground he trod. And if most of the
hundreds of thousands of visitors each year are more interested in
setting a fly or dipping in the clear waters, nonetheless Walden
Pond maintains its decorum and tranquility—the spirit of the place
still has the power to "re-create" our souls.

Thoreau moved into the little cabin he'd built just back from
Walden's shore on July 4, 1845, his personal Independence Day,
and lived there for two years, two months, and two days. The land
was owned by Thoreau's friend Ralph Waldo Emerson, who had
purchased the area to save it from the logger's ax the year before.
Thoreau's occupations during his time at the little ten-by-fifteen-
foot cabin were primarily of a solitary cast: studying the natural
world, enchanting a woodchuck, hoeing his beanfield, exploring
himself, jotting away in his journals, and writing *A Week on the*
Concord and Merrimack Rivers. Hours were spent contemplating the
light reflected off the pond or its winter ice covering, or wandering in the nearby woods or along the Sudbury River. Every
afternoon he set out to meet nature, believing, in the words of
Emerson, that "the ancient precept 'know thyself,' and the modern
precept, 'study nature,' become at last one maxim."

Yet though Thoreau's detractors, then as now, have sought to
portray him as an escapist hermit and misanthrope, the actuality
was far different—he walked into town or had visitors nearly every
day. Emerson, Channing, and Alcott, an assortment of woodsmen
and townsfolk, and young people wanting a guide for huckleberry-
ing parties spent time around the pond with Thoreau. Often his
family visited on Sundays, bringing their reform-minded friends
along for a picnic. On other days Thoreau walked to town for
dinner at home or a raid on his mother's cookie jar. Nonetheless,
Thoreau did have his limits, and if things became too social, he
would just fade off into the woods.

Thoreau, one of whose professions was surveying, was impelled by his nearly insatiable curiosity to "figure the pond out." Knowing that the pond was commonly thought to be bottomless, he took numerous depth readings from his little boat and through the ice. He found that at its deepest the pond was ninety-seven feet from the bottom to the surface. He often noted the lucidity of its waters: "The water is so transparent that the bottom can be easily discerned at a depth of twenty-five or thirty feet." At all times of year he took temperature readings of the pond. And he studied its fish and flora.

According to an Indian legend that Thoreau was aware of, Walden Pond was once the site of a hill—and perhaps it was when the Redman's ancestors arrived here behind the glacier. Geologically the pond is a kettlehole formed where a giant chunk of ice broke off from the main body of the retreating glacier. The ice was surrounded and perhaps buried by dirt and rocks pouring out in the glacier's meltwater streams. Insulated by dirt, the ice may have formed a hill with trees growing out of its cloak when the first Indians arrived in the region. But as the ice slowly melted, the hill fell, until there was only a steepsided depression to show where the ice chunk had been. Groundwater seeped into the depression, creating the pond.

The calderlike walls of the pond are mantled by trees and wildflowers little changed since Thoreau's day. The very shore of the pond is lined with innumerable white lance-leaved violets in the early spring. Sweet pepperbush, yellow birch, and red maple grow between the shore and the circuit trail. In the shade of white pine, oak, hemlock, and white birch two of Thoreau's favorite flowers, bunchberry and bluet, continue to blossom, as do such common species as starflower, Canada mayflower, huckleberry, hawkweed, and daisy. In a sedgy bog near Thoreau's cabin site, the bullfrogs are still bellowing like elephants in heat.

From his stoop and window Thoreau spent hours watching the wildlife visiting the pond: "a fishhawk [osprey] dimples the glassy surface of the pond and brings up a fish; a mink steps out of the marsh before my door and seizes a frog...." From his seat he could also see the snorting engine of the Fitchburg railroad line, its open cars loaded with lumber, cotton, and livestock going to and from the market towns along its route, calling out to the countryside with its lowing whistle. No longer quite so prosaic, now the train comes quickly into hearing distance on the far side of the pond, and after a brief roar, just as quickly passes away.

Portions of the Walden woods had surely been logged once or twice before Emerson purchased the land. During Thoreau's day the portions of the area not owned by Emerson definitely saw the logger's glinting steel. While Thoreau was living at his cabin, Tudor, the largest ice merchant in Boston, sent his crews to cut the ice on the pond. The ice was cut, hauled off the pond, stacked, and insulated with hay, but by the following summer, when Tudor's crews returned, the ice had melted clean away. Several years after moving away from the pond, Thoreau was hired by Emerson to plant trees around it. The big white pines around the cabin site may well have been planted by his hand. In 1922 Emerson's heirs gave to Middlesex County "the Walden of Emerson and Thoreau, its shores and nearby woodlands for the public to enjoy the Pond, the woods, and nature." Later the area was transferred to the state to become Walden Pond State Park.

Activities:

The pond is often crowded with boisterous children, fishermen, joggers, and romantic couples, but whether because of its associations with Thoreau, or because it has been well maintained by the state in recent years, there is still something mystical waiting to be discovered in the shady hillsides and the glimmering waters. Spring and fall are the best times of year to experience the pond as Thoreau did. The early morning and late afternoon are also tranquil times here. Be sure to look at the cabin site with its pile of stones brought by pilgrims from Europe, Japan, and India. Park rangers provide interpretive talks and guided walks through much of the year: check at the Contact Station or call for information.

Walking: A 1.7-mile circuit trail skirts the shore along the hillside, a leisurely hour's walk with a stop at the cabin site. Numerous trails wind out of the kettlehole and into the woods that surround the pond.

Swimming: The water is still crystal clear and cool. The beach is crowded and heavily used during the summer, but constant raking by the staff keeps it immaculate. Lifeguards, bathhouse, toilets, snack bar, and first aid station. Short sandy beach without much room to put down a blanket, but plenty of territory around the pond to stretch out.

Picnicking: Only a few tables so plan to bring a blanket or chairs for a picnic on one of the wooded knolls overlooking the pond. Toilets, bubblers, and snack bar at beach.

Fishing: Heavily stocked with rainbow trout, which thrive in the pond's cool deep water. Big fish, weighing five and six pounds, are pulled out of the pond year after year. Fishing is great from the shore and even better from a boat.

Boating: Launching ramp for cartop boats. No gas motors permitted, Lots of quiet canoe action.

Ski touring: Circuit trail open for skiing but heavily used by walkers and snowshoers. Make a quick circuit and then head out into the extensive backcountry.

Thoreau's cabin: A full-size replica of Thoreau's cabin has been erected behind the Thoreau Lyceum at 156 Belknap Street in Concord. The Lyceum itself has delightful displays of materials relating to Thoreau, a bookstore, and a gift shop. It is a place everyone who has read *Walden* must visit.

Reading:

Walden. An excellent biography of Thoreau by Walter Harding, *The Days of Henry Thoreau,* is available at the Thoreau Lyceum.

Directions:

Public Transportation: Take train to Concord from North Station. Half-hour walk from Concord Station to Walden. From station turn east on Thoreau Street to end, then right on Walden Street. Cross over Route 2, then walk through woods to pond.

Bicycling: Mount Auburn Street in Cambridge to right on Belmont Street. Bear right at the fork to Trapelo Road, which you follow to Lincoln Center. Bear left on Baker Bridge Road and then right on Route 126 to Reservation.

Auto: Route 2 to Concord; continue on Route 2 where it jogs left for one mile to left on Route 126. Reservation entrance just ahead on left.

Parking: Very large lot; cars very seldom turned away except on hot summer weekends.

Telephone: 369-3254

Nearby:

Fairhaven Bay: A series of trails begin over the railroad tracks at the southwest end of the pond and head southwest through the woods to Fairhaven Bay, a widening of the Sudbury River. This was a favorite walk of both Emerson and Thoreau.

Lincoln: Several trails begin at the Walden Reservation parking lot and connect to Lincoln's very extensive trail system. Hikers and cross-country skiers can do a circuit of Sandy Pond or Mount Misery from here.

Map of Lincoln hiking and ski-touring trails: Available at Lincoln Town Hall or by writing Lincoln Conservation Commission, Lincoln, MA 01773.

103. GREAT MEADOWS NATIONAL WILDLIFE REFUGE
Weir Hill Road, Sudbury, MA 01776
2,900 acres   U.S. Fish and Wildlife Service   1944

Activities: birdwatching, walking, nature study, ski touring, photography

Map: free folder with map available at Monson Road leaflet dispenser (at base of observation tower) or at the Visitor Center

Hours: sunrise to sunset

Admission: no charge

A tender place in Nature, an exposed vein, and Nature making a feint to bridge it quite over with a paddy film, with red-winged blackbirds liquidly warbling and whistling on the willows, and kingbirds on the elms and oaks. . . .

> Thoreau
> *Journal* 1852

As we stood on the observation tower here, our binoculars focused on a family of geese grazing the flooded meadows and a black-crowned night heron just beyond them spearing a fish, we were distracted by a rustle in the leaves of a black cherry tree next to us. About six feet away a goldfinch was sitting on a limb cracking a seed. As we studied his bright color, we noticed the tree was in fact

filled with birds: a pair of black-masked yellow-throated warblers
were chasing each other around the crown, a purple finch was
singing in the foliage, and a nuthatch was moving upside-down
along the trunk. Hearing a splash below the tower, we found
ourselves staring down at a muskrat, tail swishing from side to
side. Here we were, not far from Boston, yet every two minutes of
watching revealed another flash in the trees or glint of movement
in the flooded meadows—another ornithological treat.

Great Meadows is as close to a city as any National Wildlife
Refuge in the country, and the abundance of birdlife here will
thrill any birdwatcher. Though only 400 acres of the refuge's
2,900 acres are open to the public, more than one hundred and
fifty bird species may be sighted during the year. Almost two
dozen species of warbler have been seen migrating through in the
spring when their colors are most spectacular, and also in the fall;
six or seven species nest here. Two species of long-legged rail,
which Peterson describes as "somewhat chicken-like marsh-birds
of secretive habits," are regularly sighted from the strategically

placed photo blinds. Sharp-shinned, red-tailed, Cooper's, red-shouldered, and broad-winged hawks, as well as ospreys, have all been thought to nest here—you are almost sure of seeing some sort of hawk no matter what time of year you visit the refuge. Perhaps the most outstanding times to visit are the early spring and during late September and October when sizable numbers of Canada geese, mallards, green- and blue-winged teals, gadwalls, wood ducks, ruddy ducks, and black ducks arrive.

Concord was the first inland town away from the Charles River settled in Massachusetts Bay Colony. The early settlers, who arrived in 1635, were particularly attracted by the wide grassy meadows that fringed the Concord River, giving the meandering stream its Indian name, Musketaquid, "grassy banks." Local farmers immediately moved to the river's edge to cut the hay as winter feed for their animals.

But the meadows did not follow any merely human regimen: as early as 1636 the hay-gatherers were complaining about spring flooding, which made the hay too wet to harvest. They appealed to the General Court to improve the river's drainage in 1644, hoping to overcome their "problems," but then, and for the next two hundred years, the government was unresponsive to their pleas. Nonetheless, hay was regularly gathered from the meadows until the beginning of the nineteenth century. At that time a milldam was built in North Billerica, backing the river up and keeping the meadows almost continuously flooded.

When the farmers left the meadows, wildlife returned. In 1928 Samuel Hoar, a hunter whose family had lived in Concord for generations, began acquiring the meadows as a personal reserve. To encourage waterfowl to nest and visit, he diked the meadows, creating habitat. In 1944 he donated his reserve, including the diked impoundments, to the Fish and Wildlife Service, which purchased additional river meadows to make the large refuge we have today.

Activities:

There are two points of public access to the refuge: the Dike Trail area in Concord and the Weir Hill area in Sudbury. The Dike Trail goes around the refuge impoundments and out along the slow-moving Concord River. Facilities include an observation tower, two photo blinds, and display panels geared to the season. The Weir Hill site includes the newly opened Visitor Center that offers displays and interpretive programs, and a self-guiding trail with a fine river overlook. Bring your binoculars and field guide.

Walking: One-and-a-half-mile trail at Dike area. One-mile trail at Weir Hill. Both places are easy walking. Wear boots during spring flood season.

Ski touring: Most trails available for ski touring.

Visitor Center: Interpretive programs and displays. Open weekdays year-round and weekends from March to Thanksgiving, 8:00 A.M. to 3:30 P.M.

Reading:

Concord River by Laurence Eaton Richardson.

Directions:

To Weir Hill and Visitor Center: Route 27 north from Wayland Center, right on Water Row Road, right on Lincoln Road, left onto Weir Hill Drive, then right into Visitor Center.

To Dike area: Bedford Road (Route 62) north from Concord Center, one and a half miles to left on Monson Road; follow signs to refuge.

Parking: Dike area lot may be filled in the spring and fall. Weir Hill parking is adequate.

Telephone: 443-4661

103A. CONCORD RIVER CANOEING

The Concord River is as peaceful as its name implies. Join Thoreau and Hawthorne or the Alcotts for a voyage on the calm dark waters. The Assabet and Sudbury rivers meet just above Concord Center and become the Concord River for the fifteen-mile stretch to the Merrimack. Though these waters are somewhat polluted by upriver industries and towns, they flow past pleasant hills, bird-filled marshes, and North Bridge, where the Minutemen stood their ground against the Redcoats in 1775.

Launching ramps:

Lowell Street Bridge: One-half mile north of Concord Center on Lowell Road. Limited parking at the ramp, but easy walk from several nearby parking areas.

Route 225 Bridge: Two miles northwest of Bedford Center

on Route 225 (Carlisle Road). Launching and parking on both sides of river.

Canoe Rentals:
South Bridge Boat House: Complete canoe service, including hourly and daily rentals, instruction, guided tours, and sales. South Bridge Boat House, 496-502 Main Street, Concord, MA, 01742. Telephone: 369-9438.

Directions:
To SBBH: Route 2 west to Main Street exit to Concord; turn right off Route 2. Or: Main Street west from Concord Center.

104. GREAT BROOK FARM STATE PARK
North Street, Carlisle
934 acres   *State Park   1974

Activities: picnicking, hiking, fishing, ski touring, nature study, canoeing
Map: free at Headquarters or send SASE
Hours: 9:00 A.M. to dusk
Admission: free

Great Brook is one of Massachusetts' newest state parks, acquired in 1974 from Farnham Smith, a gentleman farmer, railroad financier, and conservationist. Between 1942 and 1955 Smith purchased six farms and combined them into one large farm that he called Fernhame after a great English estate of that name. In 1946 he began raising and breeding Holstein milk cows, eventually developing a nationally famous herd that included many gold medal and blue ribbon winners. Smith and his wife built dams to impound little ponds on the property and cut many trails through the woods. Before the state bought the farm, the herd was auctioned off to dairymen and breeders from all over the country. Several of the fields are kept under cultivation or mown to maintain the farm atmosphere and it was renamed Great Brook Farm after the stream that cuts across the property.

Apparently Indians once used the fertile fields to raise corn, for a depression in a rock on a hilltop across North Street has been

319

worn from use as a mortar. Near the entrance to the state park, where Great Brook passes under the road, one of the first fulling mills in America was built in 1691 by John Barett "to dress homespun cloth." By 1730 a sawmill and a grist mill were operating on the brook where it crossed under North Street and a small community known as "The City" had developed nearby. The grinding wheel of the grist mill is now a monument in Concord's Sleepy Hollow Cemetery. A stone fort was built on a nearby hill to watch for and defend against Indian attack. Around 1800 one of Carlisle's first one-room schoolhouses was built on the farm, now the office of the state park. Lime kilns operated on the property until 1830, when the higher prices that the new mills in Lowell were willing to pay for fuelwood drove the kiln owners out of business.

In 1842 Zebulon Spaulding purchased one of the farms and began work on a house for himself and his betrothed. Just as he was completing the construction he caught a cold, which turned into pneumonia, and he died. His sister and brother-in-law took over the house, still standing on Lowell Street, and the farm.

Meanwhile, in 1840 Henry Hoar acquired the mill site and began operating wheelmaking and paint-grinding mills on Great Brook. Some years later the mill site was sold to Elmon Rose. Rose remodeled Hoar's works into a hoop shop where he made birch hoops and nail kegs. His primary customers were Somerville meatpackers and Florida orange growers who used the hoops to hold their shipping crates and barrels together. Hoops were also sold for binding wooden shoeboxes together.

Great Brook Farm includes an extensive wetland, known as Tophet Swamp. According to Webster, Tophet was another name for "Hell . . . ; utter chaos, darkness," giving us more than a hint of what the old-timers thought of swamps. Today we can appreciate the beauty of the cattails, blue flag irises, swamp honeysuckles, sedges, spotted turtles, and the constant calling of birds here—at least if we can get by summer's devilish mosquitos.

In the second-growth pine and oak woodlands, the wildflower hunter will find wintergreen, starflower, lambkill, highbush and lowbush blueberry, musky-smelling withe rod, and vivacious hummingbird-pollinated wild columbine. Rock formations and short eskers add some variety to the topography of the park.

In the old fields, growing up with red cedar, you will find purple, white, and yellow clover, blue-eyed grass, wild indigo, hoary alyssum, and buttercup. All in all, Great Brook Farm has an interesting variety of habitats making for wide biological diversity. It is a beautiful place, to boot, making it an excellent addition to our state-park system.

Activities:

This is a fine place for picnicking, nature study, or wandering, with wide-open fields, needle-carpeted pine groves, ponds, streams, and miles of woodland trails. Particularly beautiful in the spring and fall. Portable toilets are the only facilities.

Hiking and walking: Six or seven miles of nicely laid-out trails. Mostly easy walking.

Picnicking: Picnic by the pastoral pond near the farm buildings and parking lot, in the pine groves, or on the open fields. No tables; bring your own blanket and chairs. Open fields for playing games or running around.

Fishing: Pond and stream occasionally stocked with trout. Also perch, pickerel, sunfish, and catfish.

Canoeing: Launch your own canoe in the big pond for exploring or fishing. Best in the spring when the water is deep.

Ski touring: Formerly the site of the North Country Touring Center, the trails are graded and well maintained but not groomed; nonetheless, this is another one of the really fine places for ski touring in the region. A new touring center may open in the near future. Toilets open all winter and parking lot cleared. Novice to intermediate.

Directions:

From Lexington or Route 128 take Route 225 northwest to Carlisle Center, turn right on Lowell Street, proceed two miles to park entrance on the right.

Parking: Plenty; plowed lot for ski touring.

Telephone: 369-6312

**RECREATION
APPENDIX**

WALKING

I have met with but one or two persons in the course of my life who understood the art of Walking, that is, of taking walks,—who had a genius, so to speak, for sauntering: *which word is beautifully derived "from idle people who roved about the country, in the Middle Ages, and asked charity, under pretense of going* à la Sainte Terre,' *to the Holy Land, till the children exclaimed, "There goes a* Sainte-Terrer," *a Saunterer, a Holy-Lander. They who never go to the Holy Land in their walks, as they pretend, are indeed mere idlers and vagabonds; but they who do go there are saunterers in the good sense, such as I mean. Some, however, would derive the word from* sans terre, *without land or home, which, therefore, in the good sense, will mean, having no particular home, but equally at home everywhere. For this is the secret of successful sauntering.*

Henry David Thoreau
Walking

NATURE STUDY

We can never have enough of nature.
Henry David Thoreau

Exploring the flora and fauna of our parks, beaches, and natural areas can be a lifetime occupation and source of recreation at minimal expense. Read the landscape. Identify hundreds of wildflowers that grow in the region largely unnoticed. Study a chipmunk or a squirrel. Nature study can be both educational and pleasurable for the entire family. Even a relatively small park can provide endless fascination once you begin to look closely.

Nature Education: The following facilities owned by Massachusetts Audubon Society provide outstanding courses and lectures for children and adults on the natural history of the region: Trailside Museum at Section 16, Blue Hills; Section 101, Drumlin Farm; Section 74, Ipswich River Wildlife Sanctuary; Section 57, Moose Hill Sanctuary; and Section 89, Stony Brook and Bristol-Blake State Reservation.

Two other organizations that offer excellent courses in natural history and environmental studies for children and adults are: Habitat Institute for the Environment, 10 Juniper Road, Belmont, MA 02178, telephone 489-3850; and South Shore Natural Science Center, Jacobs Lane, Norwell, MA 02061, telephone 659-2559.

Basic Naturalist's Library

A Sierra Club Naturalist's Guide to Southern New England by Neil Jorgensen is the most complete book about the natural history of the region and also a perfect companion to this book. It includes sections on the geology, ecology, forest succession, flora, and fauna of the region; where to find and how to identify various wildflowers, ferns, and animals. Many illustrations.

A Guide to the New England Landscape by Neil Jorgensen describes in layman's words the geology and topography of New England. It has fine illustrated descriptions of such features as eskers, drumlins, moraines, and erratics.

Puddingstone, Drumlins, and Ancient Volcanoes by James W. Skehan, S.J., provides a series of self-guided field trips to the geologic features of Boston.

Newcomb's Wildflower Guide by Lawrence Newcomb is a profusely illustrated and easy-to-use field guide to the identification of the region's wildflowers, flowering shrubs, and vines.

A Field Guide to Trees and Shrubs by George A. Petrides provides a simple method for identifying the trees and shrubs of the region.

A Field Guide to the Atlantic Shore an excellent guide to the flora and fauna of the coast, including beaches.

The Barrier Island Handbook by Stephen P. Leatherman explains the coastal geology and vegetative succession that created most of our beaches.

BIRDWATCHING

Interesting birds are all around us—sparrow hawks flutter over the grassy median at the urban intersection of the Massachusetts Turnpike and the Southeast Expressway, egrets and orioles lurk in the Fens, goldeneyes and cormorants glide by Waterfront Park. With a pair of binoculars and a field guide fascinating hours fly by, inexpensively at that. Birding is a good excuse to get "out there" at any time of year. The better birding sites are listed here, but birds will be found at nearly every site in this book.

All the beaches listed in the book, including Section 12, Boston Beaches, provide good all-season birding: sea and bay ducks, cormorants, gulls, sandpipers, plovers, and other shorebirds.

A few of the best birding spots in the region: Section 8, Arnold Arboretum; Section 16, Blue Hills and Fowl Meadows; Section 19, Neponset Marshes; Section 25, Boston Harbor Islands; Section 28, Nahant Beach; Section 29, Cutler Park; Section 41, Mount Auburn Cemetery; Section 52, North River; Section 55, Ames Nowell State Park; Section 56, Borderland State Park; Section 57, Moose Hill Sanctuary; Section 59, Massasoit State Park; Section 61, Horseneck Beach Reservation; Section 62, Demarest Lloyd State Park; Section 68, Malachi Brook Wildlife Sanctuary; Section 70, Ward Hill Reservation; Section 72, John C. Phillips Wildlife Sanctuary; Section 74, Ipswich River Wildlife Sanctuary; Section 77B, Marblehead Neck Wildlife Sanctuary; Section 82, Dogtown; Section 85, Crane Beach Reservation; Section 87, Plum Island; Section 89, Stony Brook and Bristol-Blake State Reservation; Section 90, South Medfield; Section 95, Callahan State Park; Section 99, Upper Charles River; Section 101, Drumlin Farm Sanctuary; Section 103, Great Meadows National Wildlife Refuge.

Massachusetts Audubon Society publishes a current *Birder's Kit,* which provides information on numerous regularly conducted birdwatching trips around Greater Boston. Available from Massachusetts Audubon Society, South Lincoln, MA 01773; five dollars.

Books: *Audubon Field Guide to Birds* (Eastern) by National Audubon Society.

Peterson's Field Guide to the Birds by Roger Tory Peterson.
Where to Find Birds in Eastern Massachusetts by Leif J. Robinson and Robert H. Stymeist provides detailed information on bird-watching sites in the Greater Boston region. It is available from: Bird Observer of Eastern Massachusetts, Belmont, MA 02178.

Magazine: *Bird Observer of Eastern Massachusetts,* published several times a year, provides detailed information on birdwatching sites and special features on such topics as hawkwatching and the heron populations of Boston Harbor.

BICYCLING

The Explorer Recreation Map (see "About Maps" in Introduction) is a must for bicycle exploring around Greater Boston. *Short Bike Rides in Eastern Massachusetts* by Howard Stone includes excellent details on some fifty rides in the region. Check the "Quick Guide to Outdoor Activities" at the beginning of each section for sites with bike trails.

Guided Rides: Charles River Wheelmen, one of the oldest bicycling clubs in the region, conducts two group rides every Sunday except when there is snow on the ground. One ride is fifteen to twenty-five miles of fairly easy riding; the other trip is a more strenuous thirty- to sixty-mile trip. For more information write: Charles River Wheelmen, 3 Bow Street, Cambridge, MA 02138. Telephone: 625-0610.

JOGGING

Park sites with jogging courses and approximate mileage: Section 4, Back Bay Fens, 1.7 mi.; Section 6, Riverway, 2 mi.; Section 7, Jamaica Pond, 1.7 mi.; Section 9, Franklin Park, 2 mi.; Section 37, Brookline Reservoir, 0.7 mi.; Section 35, Chestnut Hill Reservoir, 1.5 mi.; Section 33f, Commonwealth Avenue in Newton, 5.7 mi.; Section 42, Charles River Basin, 18.5 mi.; Section 43, Fresh Pond Park, 2.5 mi.; Section 44, Mystic River Reservation, 3 mi.

All the bicycle trails in the region are suitable for jogging.

Reservations and parks listed as having woodland jogging have wide woods roads, easy grades, and fair running surfaces.

SKI TOURING

A few of the best places for ski touring: Section 9, Franklin Park; Section 16, Blue Hills and Fowl Meadows; Section 29, Cutler

Park; Section 50, Whitney and Thayer Woods; Section 51, Wompatuck State Park; Section 56, Borderland State Park; Section 59, Massasoit State Park; Section 70, Ward Hill Reservation; Section 73, Bradley W. Palmer State Park; Section 74, Ipswich River Wildlife Sanctuary; Section 79, Ravenswood Park; Section 87, Plum Island; Section 91, Rocky Woods Reservation; Section 95, Callahan State Park; Section 102, Walden Pond State Reservation; Section 104, Great Brook Farm State Park.

Weston Ski Track: The Weston Ski Track, operated by Lincoln Guide Service at the Martin Golf Course in Weston, is the most complete ski-touring center in the Boston area. Several miles of prepared trails run over the course and along the river. Instruction and waxing lessons. Rentals, repairs, and snack bar. Open December through March until 10:00 P.M. every night except nonholiday Sundays, when the track closes at 6:00 P.M. Weston Ski Track, Box 426, Weston, MA 02193. Telephone: 894-4903. Directions: Route 30 (Commonwealth Avenue) west, over Route 128, left on Park Road to Martin Golf Course.

Reading: *Ski Touring Guide to New England* by Katey Ziegler. *Guide to the Ski Touring Centers of New England* by Rod Lousteau. *The Complete Guide to Cross-Country Skiing and Touring* by Art Tokle and Martin Luray.

FISHING

A fishing license is required of all persons fifteen years of age or older to fish in ponds, streams, lakes, rivers, and other inland waters. Licenses are available from town and city clerks, at sporting-goods stores, or from the State Division of Fisheries and Wildlife.

The following sites have waters stocked with trout: Section 7, Jamaica Pond; Section 16, Blue Hills; Section 73, Bradley W. Palmer State Park (Ipswich River); Section 93, Hopkinton State Park; Section 94, Ashland State Park; Section 97, Lake Cochituate State Park; Section 99, Upper Charles River; Section 102, Walden Pond State Reservation.

The following sites are known to contain northern pike: Section 16, Blue Hills (Ponkapog Pond); Section 34, Hammond Woods (Hammond Pond); Section 99, Upper Charles River.

The following site is stocked with tiger muskie: Section 97, Lake Cochituate State Park.

The State Division of Fisheries and Wildlife, Westboro, MA 01581, publishes the following free publications about Massachusetts fishing: "Stocked Trout Waters," "Best Bets for Bass," "Maps of Fishing Ponds," and "A Guide to Fresh Water Fishing." Send a self-addressed, stamped envelope for each publication and request a complete list of the Division's publications.

The State Division of Marine Fisheries, 100 Cambridge Street, Boston, MA 02202, publishes *Massachusetts Salt Water Fishing Guide,* which includes town-by-town lists of bait shops, boat rentals, jetties and piers, boat-launching sites, and party boats, as well as describing the bait and season for each saltwater gamefish.

MDC SWIMMING POOLS

The MDC maintains nineteen outdoor swimming pools. They are open from the end of June to Labor Day for general swimming from noon until 7:00 P.M. or later, if the weather is hot. Pools are located in the following areas (with telephone numbers for more information):

Brighton (254-2962)	Melrose (662-5339)
Cambridge (354-9154)	Roxbury (334-9519)
Chelsea (884-9630)	Somerville (623-9321)
Cleveland Circle (277-7822)	Stoneham (438-9888)
Dorchester (436-1460)	Waltham (899-0106)
Everett (389-9401)	Watertown (923-0073)
Hyde Park (364-9731)	Weymouth (335-2090)
Magazine Beach (354-9381)	West End (523-9746)
Malden (324-9350)	West Roxbury (322-9512)

BALLFIELDS AND TENNIS COURTS

There are hundreds of ballfields and tennis courts in the region in addition to those listed in the Quick Guide to Outdoor Activities at the beginning of each section. For more information contact town or city parks and recreation departments.

The MDC owns a large number of fields and courts around Greater Boston that are open to the public. For a complete list write for the free *Recreation Facilities* published by the MDC, 20 Somerset Street, Boston, MA 02108.

ICE-SKATING RINKS

A complete list of MDC skating rinks is included in the free booklet *Recreation Facilities* mentioned above.

CANOE RENTALS

Canoe rentals are included in the following Sections: 33C, Charles River Canoe Service; 52, North River; 73, Bradley W. Palmer State Park; 93, Hopkinton State Park; 97, Lake Cochituate State Park; 103A, Concord River.

PUBLIC SAILING

The following sites have sailing programs for adults and children including instruction and sailing: Section 11, Castle Island; Section 42, Charles River Basin; Section 44, Mystic River Reservation.

ADDRESSES AND TELEPHONE NUMBERS

Boston Parks and Recreation Department, 1 City Hall Plaza, Boston, MA 02202. 725-3290.

Metropolitan District Commission (MDC), Public Information, 20 Somerset Street, Boston, MA 02108. 727-5215.

State Division of Forests and Parks, 100 Cambridge Street, Boston, MA 02202. 727-3180.

State Division of Fisheries and Wildlife, Westboro, MA 01581. 727-3151 (Boston).

State Division of Marine Fisheries, 100 Cambridge Street, Boston, MA 02202. 727-3900.

Trustees of Reservations, 224 Adams Street, Milton, MA 02186. 698-2066.

Massachusetts Audubon Society, South Great Road, Lincoln, 01773. 259-9500.

Appalachian Mountain Club, 5 Joy Street, Boston, MA 02108. 523-0636. Founded in 1876, the AMC is the oldest mountaineering club in America and the force behind the Appalachian Trail. The club sponsors hikes, rock climbs, and other outdoor activities in the area.

Massachusetts Environmental Lobby, 3 Joy Street, Boston, MA 02108. 742-2553. Founded in 1898 as the Massachusetts Forest and Park Association, this is the organization which fought for the creation of our state forests and parks. Today MEL is devoted to lobbying for conservation legislation.

Sierra Club (New England Chapter), 3 Joy Street, Boston, MA 02108. 227-5339. America's largest organization of environmental activists, the local chapter wades into innumerable battles to protect our natural resources and conducts many outdoor activities in the region.

Index

Goddard Hill, 138
Gooch's Caves, 134
Good Harbor Beach, 258–259
Gooseberry Neck, 210
Governor Hutchinson's Field,
    85–86
Grape Island, 98, 99, 103, 104,
    107–108
Gray, Asa, 2, 26, 43, 148
Great Blue Hill, 72, 74, 76, 77,
    78, 79, 84, 291
Great Blue Hill Observation
    Tower, 77
Great Brewster Island, 104,
    108–109
Great Bridge, 151
Great Brook Farm State Park,
    319–321
Great Cedar Swamp, 79
Great Dome Footpath, 79
Great Elm, 13, 14, 15–16
Great Esker, Park, 96–97, 98
Great Hills, 75
Great House, 270, 271
Great Meadows National Wildlife
    Refuge, 315
Great Ocean Pier, 112
Great Plains, 117
Grey, Horace, 18, 21
Gurnet, 222, 223, 224

Hagbourne Hill, 49
Hager's Hill, 308
Halibut Point Reservation,
    263–265
Hammond Pond, 120, 133
Hammond Pond Woods, 131–135
Harold Parker State Forest,
    130–232
Hatch Shell, 156–157
handicapped, recreation for
    Thompson Center, 84
Hatheway School of
    Environmental Education, 309
Head House, 54, 55
Heartbreak Hill, 129–130
Hellcat Swamp Trail, 278
Hemlock Gorge, 71, 121–123,
    125, 143
Hemlock Grove, 134

Hemlock Knoll Natural Trail,
    289–290
Hemlock Ridge, 174
Henry Cabot Lodge Wildlife
    Sanctuary, 116
Hermitage, 141
Highlands, 110
Hog Islands, 271
Holt Hill, 232, 233, 234
Holt Pond, 287
Hopkinton State Park, 292–293
Hormel Stadium, 163
Horseneck Beach Reservation,
    208–211
Houghton Garden, 133, 134
Houghton's Pond, 77–78, 79, 80
Humarock, 186, 190
Hunnewell Park, 303–304
Hunnewell Visitor Center, Arnold
    Arboretum, 46
Hutchinson, Governor Thomas,
    61, 85–86, 87
Hutchinson's Ha-Ha, 86

Indian Brook, 300
Indian burial ground, 96
Ipswich River, 239, 240
Ipswich River Wildlife Sanctuary,
    241–246
Isles of Shoals, 272

Jamaica Pond, 24, 38, 39, 40–43
Jamaicaway, 38
Japanese Lantern, 18
Jones River, 268
June Pond, 289

Kelly Park, 302–303
Kendrick Farm, 125
Kettle Cove, 266
Kingfisher Pond, 285
King's Beach, 71, 176
Kingsley Park, 161
Knight's Flume, 299, 300

L Street Bathhouse, 57
Lafayette Mall, 14, 16
Lagoon
    Boston Public Garden, 18, 20
    Charles River Basin, 157
Lake Cochichewick, 235

Ward's Pond, 38
Washburn's Pond, 193
Washington Tower, 148
Waterfront Park, 58–59
Watson Pond State Park, 203–204
Waverly Oaks, 69, 143–145
weather station, 76–77
Webb State Park, 98–99
Webster, Edwin, 133
Weir Hill, 317–318
Weir Hill Reservation, 234–235
Weir River, 92–93
Weld, 138
Wellington Lake, 163
West Boston Bridge, 151, 153
Westport River, 209
West Roxbury Park, 48
Whale's Jaw, 262
Wharf Road, 262, 263
Wheelwright Edmund, 41, 55, 136–137, 138
White, George R., 61

White Horse Beach, 219
Whitney Woods, 180–181
Wigwam Hill, 269, 270
Wilderness, 48–49, 50, 51
Willowdale, 238, 239
Willowdale Hill, 239, 240
Willowdale State Forest, 238, 241
Wilson, Ernest H. "China", 45, 242
Winchester reservoirs, 167
Winchester Street Recreation Area, 125
Wingaersheek Beach, 266–267, 268
Winthrop Beach, 71, 109–111
Wollaston Beach, 71, 99–101
Wompatuck State Park, 101, 103, 180, 181–183
Wood Island Park, 57
World's End Reservation, 92–95
Wright, Elizur, 164–165, 167
Wright's Pond, 167